Spanish Screen Fiction
Between Cinema and Television

PAUL JULIAN SMITH

LIVERPOOL UNIVERSITY PRESS

First published 2009 by
Liverpool University Press
4 Cambridge Street
Liverpool
L69 7ZU

Copyright © 2009 Paul Julian Smith

The right of Paul Julian Smith to be identified as the author of this book
has been asserted by him in accordance with the Copyright, Designs
and Patents Act 1988.

All rights reserved. No part of this book may be reproduced,
stored in a retrieval system, or transmitted, in any form or by any means,
electronic, mechanical, photocopying, recording, or otherwise,
without the prior written permission of the publisher.

British Library Cataloguing-in-Publication data
A British Library CIP record is available

ISBN 978-1-84631-201-4 cased
ISBN 978-1-84631-202-1 limp

Typeset in Borges by
Koinonia, Manchester
Printed and bound by
Bell and Bain Ltd, Glasgow

In memory of my mother, Margaret
1926–2006

Contents

List of Illustrations	*page* viii
Acknowledgements	ix
Introduction: Between Cinema and Television	1
1 City Girls I: Almodóvar's Women on Film and Television	17
2 City Girls II: Television's Urban Women, Pre- and Post-Almodóvar	38
3 Crime Scenes: Police Drama on Television	65
4 Dramatic Professions: Workplace Fiction on Television	85
5 Two Suicides and a Funeral: The Euthanasia Debate on Film and Television	105
6 Transnational Telenovela: From Mexico to Madrid, via Barcelona	122
7 Auteur TV: Case Studies in Creativity	145
8 Sitcom Cinema: Case Studies in Convergence	175
Index	195

List of Illustrations

1	Pepa (Carmen Maura) awakes: *Mujeres al borde de un ataque de nervios*	24
2	Irene (Chiqui Fernández) awakes: *Mujeres*	25
3	Walking in the city: *Chicas en la ciudad*	39
4	Running from the city: *La mujer de tu vida*	52
5	Shoes in the city: *Con dos tacones*	57
6	The ensemble cast of *Policías*	71
7	Pope (Marcial Alvarez, left) and Charlie (Juanjo Artero): *El comisario*	72
8	Esther (Fátima Baeza, far left), Rusti (Angel Pardo, centre): *Hospital Central*	90
9	The ensemble cast of *Al filo de la ley*	91
10	Ramón Sampedro (Javier Bardem) faces the camera: *Mar adentro*	111
11	Marta Cuesta (Amparo Valle) faces the camera: *Periodistas*	114
12	Luis (José Coronado) and Laura (Amparo Larrañaga) watch the screen: *Periodistas*	115
13	Margarita (Litzy) and Ignacio (Maurico Ochmann): *Amarte así*	127
14	Camila on the train (Tamar Monserrat): *Los Plateados*	130
15	Andrea (Ana Turpin) and Antonio (Rodolfo Sancho) on the roof: *Amar en tiempos revueltos*	137
16	The devil child of 'El muñeco': *Historias para no dormir*	159
17	The angel child Tito (Miguel Joven) and Julia (María Garralón): *Verano azul*	164
18	Narciso Ibáñez Menta, trapped in *El asfalto*	168
19	José Luis López Vázquez, trapped in *La cabina*	169
20	Laura (Paz Vega) on the small screen: *7 Vidas*	187
21	Sonia (Paz Vega) and Pedro (Guillermo Toledo) on the big screen: *El otro lado de la cama*	188

Acknowledgements

I would like to thank the staff and students of the University of Cambridge during the time this book was written (especially the finalists who chose Sp8: Spanish Cinema and Television). The University has been particularly generous with me in granting research leave. Special thanks for support beyond the call of duty go to Michael Minden, Angela Myers, and, above all, Coral Neale, for many fruitful years of working life together. Intellectually I have been most grateful for close contact with the team of media scholars at the Universidad Carlos III, Madrid, headed by Manuel Palacio. Thanks also to Saimon Clark for generous technical assistance with the illustrations and to Anthony Cond at Liverpool University Press for the very welcome initiative of a new series in Hispanic Studies.

Earlier versions of Chapters 3 and 6 were published in a shorter form in *Journal of Spanish Cultural Studies* 8.1 (2007), 55–70, and *Critical Studies in Television* 3.2 (2008), 4–18. Unless otherwise credited all translations are my own.

PJS
London

INTRODUCTION

Between Cinema and Television

On 28 October 2007 *El País*'s Sunday supplement carried a lengthy fashion spread showcased on its cover under the title 'Gran estreno' (Cueto). The 'grand premiere' thus announced was somewhat ironic. Although the 25 actors in the lavish shoot are parodying a Hollywood film melodrama of the 1950s, complete with homburgs and Chevrolets, they have been chosen because they are the local stars of what the accompanying feature calls the 'Golden Age' of series television. In its self-conscious and frivolous way, the spread thus points to the newly elevated status of Spanish television, even in relation to classic cinema, and to the increasing convergence between the two media.

This book is the first to examine and argue for the inextricability of cinema and television as twin vehicles for screen fiction in Spain. The Spanish audiovisual sector is now one of the most successful in the world, with feature films achieving wider distribution in foreign markets than nations with better-known cinematic traditions and newly innovative TV formats, already dominant in prime time at home, now widely exported. Beyond the industrial context, which has seen the coming together of the two media in joint enterprises such as Tele 5/Estudios Picasso, this book also examines the textual evidence for aesthetic crossover between cinema and television at the level of narrative and form. While this detailed proof remains to be demonstrated through the eight chapters that follow this introduction, an initial hypothesis would be that the Spanish audiovisual sector is an excellent illustration of that crucial process of media convergence (between cinema and television, if not Internet) to which the London *Financial Times* devoted a 16-page special report in its Creative Business section (28 June 2005).

The first two chapters of this book look at urban women as subjects and viewers. Chapter 1 compares Almodóvar's classic feature *Mujeres al borde de un ataque de nervios* ('Women on the Verge of a Nervous Breakdown', 1988) with his production company El Deseo's first venture into television production, the 2006 series also known as *Mujeres* ('Women'), which has yet to attract any academic attention. Chapter 2 complements this study of urban women by reclaiming the lost history of female flat-share comedy on Spanish television from the 1960s (*Chicas en la ciudad*, 'Girls in the City') to the present-day (*Con dos tacones*, 'On Two Heels') via the 1980s and 1990s (*La mujer de tu vida*, 'The Woman of Your Life').

The next two chapters treat dominant quality forms of drama on Spanish television, which have no equivalents on film. Adopting a social science approach that appeals to Durkheim, Chapter 3 examines two prominent police dramas, *Policías* ('Police Officers', 2000-2003) and *El comisario* ('The Police Commander', 1999-), arguing that they dramatize the conflict between the individual and the collective. Chapter 4 discusses a long-running and much-loved medical series, *Hospital Central* ('Central Hospital', 2000-), and a failed legal drama, *Al filo de la ley* ('At the Edge of the Law', 2004-2005), reading them, beyond the 'effects' debate, for the way they conjoin real and fictional discursive fields in an institutional format.

Chapters 5 and 6 go beyond Spain to address transnational relations in screen narrative. Amenábar's *Mar adentro* ('The Sea Inside', 2004), an Oscar-winning film on the theme of euthanasia, is contrasted with its vital, but forgotten, antecedent, an early episode of national network Tele 5's top-rated, innovative drama *Periodistas* ('Journalists', 1998-2002). The latter was shown simultaneously with the real-life case of assisted suicide that provides the common source for both narratives. Chapter 6 traces the troubled attempt to establish a Latin American genre, the telenovela, in the very different context of Spanish daytime scheduling, which culminated in TVE1's critical and commercial success *Amar en tiempos revueltos* ('Loving in Troubled Times', 2005-), a drama set in Madrid, which was based (surprisingly perhaps) on a Catalan original.

The final pair of chapters examine two cases of media crossover, which (I argue) have established new genres. 'Auteur TV' charts the careers of two consecrated creators, Narciso Ibáñez Serrador and Antonio Mercero, who have established distinctive profiles in television over decades in a way once considered unique to feature film. 'Sitcom Cinema' charts, conversely, the incursion of television aesthetics and economics (narrative, scripting and casting) into film comedies such as *El otro lado de la cama* ('The Other Side of the Bed', 2002), which have proved among the most popular features at the Spanish box office in the last decade.

In spite of the rhetoric of 'crisis', which pervades discussion of Spanish cinema, and of 'trash', which plays a similar role in discourse on Spanish television, official figures reveal the good health of both media. According to the Ministry of Culture website, feature film production in Spain was 107 in 1975, the year of Franco's death (Ministerio de Cultura). After plunging to 47 in 1990, when the PSOE's misguided quest for 'quality' failed to connect with local audiences, production first broke the 100 barrier in 2001 and has continued to rise, to a peak of 150 in 2006. In the same year Spanish cinema reached a historically high 20 per cent audience share in its own market.

Of this total number (which included co-productions), 109 films are held to be 'fully Spanish', fulfilling all three criteria required for a 'certificate of nationality': 75 per cent of the cast and crew must be citizens of Spain or the EU; the original version should be in Spanish or any other official language of the state; and the shooting location should be in Spain, or, again, the EU, unless the script demands otherwise (Ministerio). Such production figures were only possible because of the funding provided, albeit under legal compulsion, by television stations such as Tele 5. Moreover, the renewed success with audiences of the resulting films was, as I argue in my final chapter, to some extent dependent on the use of the small screen as a launch pad for young actors who were eager to make parallel careers in both media.

The Eurofiction Working Group, led by Milly Buonanno and based at the European Audiovisual Observatory, charted a similar rise in the fortunes of Spanish television drama. In 2002 Spain reached the 'highest production level [yet] in a turbulent environment' (i.e. during the threatening rise of unscripted reality programming). Development of first-run domestic fiction programming rose from 459 hours in 1996 to a peak of 1,465 hours in 1999, falling slightly to 1,306 in 2001. This is substantially higher than the figures for France and Italy, which are just 553 and 761 respectively for the same year. Spain also has a higher 'seriality index' than the other big European territories, meaning that it produces larger numbers of episodes of fewer individual titles. This suggests that, unlike elsewhere in Europe, Spanish producers have successfully secured the fidelity of domestic audiences to long-lasting dramas that have found a secure place in national affections and living rooms.

The Working Group also notes that 'European fiction continues to be local and specifically tailored to domestic audiences'. In the case of Spain, domestic drama occupied 51per cent of prime time in 2000, with the US at 37 per cent, and 'other' (namely, Latin American) at 12 per cent. Moreover, it is these prestigious prime-time slots that are domestic, while the less-prized off-prime-time slots are relegated to foreign shows. The figures for 2006 from Lorenzo Vilches' invaluable and more recent survey of Spain in the Iberoamerican Television Observatory report on TV fiction are somewhat different. But, alluding to the title of the rare domestic telenovela success that I cover in Chapter 6, Vilches also stresses how Spain has preserved its position 'in troubled times' of increasing market fragmentation (159). He also cites workplace dramas such as *El comisario* and *Hospital Central* among the top ten watched programmes for 2006, and female-based comedies *Mujeres* and *Con dos tacones* among the most creatively innovative of the same year (184; 188). All of these shows are closely analysed in this book.

These programmes tend to contradict the generalizing claims of scholars such as Rueda Laffond and Chicharro Merayo who, in their recent study of Spanish television, cite industry sources of some twenty years ago on the supposed repetitiveness and banality of content (349). This negative attitude is also contradicted by the data reproduced by Rueda and Chicharro themselves, which show that television-watching has risen year on year in Spain from 197 minutes per day for men in 1993 to 205 in 2005 – the equivalent figures for women are 223 and a massive 246 minutes (449). Given the increasing competition from other media such as the Internet, it seems unlikely that Spanish viewers would choose to spend such lengthy periods in the company of their television sets unless they were increasingly happy with the content on offer.

While the main focus here, then, as in my previous two books (*Spanish Visual Culture*; *Television in Spain*), is on close textual analysis, I have also investigated production and consumption. Thus each chapter begins with a survey of the chosen topic, generally taken from the trade press, in which trends in the US, the UK or Latin America are used to throw the situation in Spain into relief. I then proceed to give an account of corporate mentalities (e.g. how did El Deseo's move into television production mesh with the vision set out by their financial director?) or of production history (e.g. how did the first female flat-share sitcom come to be made in the Francoist period?). The two chapters on workplace drama (police, medical and legal) appeal also to functionalist models drawn from the social sciences. Durkheim appears once more in the chapter on screen narratives of assisted suicide. The telenovela chapter is the most detailed on a crucial aspect of television, namely scheduling, in that it examines a unique Spanish programme in the light of its neighbours in the afternoon grid, more generic and familiar Mexican shows. Finally 'auteur TV' attempts to recontextualize one of the most venerable debates in film studies in the new setting of television, while 'sitcom cinema' juxtaposes the distinct theories of comedy in the two media. Hence, while the book's methodology is eclectic and qualitative, the focus on production processes is consistent throughout.

Consumption is, of course, more difficult to address, and I have not appealed to focus groups or informant interviews as my colleagues in communication studies would. I have, however, researched press archives, where appropriate, for evidence of reception, particularly for earlier periods, and have consulted Internet forums for audience responses to more recent shows. Clearly also quantitative data, readily available from official sources, such as box office and admission figures for cinema and ratings and share for television, offer invaluable proof as to which screen fictions strike a chord with mass audiences and which pass relatively unnoticed.

Finally, the texts that are studied here will be of varying familiarity. I have chosen some celebrated and much-analysed films (*Mujeres al borde*, *Mar adentro*) as test cases, in order to argue that their meaning is transformed when placed in a televisual context. Conversely, I have also devoted a chapter to the hugely popular film comedies (such as *El otro lado de la cama*) which are generally ignored by cinema scholars, whose canon seems ever more restricted, perhaps because of the aesthetic and thematic proximity of such popular films to television. One chapter argues, perversely perhaps, that Narciso Ibáñez Serrador and Antonio Mercero, who have worked in both media, deserve the title of auteur more for their television work than for their feature films. All of the television dramas studied here (most of which remain available on DVD and have clips posted by fans on YouTube) have been chosen for both their artistic and popular interest. Of course, a critical or commercial failure (such as El Deseo's *Mujeres*) can be of equal academic interest to the most resounding success.

While I have undertaken some media archeology in investigating Francoist television (from *Chicas en la ciudad* to *Historias para no dormir*, 'Stories to Keep You Awake', 1964–82), I have also focused on series that continue to play an intense role in current national life. As I write (November 2007), *Hospital Central* and *El comisario*, professional dramas that take pride in their authenticity and verisimilitude (see Gallo), are still playing to audiences of millions in prime time; and the second season of *Amar en tiempos revueltos* is still seducing afternoon viewers with its oddly successful blend of traumatic history and reassuring romance.

When actress Belén Rueda presented her horror film *El orfanato* ('The Orphanage', Juan Antonio Bayona) at the Sitges film festival, she lamented (5 October 2007) that in Spain those who work in television are thought to be incapable of delivering the goods in film (Costa). Whether directors or actors, such artists are 'pigeonholed' within a single genre or medium. She claimed that someone needs to take the first step for this 'prejudice' to collapse. Rueda is herself exemplary of the movement between cinema and television, starring as she did in both *Periodistas*, the series that pioneered the wave of quality TV drama in Spain, and in *Mar adentro*, Amenábar's self-consciously cinematic feature film. Lorenzo Vilches has also noted that, while Spanish-language TV fiction is a 'powerful cultural industry', punching its weight in global markets, it still has a 'low profile' in audiovisual culture (163). This book is intended to help undermine a prejudice that remains strong in the academy and beyond. It aims to demonstrate that it is only by charting the conflictive but necessary cohabitation of cinema and television that we can truly understand the two media in both their specificity and their mutual constitution.

Works Cited

Costa, Jordi. 'Belén Rueda/actriz'. *El País* 5 Oct. 2007: 57.
Cueto, Juan. 'Gran estreno: 25 actores ruedan una serie de amor y suspense en exclusiva para este número'. *El País Semanal* 28 Oct. 2007: 54–72.
Eurofiction (Milly Buonanno and the European Audiovisual Observatory). 'Television Fiction in Europe'. 18 Nov. 2007. <http://www.obs.coe.int/oea_publ/eurofic/>
Financial Times, The. 'FT Creative Business. Cracking Convergence'. Special Report 28 June 2005.
Gallo, Isabel. 'Detectores de gazapos'. *El País* 17 June 2007: 90.
Ministerio de Cultura. 18 Nov. 2007. <http.www.mcu.es>
Rueda Laffond, José Carlos and María del Mar Chicharro Merayo. *La televisión en España (1956–2006): Política, consumo, y cultura televisiva*. Madrid: Fragua, 2006.
Smith, Paul Julian. *Spanish Visual Culture: Cinema, Television, Internet*. Manchester: Manchester UP, 2006.
—. *Television in Spain: From Franco to Almodóvar*. London: Boydell and Brewer/Támesis, 2006.
Vilches, Lorenzo, ed. *Culturas y mercados de la ficción televisiva en Iberoamérica: Anuario OBITEL 2007*. Barcelona: Gedisa, 2007.

CHAPTER ONE

City Girls I:
Almodóvar's Women on Film and Television

Women on the verge of an urban breakdown

Picture this: the main character is a middle-aged, working-class housewife in one of the grittier outlying areas of Madrid. She struggles to cope with the problems of her family: her teenage daughter has personal problems, while her eccentric mother is in another realm altogether. In the absence of support from a husband, she can rely only on the female solidarity of family and friends to pull through.

The plot is, of course, familiar. Almodóvar's sixteenth feature film, *Volver*, was released in Spain on 17 March 2006 and starred Penélope Cruz as the desperate housewife Raimunda and Carmen Maura as the eccentric mother Irene, apparently returned from the dead. But I was in fact describing another project by Almodóvar's independent production company El Deseo, released in the same year as *Volver*: the TV series *Mujeres* ('Women'), which premiered on national public channel TVE2 on 18 September 2006, starring relative unknowns Chiqui Fernández as the housewife heroine (also given the uncommon name Irene) and Teresa Lozano as her eccentric mother Palmira (here consigned to the living death of dementia). As the very first TV series produced by El Deseo, *Mujeres*, directed by Almodóvar's twin protégés Dunia Ayaso and Félix Sabroso, is clearly worthy of close study. And as is signalled by the title, which cites Almodóvar's breakthrough 'high comedy', *Mujeres al borde de un ataque de nervios* ('Women on the Verge of a Nervous Breakdown', 1988), his first massively popular hit and his first work to be nominated for an Oscar), *Mujeres* has many plot elements in common with Almodóvar's feature films. Given these industrial and thematic similarities, it is thus possible to use the two *Mujeres* as a test case for comparing cinema and television and for exploring the differences between the two media at a textual level.

But almost twenty years separate *Mujeres al borde* from *Mujeres* tout court. During that period the first *Mujeres* established itself as a pioneer, or prototype, setting the generic boundaries for the crazy and often camp film comedies that can clearly be categorized as 'post-Almodóvarian'. Less well known is the television tradition of 'city girls', which both preceded and followed Almodóvar. As we shall see in the following chapter, this television genre began as early as 1961 with Jaime de Armiñán's long-lost flat-share sitcom *Chicas en la ciudad* ('Girls in the City') and continued from the 1980s to the 2000s with what we might baptize 'post-Almodóvarian TV': from the series of one-off dramas *La mujer de tu vida* ('The Woman of Your Life', 1988–94) through comic serials *Chicas de hoy en día* ('Girls of Today', 1991–92) and the failed *Con dos tacones* ('On Two Heels', 2006). The TV *Mujeres* thus inscribes itself in a historical tradition both cinematic and televisual, and one that is dominated by the uniquely successful and influential figure of Almodóvar himself. As we shall see in this first chapter, it is precisely this sense of familiarity that engages the show most closely with television as a medium, yet calls into question its value as an audiovisual product.

Industry of desire

El Deseo, perhaps the most consistently successful small production company in Europe, is itself highly aware of Almodóvar's status as a 'figure' and of the economic value of 'quality' in audiovisual commodities. An invited presentation by the company's financial director, Diego Pajuelo Almodóvar (a nephew of Pedro and Agustín), given at Madrid's Universidad Complutense on 1 December 2005, offers unique access to the economic criteria involved in the production process. Pajuelo began by noting that since the first *Mujeres* Pedro had not made a feature using his own (i.e. El Deseo's) finance, but had relied on sources such as French company CIBY 2000 for relatively high budgets such as the €7 million of *Hable con ella* ('Talk to Her', 2002). However, El Deseo had itself also aimed to sponsor first-time or inexperienced directors, who were not followers or disciples of Pedro but rather made 'quality' films. The examples he gave were features by now-established Spanish and Latin American directors such as Alex de la Iglesia (*Acción mutante*, 'Mutant Action', 1993), Guillermo del Toro (*El espinazo del diablo*, 'The Devil's Backbone', 2001), Isabel Coixet (*Mi vida sin mí*, 'My Life Without Me', 2003), and Lucrecia Martel (*La niña santa*, 'The Holy Girl', 2004). This policy of 'diversification' would also lead, he claimed, to the making of two or three feature-length documentaries a year.

What is the 'business mission' of El Deseo? The first priority is, unsurprisingly, 'to produce, promote, and preserve the work and figure of Almodóvar' (Pajuelo Almodóvar); the second, to promote new talents and independent creators; and the third, to 'develop other audiovisual products of high quality'. The 'organizational vision', related to but distinct from the 'mission', is to 'guarantee the continuity of production in the long term, assessing risks, improving organization, and refining [*depurar*] activities that are already completed'. This last process of added value does not extend to merchandising: Pajuelo claimed that he had rejected offers to lend Pedro's name or face to mugs and mouse mats (which would harm the brand's perceived 'prestige'); that of the 150 scripts submitted to El Deseo each month, only the most professional (those with a 'believable plot' and 'well rounded characters') went into production; and that Pedro himself had refused many offers to direct other people's projects, such as gay Western *Brokeback Mountain* (Ang Lee, 2005).

As this last example suggests, El Deseo's context is global, not national. Of the €21.5 million of income the company received in 2004, 70.2 per cent came from abroad. Yet if El Deseo is not dependent economically on its home market, still it and its assets are wholly based in Spain, with a back catalogue of 26 works valued at €45.3 million and 15 permanent employees, rising to 18 during periods when a new feature is in production. And if El Deseo does not risk its own capital in the production process, it remains reliant on some Spanish sources of funding: 33 per cent of a typical feature budget comes from government subsidy and a similar figure from pre-sales of television screening rights.

After release, any new film from El Deseo would go through a 'first cycle of exploitation', passing through a series of time-delayed 'windows': four months on cinema screens before the DVD release; eight months on pay per view; a year on Canal + (then a premium channel); and up to five years on free-to-air TV. This cycle produces 80 per cent of the feature's total revenue. The general aim of the company, however, is not to maximize such short-term profits but to 'preserve and maintain' Pedro's legacy. To this end it has recently bought back the rights of early features such as *Entre tinieblas* ('Dark Habits', 1983) and *Qué he hecho yo para merecer esto?* ('What Have I Done to Deserve This?', 1984), in order to restore the negatives. Yet the preservation and promotion of the entire corpus of Almodóvar's oeuvre sometimes founders on economic obstacles that even El Deseo cannot control: Pajuelo said that *Tráiler para amantes de lo prohibido* ('Trailer for Lovers of the Forbidden', 1985), a rarely seen mid-length project originally made for television, would not be re-released on DVD as it featured too many musical numbers whose rights could not be cleared (as I write it is, however, available in three instalments on YouTube).

What is striking about El Deseo's business plan and practice is its twin commitment to diversification and to quality, ends that may potentially come into conflict. Indeed, Pajuelo called attention to the TV *Mujeres*, then in production, in precisely this double context, citing the names of creators Ayaso and Sabroso as he did so. Interestingly he did not refer to the features they had previously made with El Deseo. As its campy title suggests, *Perdona, bonita, pero Lucas me quería a mí* ('Excuse Me, Darling, but Lucas Loved Me', 1997) is a post-Almodóvarian urban farce in which a gaggle of gay men, queer imitators of Almodóvar's luckless, loveless women, argue over a cute dead guy. More cheekily, *¡Descongélate!* ('Chill Out!', 2003) bites the hand that feeds it, satirizing

Pedro's celebrity and influence: an out-of-luck actor, desperate to secure a role in a film, goes so far as to preserve in his bath the corpse of the most famous film director in Spain, who has succumbed to a drug overdose in his flat.

These comedies, which received a mixed reception from critics and audiences alike, do not display the wit and visual imagination of the reworkings of popular culture by de la Iglesia or del Toro, much less the sensitivity and sophistication of the highly crafted art movies of Coixet and Martel. Far from being original creations, *Perdona, bonita* and *¡Descongélate!* are clearly the works of disciples, even camp followers, of Pedro. Contradicting one aspect of El Deseo's mission statement (the 'quality' that enhances the brand's overall cultural prestige), these features nonetheless reinforce another (the diversification that spreads the company's financial risk). Moreover, the fact that, unlike other genuine auteurs sponsored by El Deseo, Ayaso and Sabroso are content to echo their master's voice means that a case can be made for their work, in television as in film, as an officially authorized extension of Pedro's, in much the same way as a painting is said to be 'from the studio' of an old master. Ayaso and Sabroso will have some trouble escaping from Almodóvar's long shadow, but, paradoxically perhaps, they remain spotlit by the celebrity of their patron.

Women: Take 1

Let us return to the more familiar *Mujeres al borde de un ataque de nervios*, the film that established the cinematic genre of the urban female comedy in Spain and was for many years the highest-grossing feature in the country's history. As the second self-produced feature from El Deseo, and the first with a comfortable budget, *Mujeres* exploits, or more properly revels in, the specificity of cinema as a medium. From the expertly drawn titles by Juan Gatti (with their fragmented collage of fashion spreads, see D'Lugo 60–61) to the stylish costumes in primary colours by José María Cossío and the expert music by Bernardo Bonezzi (all frequent collaborators with Almodóvar in the period), the film is a perfectly consistent, indeed unique, aesthetic creation. Most striking and novel in Pedro's filmography to that date is the large studio set, built for the main location (Pepa's penthouse), with its expensive recreation of the Madrid skyline that figures so prominently beyond the terrace. Quite literally an 'alta comedia' (Smith, *Desire Unlimited* 94), in that most of the action takes place high above the street where Almodóvar had shot his earlier, grungier features, the hermetic universe of *Mujeres*, which is 'highly coloured', both aesthetically and emotionally, offers film-goers in abundance the visual and affective pleasures peculiar to cinema: those of dream and fantasy.

But *Mujeres* also engages to some extent with history. As the quintessential 'modern' film of the period (see D'Lugo 63), it represents the consumerist boom of the Socialist era that would end in bust after the climax of the annus mirabilis of the Barcelona Olympics, the Seville Expo and Madrid's selection as European Capital of Culture in 1992. But *Mujeres* avoids reference to topicality, even as it playfully invokes current themes. It is characteristic that the terrorists cited, but not seen, in the film are Islamists (not then seen as a real threat to Madrid), rather than the ETA commandos who were making headlines at the time.

More often the history referenced is cinematic: Hollywood sex comedy (the penthouse terrace is borrowed from *How to Marry a Millionaire*, Jean Negulesco, 1953), and Hitchcock (the playful recreation of *Strangers on a Train* (1951), when the camera shoots through Pepa's glasses after they have fallen on the floor of the dubbing studio, and of *Rear Window* (1954), when the camera takes up Pepa's perspective as she surveys the windows of Lucía's building). The retro credits, source music (Cuban bolero and Mexican ranchera), and costume (epitomized by Lucía's Courrèges leopard-print hat) point to an anachronistic cinematic temporality that was frequently called 'postmodern' (see Sánchez Biosca). Even when Almodóvar recreates that most immediate and contemporary of genres, TV news, it is ironically distanced in time: it is his own aged mother who haltingly reads the bulletin on the Shiites.

Mujeres thus extends beyond the national into the international. Although some of its references are domestic, even parochial (the corral of chickens and rabbits that the modern urban woman keeps on her luxury terrace; the fake city skyline that memorializes icons of Madrid such as the Telefónica tower), the film places itself and its characters in a much wider, more ambitious context. It is characteristic that, with some implausibility, the film that Pepa and Iván are dubbing, separately and together, is Nicholas Ray's problem Western *Johnny Guitar* (1954), very distant in time and space from 1980s Madrid (D'Lugo 63–64). It is a fierce-faced Joan Crawford whom Pepa is forced to voice and whose disappointments in love she echoes. Only much later (in *La mala educación*, 'Bad Education', 2004) will Almodóvar supply a Spanish star for similar purposes of filmic projection and identification: his pair of lovelorn tweens gaze up at a regal Sara Montiel in Mario Camus' *Esa mujer* ('That Woman', 1969).

The textuality of *Mujeres* is thus, as I mentioned earlier, highly cinematic. In spite of a wordy script and a great deal of difficult-to-translate verbal humour, the film exploits to the full the potential of the image and of the big screen. Wide framings enable crowded group shots (the penthouse is crammed with ever more visitors), while (conversely) the camera cuts in for extreme close-ups of perfectly realized items of *mise-en-scène* (a pair of high heels clicks back and forth over a parquet floor, a sharp knife slices through the reddest of tomatoes). A tragicomedy complete in a brisk and condensed 95 minutes, *Mujeres* compresses a wide range of time, space and affect into its strictly delimited filmic text.

Much of *Mujeres* is domestic, an important aspect of its female-centredness. The penthouse, with its views and memories, is finally a safe house for Pepa, the abandoned woman who is a victim of the war between the sexes. In the last sequence she resolves both to carry her baby and keep her apartment, in the company of and in complicity with Marisa, played by the extraordinary Rossy de Palma. While external space is invariably confrontational (the tense scenes with the chemist and lawyer, the fraught encounters in the street), internal space is sacrosanct. However, home is by no means *heimlich*. *Mujeres* parodies domesticity: if Pepa uses a garden hose it is to put out the bed she has accidentally set on fire; and if she makes gazpacho it is to knock out her faithless boyfriend (in the event it is Marisa and the police who fall victim to the drug-spiked dish). As a highly stylized Spanish event movie (a fictional universe suspended outside time, a prestigious feature film that had no equal), *Mujeres* turns its back on everyday life, even as it gestures towards domestic labour (that gazpacho in the blender once more).

This question of the everyday raises, in turn and finally, that of value. Almodóvar's defenders (e.g. Hergueta 11) at this key point in his career (and critics were by no means unanimous in Spain or out of it) claimed to identify what was by now a unique style and vision from a modern maestro. Conversely, detractors (e.g. Caparrós Lera 324) claimed he was just recycling familiar tropes and was no match for the old masters he sought to imitate. Whatever their position, positive or negative, critics relied on the Romantic conception of value that identified the work of art with the unique and the original: it was the film's bid for creative difference that was at stake in *Mujeres*' battle to achieve that artistic distinction or quality that El Deseo would later so single-mindedly set their sights on.

Opening nights

The distinctively cinematic creative ambition vindicated by critics such as José Arroyo, who praised the film's 'visual poetry', is clear in *Mujeres*' opening sequence, which far surpasses in technique what might be expected from a crazy comedy. The lengthy credits (more than two minutes long) showcase Juan Gatti's exquisite objets trouvés: fragments of fashion shots from the late 1950s and early 1960s tinted in primary colours (especially red) or hot pink. Female body parts (hands, feet and eyes) and accessories (shoes and jewellery) are cut and shuffled to suit each title. For example, the design for Almodóvar's faithful editor José Salcedo is of multiple eyes cut and arranged to form a surreal flower. On the soundtrack we hear Lola Beltrán's slow, sultry 'Soy infeliz', set to a Mexican brass backing.

The first (inexplicable) shots are of (what later turns out to be) an architect's model of main character Pepa's luxury apartment building and of the ducks and chickens she keeps in a coop on the terrace. Pepa's voice-over, spoken from an unspecified point in the future, soberly relates that, unlike Noah (an earlier collector of animal pairs) she was unable to save the couple she cherished the most: herself and Iván. Almodóvar cuts to an extreme close-up of an overflowing ashtray (yellow), papers (red and blue), and an LP sleeve (white) featuring the title of the song we have just heard, this last customized by a handwritten scrawl in which faithless Iván claims he never wants to hear Pepa say she is unhappy. A slow pan, also in extreme close-up, over Pepa's magenta pyjamas comes to rest on her auburn hair, hiding a head buried in a pillow.

We dissolve to a black and white sequence in another unestablished location. Lingering in extreme close-up on a Moorish-style, star-pierced screen, the camera pulls back to show the lower half of a mature man's face in profile. Iván squirts two doses of throat spray into his mouth and we cut to a full-figure framing that will prove to be an extended lateral tracking shot. As Iván strolls through what is now revealed to be an alienating modern setting (glass and concrete high-rises are reflected in passing windows) he addresses a parade of female stereotypes, speaking into an oversize microphone the words that each wishes to hear: a frumpy hausfrau is told that he wishes to marry her again; a turbaned African that 'our night in the jungle was unforgettable'; a cheerleader that 'some things are quintessentially American'; and a rope-wielding dominatrix that he is 'at [her] disposal'.

The final figure is a sarcastic drag queen posed under a traffic light. In a subtle graphic match, the monochrome light turns into the red warning light of a recording studio. Once more we see Iván's mouth in extreme close-up next to a microphone. As he voices the male character's dialogue, we cut to Joan Crawford on-screen (black brows and face framed by darkness) as her scarlet lips move in silence. We next see Iván in full-face profile: 'Tell me you've been waiting for me all these years ... tell me'. Cross-cutting between the male dubber and female mute gives way to a high-angle shot of Pepa, face still hidden, sprawled on her bed. We cut back to Iván in the studio. Now out of focus, Crawford looms behind him – she smashes a glass on-screen. A red alarm clock now fills the frame and Almodóvar switches giddily between Iván in the studio and a series of clocks in the bedroom (red, yellow and white), before coming to rest once more on Pepa's magenta shoulder. Next, Iván is shown placing a call through the studio's chatty receptionist: the fire engine-red phone contrasts with the saturated blue of the translucent canopy that screens his head. Back in the flat, Pepa hears his voice on the answerphone and, in a series of quick cuts and rapid camera movements, sprints to her (matching red) phone just too late to take her errant lover's call.

Gatti's hyper-aestheticized and historically distanced credits had already primed the audience for a drama that was not naturalistic or contemporary. This opening sequence of the film itself plunges us into a highly stylized world

1 Pepa (Carmen Maura) awakes: *Mujeres al borde de un ataque de nervios*

in which fantasy and reality are inextricable. The dream sequence (as it is now clearly seen to be) is formally distanced from the rest of the film's cinematography and editing through monochrome and dissolves. Yet the primal scenes of Pepa's bedroom and Iván's studio are equally abstracted, glimpsed only through the fragments of extreme close-ups (record sleeves and clocks, mouths and mikes) that are themselves juxtaposed with unestablished and inexplicable elements (the architectural model and the Noah's ark of animals). It is a setting deprived of any history (except for that of classic or campy cinema) and of nationality (the cinema references are to Hollywood, see Evans, passim) and in which everyday life (an ashtray, a warning light) is colour-coordinated with extreme, even excessive, precision (Allinson 183). Disorientating us through scale (the cross-cutting between extreme close-up and long shots), Almodóvar weaves together a large number of locations (the model will prove to be in a real estate office) without establishing the relative position of any of them to the bemused viewer. Appealing rather to the cinematic logic of visual poetry, he exploits the fundamental formal properties of images (shape and colour) to suggest similarities and differences, equivalences and disturbances. It is a distinctive and, indeed, distinguished technique that, as José Arroyo notes once more, is simultaneously beautiful, conceptually intricate, and moving.

Let us compare this with the opening sequence of the first episode of the second *Mujeres*, which premiered on the small screen almost twenty years later. The credits are scored to a (wordless) funky urban theme, oddly reminiscent of klezmer, led by a smoky clarinet. The first frame of the title sequence, once more by Juan Gatti, gives credits for El Deseo, co-producer Mediapro, and distributor

2 Irene (Chiqui Fernández) awakes: *Mujeres*

TVE in blue and red on a black and white grid. As the grid resolves into the repeated bars of balconies, small female figures, reminiscent of cut-out paper dolls, pose theatrically on the schematic terraces. Moving in and out of frame, horizontally and vertically, the architectural elements are progressively fleshed out into a recognizable urban setting, complete with trees and chaotically parked cars. Likewise the female figures, although they remain faceless become more distinct and detailed: one housewife sports a yellow apron; another cuddles a cat. While some of the figures sport retro fashions (a billowing pink New Look gown with a cinched waist) others are clearly contemporary (jeans and sweatshirt). Attentive viewers will note familiar names in the credits: not just Gatti but also executive producer Esther García, who has worked on the production of Almodóvar's features since *Matador* (1986).

The credits thus stage a journey towards modernity and the everyday, even as they cite a postmodern graphic style familiar to Spanish audiences from decades of title sequences for Almodóvar's features, not to mention the films themselves. And the first shot is clearly contemporary. To a spacey, electronic drone the camera pans left over an urban landscape of mid-rise housing projects, the sun flaring into the lens. It comes to rest on a rooftop terrace [*azotea*], on which improbably white sheets billow into frame as puffy white clouds speed over a perfect blue sky. Main character Irene, her auburn hair pinned up and her full figure tightly fitted into a low-cut, white sleeveless dress, is hanging up the laundry. A close-up of Irene's basket leads to a tilt up behind her shoulder, revealing the presence of a middle-aged man facing her. Irene, in reverse shot, smiles and addresses him: 'Domingo'. A lengthy two shot follows in medium close-up: he asks how she is and she fills him in on her failing business (a bakery) and family problems (distraught daughters and demented mother). When he compliments her, she turns tearful and asks in turn why he looks so good. He replies: 'Because I'm dead'.

We cut to an interior (Irene's bedroom). Sleeping, in medium close-up, her brown hair spreads behind her round face on the white pillow and sheet. A voice off-screen shouts for her. She wakes and, as she leaps from the bed, a high angle reveals the whole set: an unremarkable bedroom in white and brown, with indistinct ornaments crowding the bedstead. Irene next runs towards the camera down a corridor shrouded in smoke (traditional dark wooden furniture includes a wall clock). In the kitchen is Palmira, Irene's mother. The two women are shot behind an impressive fire on the tablecloth. As Irene puts out the flames with a wet cloth, comic dialogue is heard in medium two shot: Palmira, forgetting what her daughter had told her (that 'fire is hot'), has lit a candle to Saint Pancras, whose feast day she claims it is.

We cut now to the bathroom, where in close-up a pair of chubby legs topped by red and white spotted knickers stands on a pair of scales. As Irene, off-screen, calls 'Magdalena!' the camera tilts up to show her younger daughter, her rounded figure topped by a black bra. The next sequence is breakfast in the kitchen. Beginning with a group shot of the three women (of the three female generations), the directors cut in traditional TV style to medium close-ups of each actress in turn as she speaks. They are set apart by costume: Irene's pale green robe; Palmira's black housecoat; and Magdalena's lumpy brown sweatshirt. When the phone rings, screen left, Irene speaks to her elder daughter Julia, who, we are told, has a history of trouble with men. We hear that Julia, dumped by boyfriend Jaime, will be coming back to live with the all-female family. As a parting shot, Irene warns her mother not to do any ironing (danger of fire, once more). Why doesn't she just watch TV? The old battleaxe replies that on the telly there's nothing but 'shit'.

Following on from Juan Gatti's contemporary-style graphics, this opening sequence appeals to a specific national history and to an everyday domesticity that could not be further from the first *Mujeres*. This is now a working-class setting, socially and aesthetically divorced from Almodóvar's cinematic universe. In the latter the only problems to be faced are those of love, and even those are as elegantly shod as they are shot. Conversely the TV show's first pan over the cityscape reveals familiar buildings that are recognizably contemporary and yet (unlike the first *Mujeres*' stylish skyline) impossible to identify. And here the problems that women face are as much socio-economic as emotional. Maternal Irene must care for an ageing parent and demanding children without the benefit of the high-paying and apparently undemanding media career enjoyed by childless Pepa. Significantly, part of this history of everyday life is television itself: the demented grandmother, with what will prove to be insistent insight, aligns herself with the received wisdom in Spain that television is trash. And the very precise comic reference to a saint's day is, of course, characteristic of older Spaniards' sense of the calendar. Yet more typical of the specificity of the TV text is the primacy of sound over image. While Almodóvar's visual poetry carries the burden of narrative in the first *Mujeres*, in the second *Mujeres* art design is relatively muted (colour is less intense) and rapid-paced dialogue predominates. As might be expected also, the average shot length in this opening sequence is shorter than in the film, by approximately one second.

Yet still there are features that aspire to cinematic distinction. As my shot-by-shot analyses suggest, there are several elements here that seem to cite *Mujeres al borde* directly. Thus the TV series begins, like the feature film, with a dream sequence and one that establishes that the main female character is distressed by her loss of a man. The significant difference here is, of course, that the focus is on the woman herself and her longing to see a late, loving husband, rather than on the philandering boyfriend and his many mistresses. The common theme of female abandonment is thus established more clearly and swiftly in the TV narrative. When Irene leaps from her bed (like Pepa) it is to discover (like Pepa a little later in the film) that her flat is on fire, although here a table substitutes for the film's bed. Even the series' small *azotea*, suspended above the city, is reminiscent of Pepa's ample terrace: in future episodes women will converse from one urban balcony to another.

Finally, there is some visual stylization here also. Irene's barrio is not as grungy as one might expect and the series' wardrobe will raise its game when zany Julia moves in with her Afghan coat and 'Free Winona' T-shirt. Irene's best friend, the randy Susana, will also sport a succession of highly coloured outfits. While the pervasive naturalism of television does not allow Ayaso and Sabroso the poetic licence Pedro exploits so successfully, the opening fantasy sequence of the second *Mujeres* (all white and blue) clearly aspires to a 'quality' look that viewers (and critics) might well expect from El Deseo's first TV series. And the opening also exploits memories of Almodóvar's features to heighten vicariously its own cultural distinction, even as it distances itself from a television medium dismissed within the show itself as trash.

Women: Take 2

In the first sequence of the TV *Mujeres* there are thus some very precise echoes of Almodóvar, and especially *Mujeres al borde*. Ayaso and Sabroso show themselves to be faithful disciples of the maestro. Plot synopses (laguiatv) for the first three episodes confirm the debt:

Episodio 1
Irene no puede más. Tiene que atender la panadería que le dejó su marido al morir, pero además cuidar de su madre, Palmira, que tiene principio de demencia senil, y de su hija Magda, una adolescente problemática. Para colmo Irene descubre que los papeles del negocio no están en regla y podría perderlo. Como a perro flaco todos son pulgas, Julia, la otra hija, regresa a casa, recién separada y con tendencia a visitar todos los bares del barrio. Todo este estrés hará que Irene se pelee con todo el mundo incluida su vecina Susana.

[Episode 1
Irene can't take any more. She has to look after the bakery her husband left her on his death, but also take care of her mother, Palmira, who's showing the first signs of Alzheimer's, and her daughter Magda, a difficult teenager. To cap it all, Irene discovers that the papers for her business are not in order and she could lose it. Things go from bad to worse. Julia, her other daughter, also comes home. She has recently split up with her boyfriend and likes to hang around the local bars. All this stress will make Irene argue with everyone, including her neighbour Susana.]

Episodio 2
Irene sigue peleada con su amiga Susana, Julia mientras tanto investiga obsesivamente buscando la razón por la cual su novio la abandonó y descubre así que éste es homosexual. La tensión que esto le provoca hará que Julia discuta con su abuela. Palmira, disgustada por la pelea, se escapa a Valencia, a casa de su hijo Ramón. Además Julia, con su carácter y en pleno síndrome de mujer engañada, hará lo que sus impulsos le dicten para vengarse de Jaime. Por otro lado Gabriel, que ya se ha hecho a la familia, recibe una visita de su pasado en Perú, que nos mostrará su lado más oscuro ... Mientras tanto, Manuel, el neurótico cliente de la panadería, se ofrecerá para ayudar a resolver los papeles del negocio. Finalmente Irene y Susana harán las paces y Julia, arrepentida de la discusión con su abuela y aconsejada por una psicóloga, se marchará a buscar a su abuela fugitiva.

[Episode 2
Irene is still angry with her friend Susana. Meanwhile Julia is desperately seeking the reason why her boyfriend dumped her and finds out that he's gay. Because of the pressure this puts on her, Julia argues with her grandmother. Palmira, unhappy about their fight, runs off to Valencia where her son Ramón lives. Julia, like the scorned woman that she is, will do all she can to get back at Jaime. Gabriel, who's become one of the family, has a visit from his past in Peru, which will show his darker side ... Meanwhile Manuel, a neurotic customer in the café, offers to sort out the business's accounts. Finally Irene and Susana will make up and Julia, upset by her argument and counselled by a psychologist, will set off to look for her missing grandmother.]

Episodio 3
Magda visita una ONG y allí conoce a Willy, un chico que le gusta. A partir de ese momento, su interés por la ONG se confunde con su interés por el chico, con el que empieza a salir. Su familia se entera de la relación, pero no sabe cómo reaccionar

cuando ve que Willy va en silla de ruedas ... Mientras, Julia echa de menos a Jaime y ... sale a la calle en busca de trabajo, decidida a todo. Palmira está obsesionada con el deporte y la vida sana. Necesita un chándal y no se le ocurre nada mejor que robarlo en una tienda. Gabriel se encara con el vigilante de seguridad. Cuando por fin se lo compran, Palmira sufre un accidente en su primera carrera por el parque: tropieza con Orlando, que persigue a Gabriel exigiéndole el pago de una deuda. Y una noticia: a Bea le conceden la beca que estaba esperando para volver a Londres. Raúl, a quien su madre acaba de pedirle que ponga la tienda a su nombre, se ve obligado a tomar una decisión.

[Episode 3]
Magda drops in at a charity where she meets Willy, a boy she fancies. From that moment her interest in the charity is mixed up with her interest in the boy, whom she starts to date. Her family find out about the relationship but don't know how to react when they discover that Willy uses a wheelchair ... Meanwhile Julia misses Jaime and ... goes out in search of a job, ready to do anything. Palmira is obsessed with sport and healthy living. She needs a tracksuit and goes so far as to shoplift one. Gabriel confronts the security guard. When finally they buy it, Palmira has an accident on her first run in the park: she bumps into Orlando, who is pursuing Gabriel for repayment of a debt. There is more news: Bea gets a grant to go back to London. Raúl, who has been asked by his mother to take over the shop, is forced to make a decision.

An examination of the shows themselves reveals further echoes of Almodóvar's films, which are not clear from the synopses. In the first episode, sexy Susana gives glum Irene antidepressants, and the women dreamily congratulate local junkie Nicolás on getting on to a methadone programme (drug use is, of course, frequent in early Almodóvar and the comic, shambling junkie is a distinctively Spanish figure). In the second episode Susana emerges wearing a lurid green face mask, as previously seen in the film sequence where Pepa visits the chemist in search of her antidepressants.

As in the first *Mujeres*, men are absent here. Irene has a son, Raúl, but, unlike his sisters he lives away from home. Julia's boyfriend has left her at the start of the first episode (like Pepa's at the start of the film), but in this case it is revealed in a would-be comic tag that the erring lover is gay. As Julia makes yet another late-night phone call to her ex (mobile phones are almost as prominent as landlines and the answerphone in Almodóvar) the camera pans right to show that he is in bed with an older man. The eccentric TV grandmother clearly derives from the Chus Lampreave character in *Qué he hecho yo...* (movingly re-enacted in *Volver*), although her inappropriate speech here is wearisome profanity rather than the film's more humorously incongruous teenage slang. Showy high-angle shots of Irene, with the camera looking down from on high as she sleeps, dresses, or works, echo the cinematography of both *Qué he hecho yo...* and the first *Mujeres* and remain relatively rare in TV drama. An unnervingly frequent motif in Almodóvar's filmography (girls peeing) makes itself felt in episode five.

More generally, Almodóvar's frequent tonal shifts between crazy comedy and pathos are integrated somewhat uncomfortably into the TV series, with Irene (expertly played by Fernández) shown as a strong, caring woman who is nonetheless often reduced to tears. And a reasonable budget provides a large, handsome construction, which serves for exteriors as well as interiors. The street set, based on a real-life fragment of Madrid's Fuencarral, is of a pedestrian precinct just off the main road. The apartments of Irene and Susana face each other on the first floor, while the ground floors are devoted to retail: an underwear shop (source of the sexy lingerie donned by more than one character), an accountant's office (in which Manuel, Irene's shy suitor, lives and works), and Irene's own bakery-cum-café (still named for her dead husband). This serves as a convenient point of encounter for the large cast, as well as a pretext for introducing additional characters such as the stereotypically sexy Afro-Cuban server Belinda. In frequent cinematic-style movements, the camera cranes up or down between flats and street (private and public spaces), integrating the two realms for characters and viewers. The extended viewing time of just over one hour (stretched to an hour and a half with commercial breaks) also permits more expansive plot and character development than is common in the shorter formats of other national television traditions. When, with the family reunited for dinner, Irene claims 'We're like four women in one of those old black and white films' it feels like an attenuated reference to those Hollywood women's pictures that Almodóvar has so consistently and precisely referenced.

The specificity of television, however, also makes itself felt, even in a series haunted by film. Although it begins with a dream sequence, the TV *Mujeres*, responding to the habitual naturalism of the medium and the much lower budgets, offers little material for fantasy, preferring to tell us, however inconclusively and inaccurately, about the real world. It is striking that the one non-naturalistic plot element (the appearance of the dead husband, who also pops up in Irene's bedroom) is abandoned after the first episode. It is a device used more consistently and effectively by HBO's much-praised *Six Feet Under* (shown in Spain, like *Mujeres*, on TVE2). The one unusual device that is kept up throughout the first season of thirteen episodes is the most transparently televisual in form: as the final credits roll, a character addresses the viewer directly, giving a sneak preview of plot points in next week's episode.

Unlike film, television has no stable canon, and the broad-brush history cited by the TV *Mujeres* is not of its own medium but of society. Although, unlike earlier Spanish shows such as Telecinco's *7 Vidas* ('Nine Lives', 1999–2006), *Mujeres* does not make party political jokes, it consistently invokes social and urban issues much debated in national life. Thus the opening premise involves care for the elderly in a rapidly ageing society. This theme itself leads to plot strands on immigration and racism. The crazy grandmother will be cared for by Gabriel, a too-good-to-be-true Peruvian immigrant: 'What', says the newly amorous Palmira, 'will people say in the barrio when they see me with a man who is so young ... and so dark?' (Episode 1). The introduction of a scary criminal who is extorting Gabriel for debts incurred through illegal immigration and is himself murdered in the local park (Episode 5), adds a disconcertingly sombre and violent note.

The social attitudes displayed, even in this working-class setting, are reassuringly politically correct. Julia, betrayed by her boyfriend, is anxious to reassure her friends (and the audience) that she is no 'homophobe', even when she comes across him kissing a man in a car (Episode 2). The underwritten and overworked social worker Mariana delivers some humourless dialogue on the crisis in Spanish services. When plain, studious Magda falls in love, it is with Willy, a cute disabled guy ('Sorry for not getting up') who works at an environmental NGO. Family members are sceptical about his sexual potency. She calls them 'phallocrats' (Episode 3). When he comes to visit his girlfriend's family he is shown struggling up the ramp in his wheelchair. Irene, trying to find a common interest, is keen to reassure her ecologically committed potential son-in-law that everyone in her household supports 'Mr Kyoto' (Episode 4). Even superficial Susana is granted plot strands that stray disconcertingly into seriousness. Having picked up a guy who insists on sex without a condom, she throws him out, flashing back to the dead husband who had physically abused her (Episode 5). The series thus addresses what is now called 'gender violence' in Spain, a theme that makes nightly news with a tally of deaths kept up through the year on television.

More generally, the stress on 'solidarity' (often over-explicit) echoes not just Almodóvar's female-centred films but also Spanish national media life. Spanish newspapers such as *El País* have permanent sections devoted to 'Solidaridad', as naturally as they do for domestic and foreign news, sport and television. But it should be stressed that in the Spanish televisual ecology, *Mujeres* is hardly innovative in addressing social issues. *7 Vidas*, once again, showed a gay wedding long before *Mujeres* had had Julia impregnated by a gay man (she chooses to carry the baby with the support of two fathers – Jaime and his new boyfriend). Once more television is cited in this construction of national history: the grandmother loves to re-watch on videotape the Christmas lottery draws called out by the traditional children in 'the old pesetas' (a focus for nostalgia since the introduction of the euro). The fact that the cast is relatively unfamiliar to audiences in Spain (having few credits in either film or television) enhances the everydayness of the show's texture. The movie stars who have designed to appear so frequently in quality Spanish TV drama are conspicuous by their absence here.

As all these examples suggest, the TV text of *Mujeres* is based predominantly on sound, not vision, on dialogue, not decor. The grandmother is prone to comic malapropism, demanding of the female carer who offers to help her: 'Are you one of those Lebanese (i.e. lesbians) from the telly?' and suspecting that her granddaughters have been indulging in 'drugaine' and 'vaginal sex'. But two textual resources are more complex and significant here than the verbal gags: music and montage. Often they are combined. Towards the end of the first episode, drunken deadbeat daughter Julia is in 'Peter's Pub', a late-night watering hole, where she sings a karaoke version of a defiant 'No me importa nada' ('I couldn't care less'). As the music continues (now in its original professional version) we cut in turn to Cuban Belinda, apparently insulted on her way to the metro; to the family, sans Julia, gloomily picking at their dinner in the flat; and to widowed, brutalized Susana trying on a sexy red dress in preparation for yet another night on the town.

The moral of female survival is, of course, central to Almodóvar's cinema. But the montage device here serves in typically televisual style to remind inattentive audiences of the current state of play with each of the ensemble cast. However, unlike in *Desperate Housewives* (ABC, 2004–) – the US show that was the most innovative female comedy drama at the time *Mujeres* was made, and was shown in Spain on the majority TVE1 channel – this catch-up montage recurs frequently, but not consistently, at the end of episodes. Likewise the karaoke device, in which key characters provide a musical interlude, is reminiscent of *Ally McBeal* (Fox, 1997–2002), another influential female-oriented series. In the US series, however, it served as a reassuringly regular date with the audience.

The featured source songs on *Mujeres*, which play at full length over the montages, tend, like those in Almodóvar's cinema, to be Latin American in origin. But they are more contemporary-sounding and less marked as theatrical or camp. Many, such as Pedro Marín's 'Aire' and Gato Pérez's 'Gitanitos y morenos', come from the 1980s, the period of the first *Mujeres*. The insistent musical cues of the incidental music by newcomer Arturo Soriano, however, are reminiscent of that much-debased TV genre, the telenovela, prompting in turn reverie (the spacey electronica), whimsical humour (a *Desperate Housewives*-style pizzicato), or melancholy (a plangent harmonica).

Music and montage thus attempt to stitch together the varied and indeterminate TV text, which runs parallel to everyday life and is much more flexible than the 90 minutes of a feature film. Yet, as neophytes in the series drama form, El Deseo and their chosen creators are unskilled at structuring the flow. Characters are bizarrely inconsistent: one week the grandmother is on a health kick (reciting her rosary as she does gymnastics), the next she proclaims herself a 'butter junky'. Structuring devices are introduced (the dream sequence, the karaoke bar), only to be abandoned after a couple of weeks. For one episode only Manuel (Irene's accountant suitor) is granted a self-help voice-over, which plays over the full hour and is even used as a non-musical background for the montage sequence (the show's many troubled couples are shown to the sound of Manuel's plangent plea for love). The drama is thus not consistent enough to fulfil audience expectations of familiarity (even the Almodóvar references soon fade away). But neither is it novel enough to excite audience curiosity. The most important deep-level plot strand (Irene's slow-motion, on-off romance with timid Manuel) is exhausted before it finally reaches consummation in a dreary Episode 10. While TV viewers crave familiarity, they fear mere repetition. Mujeres fails to draw the line between these two conflicting, but tantalizingly similar, properties.

This brings us to value and quality, one of the avowed ends of El Deseo's mission statement. While *Mujeres* clearly fulfilled the company's desire for diversification into other audiovisual products not helmed by Pedro, it can hardly be claimed as a success, either commercial or artistic. Long-time faithful supporters of Almodóvar such as Vicente Molina Foix praised individual elements (those Gatti credits, Teresa Lozano's performance as Palmira). But, as reported in the press, the production process of the series proved as problematic as its reception.

Desperate daughters

An account of the production and distribution context of the TV *Mujeres* will help to connect the textual analysis above to the economic criteria presented by Diego Pajuelo Almodóvar at the time the series was being shot. As *El País* reported on the day of the premiere (18 September 2006), shooting for *Mujeres* had been completed a year before, on the understanding that the much-anticipated new drama would be shown on the mass entertainment channel TVE1 (T. B. G.). Now the series was being broadcast, after a mysterious delay, on the minority cultural channel TVE2 (and scheduled on a Monday – the night with the lowest audience of the week – albeit at 10.30 pm, Spanish prime time). *El País* cited TVE's head of drama, who claimed that the project was 'riskier' than more 'familiar' programmes on the main channel. The article stresses the 'realistic' and 'ironic' tone of the show, its everyday nature ('la vida cotidiana'), and the theme of female solidarity, citing a line of dialogue spoken by Palmira: 'We're a gang of single women who need each other'. It was also claimed that the real-life family backgrounds of the novice creators (who hail, in fact, not from Madrid but from the distant Canary Islands) provided the original source for the various plot lines, thus enhancing the show's typically televisual sense of everydayness.

Curiously, given El Deseo's lack of experience in the relentless rhythm of TV production (their features typically take two years, while a television episode is shot in a week), they chose as producing partner another company without a clear track record in the medium. Mediapro is best known as co-producer of some prizewinning feature films on social issues, such as unemployment (*Los lunes al sol*, 'Mondays in the Sun', 2002) and prostitution (*Princesas*, 'Princesses', 2005). Their only substantial TV project is *España directo* ('Spain Live', TVE1, 2005–), a breathless collage of live reporting on lifestyles from around the Peninsula, which is hardly a preparation for the very different discipline of long-form fiction.

In spite of continuing loss of share (the percentage of Spaniards watching the channel night by night), TVE remained in 2006 the only public service broadcaster in Spain and one that was now fully open to independent production from companies such as El Deseo and Mediapro. A successful show such as *Cuéntame cómo pasó* ('Tell Me How It Happened', 2001–), a long-running period drama, proved that the much-reviled state broadcaster could still unite the nation around a quality fiction on TVE1, even when the show was not made in-house but was bought in from a private producer. TVE's little-watched second channel (known as 'la 2') still held fast to cultural programming, such as documentaries. But, in spite of their avowed concern for quality, El Deseo had not anticipated being marginalized on the minority channel.

As a new broom at RTVE, the Director General, academic Carmen Caffarel, professed (like El Deseo) an organizational vision that focused on 'quality' in all genres, including well produced mass entertainment. This involved her greenlighting no fewer than four new dramas screened on TVE1 in 2006, which, as Manuel Palacio has noted (76), were all female-centred. The least successful of these was the farcical flat-share comedy *Con dos tacones* (see Chapter 2), in the first episode of which a spurned wife holds her erring husband hostage with a pistol. This was scheduled on the same night as the import *Desperate Housewives*, whose Spanish translation was, significantly perhaps, *Mujeres desesperadas* (Palacio 77). Public television was thus already awash with darkly comic abandoned women when *Mujeres* made its delayed entrance. Like Julia's 'Free Winona' T-shirt, El Deseo's TV flagship was now well past its sell-by date.

Moreover, post-Almodóvar television (as I have called it), unconnected with El Deseo, had already had great successes on the private channels. Tele 5's *7 Vidas* had gone further into risky gender territory by staging a lesbian marriage well before Spanish law changed to allow such an event. Antena 3's *Aquí no hay quien viva* ('No-one Can Live Here', the most popular programme of the 2000s) had also experimented with queer comedy (two gay men plan to have a child with a lesbian) and urban issues (the show was set in a shared apartment building). In comparison *Mujeres*' exploration of these topics is timid.

Hence while the 'continuity of production' required of a TV series fits with El Deseo's organizational vision (anxious as it is to extend the first 'cycle of exploitation'), the 'risk assessment' made by executive producers such as Esther García was clearly faulty. El Deseo could hardly have anticipated TVE's lengthy delay in airing the show. But they should have seen that, in the audiovisual ecology that Pedro had himself helped to create, their new show's premise was hardly innovative. Certainly, as the episodes rolled on, the teleplays lacked the 'believable plot' and 'well rounded characters' El Deseo claims to seek in the film scripts that, when developed, also serve the business mission of diversification.

Such an end is not always easy to square with quality. After all, cultural distinction is what economists call a 'positional good'; that is to say, it is something that is necessarily in short supply (*Economist*). By definition, the majority of films or TV shows cannot be prestigious successes that promote and preserve the figure of their creators. If *Volver* has proved one of Almodóvar's greatest hits both commercially and critically, it is at the expense of many other titles in the zero sum game of art house film. The old master Pedro kept his distance from the TV *Mujeres*, which carried, nonetheless, the imprimatur of his studio and benefited from the media attention focused on him and it. While *Mujeres al borde* is now consecrated as a piece of 'classic cinema' (acclaimed by Peter Evans as a Modern Classic and presented by José Arroyo as one of the best comedies in film history), *Mujeres* tout court, even on first broadcast, seemed like 'old television', its themes and aesthetic over-familiar.

The perceived difference between 'classic cinema' and 'old television', noted by John Caughie (13), is derived to some extent from the specificity of the two media themselves: the availability of television – unlike film – and its integration into and limitation by everyday, national life, have made it much more difficult for an accepted canon of classic shows to emerge. The suspicion arises, moreover, that El Deseo, accustomed to and acclaimed in the transnational film market from which it draws most of its revenue, were not well placed to enter the domestic television scene. Not different enough to be (cinematically) distinctive and not familiar enough to be (televisually) endearing, the TV *Mujeres* thus fell between two media stools.

Yet as best friends Irene and Susana chat on their tiny balconies (the camera characteristically cranes back to a two shot at the end of Episode 11), there is no doubt that they are the TV daughters, desperate but optimistic, of Pepa and Marisa on their big-screen penthouse terrace some twenty years before. It is an urban female genealogy that deserves to be studied and celebrated.

Mujeres al borde de un ataque de nervios
('Women on the Verge of a Nervous Breakdown', 1988)

Director and screenwriter	Pedro Almodóvar
Production company	El Deseo
Executive producer	Agustín Almodóvar
Production manager	Esther García
Cinematographer	José Luis Alcaine
Costume design	José María Cossío
Original music	Bernardo Bonezzi
Credit design	Juan Gatti

Cast

Carmen Maura	Pepa
Fernando Guillén	Iván
Julieta Serrano	Lucía
Antonio Banderas	Carlos
María Barranco	Candela
Rossy de Palma	Marisa

Mujeres ('Women', TVE2, 2006)

Production companies	El Deseo, Mediapro
Executive producers	Esther García, Javier Méndez
Directors and chief writers	Dunia Ayaso, Féliz Sabroso
Original music	Arturio Soriano
Credit design	Juan Gatti

Cast

Chiqui Fernández	Irene
Teresa Lozano	Palmira
Carmen Ruiz	Julia
Inma Cuevas	Magda
Bart Santana	Raúl
Gracia Olayo	Susana
Antonio Gil	Manuel
Marilyn Torres	Belinda

Works Cited

Allinson, Mark. *A Spanish Labyrinth: The Films of Pedro Almodóvar*. London: I. B. Tauris, 2001.
Arroyo, José. Introduction. (UK DVD) *Women on the Verge of a Nervous Breakdown*. Almodóvar: The Collection. Vol. 1. Optimum, 2005.
Caparrós Lera, J. M. *El cine español de la democracia*. Barcelona: Anthropos, 1992.
Caughie, John. *Television Drama*. Oxford: Oxford UP, 2000.
D'Lugo, Marvin. *Pedro Almodóvar*. Urbana and Chicago: U of Illinois P, 2006.
Economist, The. 'Happiness (and How to Measure It)'. 23 Dec. 2006: 13.
Evans, Peter. *Women on the Verge of a Nervous Breakdown*. London: BFI, 1996.
Hergueta, José A. 'A vueltas con P. A'. [sic] Ed. Miguel Albaladejo, et al. *Los fantasmas del deseo: el cine de Pedro Almodóvar*. Madrid: Taller 87, 1988. 10–13.
Laguiatv. Synopses of episodes of *Mujeres*. Accessed 10 Jan. 2007.
<http://www.laguiatv.com/serie_episodios_sinop.php?id=155872&t=1&e=1>
Molina Foix, Vicente. 'A la parrilla: con y sin'. *El País* 20 Sept. 2006. Accessed 10 Jan. 2007. <http://www.elpais.com/articulo/radio/television/elpepirtv/20060920elpepirtv_5/Tes>.
Pajuelo Almodóvar, Diego. Unpublished presentation on El Deseo's financial strategy. Given at Universidad Complutense, Madrid, 1 Dec. 2005.
Palacio, Manuel. 'La televisión pública española (TVE) en la era de José Luis Rodríguez Zapatero'. *Journal of Spanish Cultural Studies* 8.1 (2007). 71–83.
Sánchez Biosca, Vicente. 'El elixir aromático de la postmodernidad o la comedia según Pedro Almodóvar'. *Escritos sobre el cine español 1973-87*. Ed. José A. Hurtado and Francisco M. Picó. Valencia: Filmoteca, 1989. 11–24.
Smith, Paul Julian. *Desire Unlimited: The Cinema of Pedro Almodóvar*. 2nd ed. London and New York: Verso, 2000.
T. B. G. 'La 2 estrena la serie *Mujeres* un año después de su rodaje'. *El País* 18 Sept. 2006. Accessed 10 Jan. 2007. <http://www.elpais.com/articulo/radio/television/estrena/serie/Mujeres/ano/despues/rodaje/elpporgen/20060918 elpepirtv_1/Tes/>

CHAPTER TWO

City Girls II: Television's Urban Women, Pre- and Post-Almodóvar

Women, television and the city

Four young women stride down a city street. Shoulder by shoulder and engaged in lively conversation, they gesture, palms outstretched, and catch each other's eyes. Three, their hair permed into place, wear fitted skirts, just skimming the knee, and modish heels. Two carry large handbags, plain and patterned, in their right hands. One, the most modern of all, sports short, tousled hair, a mannish coat and cravat, skinny cigarette pants and casual flats. Behind them we glimpse a contemporary urban building: anonymous walls, perhaps of concrete, and a glassy entrance, banded by vertical metal rails. The wide pavement beneath their elegant feet is made of modern paving stones, not traditional cobbles, but is stained nonetheless with the trace of urban traffic.

The year is 1961 and these are the four protagonists of *Chicas en la ciudad* ('Girls in the City'), a long-lost situation comedy created by veteran Jaime de Armiñán. Such production stills are all that survive of a seminal 15-minute drama that founded a genre and a character type: the story of the city girl (single, working and independent), whose narrative will be based more on her relationships with familiar and dependable female friends than with shady and unreliable male suitors. While the genre has clear contemporary echoes in recent US sitcom and drama, it is something of a shock to come across it in Francoist TV, so rigidly controlled by the regime.

As we shall see, *Chicas en la ciudad* thus testifies to, or even anticipates, social changes or contradictions set in train by the modernizing programme of the technocrats of the 1960s. But as an Ur-text for Spanish city girls on statecontrolled Televisión Española, the series can also be compared with later manifestations of the genre on the same channel in the democratic era, such as Fernando Trueba's TV movies run under the banner *La mujer de tu vida* ('The Woman of Your Life', 1990; 1994), and, most recently, the female flat-share sitcom *Con dos tacones* ('On Two Heels', 2006). Other titles, such as Fernando Colomo's serial *Las Chicas de hoy en día* ('Girls of Today', 1991–92), could clearly also be studied. The resilience or persistence of this critically neglected format on

Spanish television thus suggests that it is especially significant for the medium in general, and that it can serve as a litmus test for particular changes in the Spanish television ecology and, indeed, in Spanish society, over the decades.

But as we examine the four girls, frozen in mid-stride on the city pavement, the first association that comes to mind is not *Sex in the City* (HBO, 1998–2004) but *Women on the Verge*. Almodóvar's affection for the US female-centred sex comedies of his youth, such as *How to Marry a Millionaire*, is well known. Less cited as an influence are the TV series of his home country, which were highly successful, but ephemeral: they were broadcast live and not yet preserved on tape. It remains the case, however, that retrospectively such early television narratives take on a new significance; and, given Almodóvar's extraordinary prestige and impact it would be most unlikely that his cinema would, in turn, have had no repercussions on a television that by the 1980s and 1990s aspired to the production values of cinema. A working hypothesis, then, would be that Almodóvar's audience was

3 Walking in the city: *Chicas en la ciudad*

already schooled in the conventions of the city girl genre before he perfected it on film, thus inadvertently diverting it back onto the small screen. The dilemmas of women on the verge of an urban breakdown are thus repeatedly worked through on television, both before and after they explode into much more dramatic and highly coloured visibility on the big screen.

Women, television, and the city: it is not easy to think through the mutual interaction of these three factors and I know of no Spanish scholars who have studied this constellation of themes. In an Anglo-American context, however, media specialists have long explored women and television, with occasional forays into the question of urban space. For example, in Lynn Spigel and Denise Mann's *Private Screenings: Television and the Female Consumer* (1992), contributors explore gender and US TV from the 1950s to the present day in many genres: popular discourse on television and in domestic space; the 'spectacularization of everyday life', when Hollywood stars were 'recycled' on early TV variety shows; sitcoms and suburbs; the 'new women' of 1980s divorcee households; soap opera and the (surprisingly problematic) 'marriage motif'; and melodrama and consumer culture.

As the editors write in their introduction, 'television has always had its eye on women', the primary consumers in their households (vii). In its attempt to appeal to women consumers, television thus 'inserts itself into their everyday lives, both at home and in the marketplace'. television consumption is to be understood in two, implicitly gendered, ways: the 'display of commodities and consumer lifestyles' and 'the consumption of television itself – how audiences understand television programs and [...] how the medium defines femininity and female desire'. Integrating feminist theories of representation with methods of cultural history and interpretation, the essays attempt to 'move away from grand generalizations of television', decried as '"big bang" theories of mass culture and its social effects' (viii). 'Close analysis and historical contextualization' thus serve as a 'necessary complement and corrective' to generalizations that, interestingly enough, are here presented in spatial terms: 'whether a democratic "global village" or a ruinous "vast wasteland", television has typically been conceptualized as an amorphous geographical terrain across which people communicate only in the most abstract, reified ways' (xiii).

Four years later Bonnie J. Dow explored *Prime-Time Feminism: Television, Media Culture, and the Women's Movement since 1970* (1996). Although here the focus is more on production than consumption, Dow also gives a historical survey of American television's women, from the 'lifestyle feminism' of the 1970s, through the 'emerging woman' of prime-time divorce, to the 'post-feminist' designing and maternal women of the 1980s and 1990s. Significantly, however, like Spigel and Mann before her, Dow rejects 'big bang' theories of television as a cultural wasteland:

> [A]n unrelenting focus on television as a social problem [...] blinds us to the complexity of television programming as, simultaneously, a commodity, an art form, and an important ideological forum for public discourse about social issues and social change. (Dow: 1)

An unabashed TV fan, she believes the medium has 'contributed to the cultural conversation about feminism [...] at different historical moments over the past twenty-five years' (xiv), working 'rhetorically to negotiate social issues: to define them, to represent them, and, ultimately, to offer visions of their meanings and implications' (xv). Textual strategies ('genre, plot, character development, narrative structure') thus intersect with specific and changing cultural contexts (xvi).

This sense of 'teleliteracy' (an awareness of the relationship between television's past, present and, indeed, future) emphasizes the medium's 'role in mediating social change, in reproducing assumptions about women's "appropriate" roles, and in appealing to and constructing a subjectivity for women as a television audience' (xix). In a significantly spatial term once more, a 'woman's place' (both on and off the screen) may shift from 'specific caretaking behaviors ranging from cooking, cleaning and child-rearing [and] more general qualities of nurturance and emotional support' (xxi) to 'independence, participation in the work force, individual freedom, and self-control' (xxii). But still the latter constellation of qualities contains the ghostly remnant of the former within it.

The only theoretical account I am aware of that treats the theme of women, television and the city is the dialogue between British media scholar Karen Lury and feminist cultural geographer Doreen Massey that serves as an introduction to the special issue of *Screen* entitled 'Space/Place/City' (see Lury and Massey). The two scholars begin by exploring the 'deep historical connection between the development of cinema and a particular form and type of urbanization' (230). While agreeing with Lury that cities are characterized by 'intensity [...] the discordant, the different, the supposedly incongruous', Massey argues that this density and intensity – 'a vast variety of different human trajectories' (231) – this 'coexisting multiplicity' or 'intense and unexpected juxtaposition' (232), is the product of spatial relations, not simply the arena within which those relations are played out.

For Lury, the role of film here is to

> relate the construction of the diegesis (the 'world') of the film (emphasizing the use of framing, the use of landscape, architecture and mise en scène, the placing of characters within particular geographical locations) with the lived world of actual social relations. (Lury and Massey 233)

Unlike film, however, television is, in addition, 'embedded into the temporal and spatial routines of everyday life [and thus] presents itself as open, unfixed, multiple' (234). Not simply a 'representation of the world' but, rather, 'part of lived experience', 'watching television', argues Lury, is 'an always-unfinished process [that] mirrors the experience of the pedestrian' (236). Here Lury cites Massey's account of an urban walk down London's workaday Kilburn High Road, in which the geographer attempts to insert 'distinct groups of people' (such as 'the pensioner [...] eating British working-class-style fish and chips from a Chinese take-away, watching a US film on a Japanese television') into global relations. Television can 'change our way of thinking' about such apparently banal urban spaces, making visible the way in which they are open and interrelated and structured by power relations, which bind them together.

Lury adds a warning, however. In television studies

> the process of 'thick description' that the acknowledgement of the importance and specifics of space and place demands can become so particular, so finely grained that it becomes limited or impossible as an interpretive framework. (237)

For Massey also the incorporation of space into the analysis (of television, of gender) must be integrated with an awareness of temporality. The challenges of 'taking space seriously' are thus those of navigating the extremes of generality and specificity, and avoiding the 'freezing' or 'fixing' of spatiality outside historical change and lived experience. It is a tricky balancing act, attempted in very different ways by the three female-centred urban comedies I examine below.

Chicas en la ciudad ('Girls in the City', 1961)

In the only scholarly account of Jaime de Armiñán's career of which I am aware, Catalina Buezo makes a strong case for him as a unique auteur, successively pursuing distinct aesthetic and social interests in theatre, television, film and, finally, prose fiction. Buezo argues that the broad-brush dismissal of late Francoist culture by critics has meant that Armiñán's importance as an intermediary or bridge between dictatorship and democracy (a function that is at once political, social and cultural) has not been recognized:

> Vive este dramaturgo, guionista de televisión, cineasta y narrador en la confluencia de dos épocas. Políticamente significa el tránsito de la España del régimen a la de la constitución democrática; socialmente, la sustitución de unos valores caducos por los ideales de progreso y libertad; culturalmente, la búsqueda de nuevos soportes literarios, que suponen la incursión de este 'contador de historias' en el terreno de la televisión, el teatro y el cine.

> [This playwright, TV dramatist, filmmaker, and novelist lived at the crossroads of two periods. Politically, he marked the transition in Spain from the [Francoist] regime to a democratic constitution; socially, the replacement of outdated values by the ideals of progress and freedom; and culturally the quest for new narrative formats, which enabled this 'storyteller' to contribute to the fields of television, theatre, and cinema.]

Rejecting the escapist comedies of manners dominant in the theatre of the 1950s, Armiñán turned to television as a vital new medium for the critique of social problems. It is a critique (according to Buezo) that is not bitter, but rather sentimental in tone, seeking both to evade the restrictions of censorship and to exploit the limits of what was possible at the time. Armiñán, whether bravely or cannily, anticipated the decline of autarchism and centralism and the regime's attempt to open up the Spanish economy (including the new television industry) to the outside world. This process was to continue with the nomination of the reformist Manuel Fraga as Minister of Information and Tourism in 1962, the opening of new TV studios in Prado del Rey, and the participation of Televisión Española in foreign festivals.

As Buezo notes, Armiñán's first job in television, in 1957, was as 'ghost-writer' for his wife, who was the hostess of a talk show called, significantly, *Entre nosotras* ('Between Us Women') (according to IMDb, the then-youthful Chus Lampreave, a future Almodóvar regular, was a co-host). After initial failures in children's programming, Armiñán returned with a new format for adults. *Galería de maridos* ('Portraits of Husbands', 1959) depicted in an economical fifteen minutes a typology of different husbands: examples included the shy, the old-fashioned, the gloomy, the football fan, the mummy's boy and the forgetful. *Galería de esposas* followed the next year ('Portraits of Wives', 1960) with vignettes of jealous, pretentious, pessimistic, fantasizing, and hysterical wives, among others. Buezo briefly mentions that Armiñán's unique analysis of the 'woman's world' on early television will continue with his *Mujeres solas* ('Single Women', 1961), later rebaptized *Chicas en la ciudad*, and subsequently *Trío de damas* ('Three Queens', 1962), *Las doce caras de Eva* ('The Twelve Faces of Eve', 1971) and *Tres eran tres* ('Three in a Row', 1972). The question of gender was thus intimately, if discreetly, linked to that of modernization and, indeed, of television itself.

Clearly, it is difficult to analyse early television drama that was transmitted live. In the case of Armiñán, however, there is a unique record: published scripts of a selection of no fewer than four of his strands of micro-dramas, complete with production stills. Indeed, the very fact of publication shows that, far from dismissing television as trash, in the style of current commentators, Spaniards respected early production in the medium: *Guiones de TV* was published in 1963 by a Barcelona film club in the same series as studies of Soviet, neo-realist, and French New Wave cinema. The anonymous foreword to the volume laments the lack of bibliography on the medium in Spain (a complaint that would echo down the decades) (Armiñán 9). It also raises, via Bazin, the quest for the specificity of television (10), and anticipates the book's multiple readership: student screen-writers who require an example of good practice in the new medium; avid viewers who need a reminder of a 'fleeting' moment, now preserved for posterity; and ordinary readers (presumably those without access to a still relatively rare TV set), who simply wish to educate and entertain themselves (11).

In his own introduction Armiñán gives a somewhat ironic account of his 'five years in television', recounting in a self-deprecating key some of the story retold by Buezo 40 years later. Armiñán, creator and director of so many series, generously stresses the contribution made by his skilled actors, many with theatrical experience, who would soon become a surrogate family: established star Adolfo Marsillach played the multiple husbands in the TV 'galleries', while the wives were impersonated by newcomer Amparo Baró (soon to be the spiky-haired, trouser-clad gamine in *Chicas en la ciudad*) (16). Armiñán stresses the double difficulty of live TV for the actor: unlike theatre there is no audience to feed off and unlike cinema there is no possibility of reshooting a fluffed take (18). Moreover, he is clearly aware of the distinctively domestic nature (and, indeed, power) of the new medium. Invited into the home to share a meal with the family, the TV actor labours under the new burden of not making a bad impression [*caer mal*] (18). Those whose invitation is welcome, however, already benefit from a unique national presence and reach: at the San Sebastian film festival, where Marsillach won best actor, he was asked for autographs by TV fans who, heedless of his cinematic success, requested him to sign not his own name but that of his small-screen character, Bruno (19).

The essay that follows Armiñán's professional biography, by critic Enrique del Corral ('Viriato'), complements his production-led account with a more theoretical analysis giving valuable evidence for debates around television at this crucial time. Del Corral cites (like Armiñán himself elsewhere) Paddy Chayevsky (creator of the mythical *Marty*, 1953) on television drama, defined as 'the wonderful world of everyday things' (25). Television, del Corral goes on, explores new and unexpected territory: man himself, caught on the horns of a psychological dilemma (26). The then technical limitations of the medium (the reliance on close-ups, a small cast and a single set) heighten this sense of concrete, social reality. While cinema has conquered space, television has moved in the opposite direction: from the environment to the individual (27). The uniqueness of Armiñán is that, unlike others who have come from theatre or film, he has understood the specificity of the medium. In spite of the brevity of his dramas, their 'types' are rooted in reality, playing successfully week after week in the domesticated *sobremesa* time slot (30). The 'prefabricated dream' of television has thus become 'one of the realities of our world, increasingly stuck and attached [*pegado, apegado*] to those realities'.

When we turn to the scripts, we note that the most striking formal device is direct address to camera. Thus the shy husband, discovered by the viewer hidden behind an ample armchair, begins his piece by greeting the audience, introducing himself, and excusing his embarrassment at talking 'in public'

(39). As Bruno reluctantly reveals his love for Paula (the names are repeated throughout the series, even as the characters and situations change) a stage hand sets up the single set: a café in which, in spite or perhaps because of his timidity, his girlfriend will ultimately declare her love for him (48). In another episode the 'old fashioned' husband, who is, we are told, 'severely dressed', speaks to the audience with yet more formality and from a domestic interior described as 'anachronistic and antiquated' and decorated with faded curtains and uncomfortable furniture: 'Buenas tardes, señoras. Buenas tardes, señores. ¿Están ustedes bien? Yo bien, muchas gracias.' [Good afternoon, ladies. Good afternoon, gentlemen. Are you well? I'm fine, thank you.] (Armiñan 49). Note that he addresses women and men separately and presumes, in turn, a polite response from attentive viewers. This Bruno even presents his business card to camera, thus facilitating a shift back to the single set, where Paula is busy cleaning the furniture, but dressed in (scandalous) slacks (50). Unusually, in this episode it is she who signs off direct to the viewers, hoping to see them next Sunday and apologizing for her casual clothing (although she is, she says, so 'cute' in slacks) (59).

Elsewhere, the football fan offers the audience a nonsensical chant direct from the stand ('¡Alabí, alabá, alabimbombá, señores!') (70), while the mummy's boy speaks from a flat full of photos of the matriarch he will invite to an intimate dinner on his wife's birthday (85). A more ambitious studio set, intended for the forgetful husband, contains three urban exteriors in one: a tram window and seat, a café table and a park bench (88). By the end of the playlet this last Bruno has no appointments left to remember: now he is married, he and Paula can just spend the whole weekend together. The couple both bid farewell to the audience, looking forward to seeing them (to seeing us) next Sunday (97).

It seems plausible that this now obtrusive device of direct address to camera was intended to school novice audiences, unskilled in entertaining uninvited electronic house guests, in the conventions of TV drama. Whatever the case, there is no doubt that direct address is a specifically televisual technique that serves quite explicitly to relate the construction of the fictional diegesis to the lived world of actual social relations. Such a relation is embedded not only in the temporal routines of everyday life (the repeated and precise references to the now distant Sunday afternoons when the show was both performed and transmitted), but also in the representation, however schematic, of specific geographical and urban locations that are often exteriors (the café, the stadium, the park). Even the interiors are explicitly located according to class and taste. We have a glimpse here of a medium new in Spain that was produced and, we may assume from its immense popularity, consumed in such a way that it was no mere representation of the world but rather a newly possible part of lived experience.

But whose experience? While the adaptable wives frequently get the better of their inflexible spouses (the successive Paulas propose marriage to a shy suitor or refuse to take off their modern slacks for an 'anachronistic' spouse), it is striking that the women are rarely permitted the direct address device even in the pendant series, *Galería de esposas*, that followed on from the 'typology' of the husbands. Here it remains the men who complain to camera of their wives' jealousy or pretentiousness (99; 108). While the fantasist and the hysteric do introduce themselves directly to viewers (128; 139), these are stereotypical representations that no longer mediate social change, but rather reproduce traditional assumptions about women's appropriate roles. The construction of subjectivity for women as a TV audience is thus left until the 'galleries' immediate successor, *Chicas en la ciudad*, the series that Armiñán himself claims as the beginning of his experiment with elements of social critique that would, nonetheless, remain acceptable to censors and audience alike (cited by Buezo).

The surviving scripts, a precious remnant of an evanescent cultural form, are six in number. The four single 'girls' live first in a women's hostel in Madrid, later in a shared flat served by a homely maid (played by already veteran character actor Rafaela Aparicio). Armiñán describes each in turn. Paula (Amparo Baró) is sentimental, but with hidden strength (a 'steel butterfly' [*mariposa con garras*] (21)). Ester (Alicia Hermida, still working on TVE some 40 years later in period drama *Cuéntame*) is an optimistic nurse. Flirty Verónica (Elena María Tejeiro) studies law. Laura (Maite Bisco) is a valiant immigrant from a rural village. Scheduling problems meant that in the second season the last two were replaced by Erika (Irán Eory), a model from exotic Hungary, and Coro (Paula Martel), who works in a bookshop (22). It is this definitive cast that is strolling in the street in the image with which I began this chapter, the still used on the cover of the published version of the scripts.

The first episode ('Un viejo tema', 'The Same Old Story') treats the battle of the sexes. Relaxing in the library of the young ladies' hostel named for Mary Queen of Scots (it is summer and the windows are open), exile Erika is reading *Don Quixote* in her native language, a work the local Verónica, a girl 'of her time', has not troubled to read herself (150). Enter Ester, still in nurse's uniform, with a bottle and glasses: her doctor boyfriend has broken off their date (a trip to the cinema) just to perform a tonsil operation! Men should be wiped from the face of the earth. When Verónica and Erika claim that what women want is marriage, Coro joins the fray: who can believe women still think like this in Spain? The girls drink and argue as Erika smashes glasses on the floor with pseudo-Slavic abandon. Ester claims that women should do more than fry eggs and clean a husband's shoes; they've spent a hundred years fighting for their rights. Erika rejoins that they would do better just to let themselves be loved. The maid appears. Dinner is served and the argument must be postponed. But the friends are all agreed on one thing: that they have debated the rights of women, while the only subject men are likely to discuss over a drink is football (159).

What is striking here is the explicitness with which television is used as an ideological forum for public discourse about the new or emergent woman and the battle of the sexes. The script openly negotiates this crucial social issue: defining the problem (work or marriage?), representing it (with conflicting female opinions), and offering a certain vision of its meaning and implications. Two more factors stand out. This is a protected all-woman urban space, in which no man appears. And the dialogue (or rather, polylogue) is unfinished. Like a walk in a city street or a session of television-watching, women's everyday conversation is always unfinished, to be continued after dinner or in the next episode.

In the second script feisty Ester arranges a rendezvous with her busy boyfriend. The problem is that he is bringing a friend who needs a date (160). Bookish Coro fills in, against her better judgement. Here the action takes place outside the hostel in a city café. The friend turns out to be no doctor, like Ester's suave mate, but a loutish orderly. He tries to impress Coro by challenging her to arm wrestle and offers to stop a bus with his bare hands. Finally she is won over, not by his machismo but by his unexpected shyness: blushing hot red, he says that to look at her is like looking at the sun. Coro now wishes she could take him back to the hostel. They have no future together, but she will never forget her strange suitor.

The third script continues to chart (to create?) this changing equilibrium between the sexes in the city. Here the setting is the street, with a stone staircase behind, blocks of flats in the background, and traffic noise over the dialogue. A 'ragged' man sits on the steps. It is late afternoon (the same time that the series was aired) and Ester and Paula are waiting for their friends to go to the pictures. The girls offer the tramp money, which he refuses. His home, he says, is the world (one girl asks if he is a Communist) and his movie screen is limited only by the horizon. The ragtag philosopher claims that the cinema of nature is as dramatic as any made by man. As he wanders off the girls agree: they will never see the poetic vagabond again, but he is a real man 'in the full sense of the word' [*un hombre hecho y derecho*]. While the element of social critique is typically sentimental (although the tramp does indeed take the girls' peseta in the end), the playlet presents the city as a place of intense and unexpected juxtaposition, and one that young women can enjoy without let or hindrance.

The next urban location is an optician's waiting room. Here, inexplicably, the definition of femininity and female desire is much more retrograde: all four girls compete for the attentions of the handsome specialist, who, horror of horrors, turns out to be married. The broad humour comes not from the subtle irony or open conflict of previous episodes but from the vain and farcical pretence that pretty girls don't need glasses. The following episode treats the equally unpromising topic of fashion, with one girl slavishly following French trends and another saying women should wear what they like. Each of these immigrants to Madrid is agreed, however, that the best dressers are in their own home regions (the Basque Country, Catalonia and Asturias) or, indeed, Erika's Eastern Bloc (197). But there follows a unique moment of direct address to camera: Coro recounts how the four friends have found a flat of their own in a distant district, to which they had to walk, braving the catcalls of local men (200). It is a profession of female independence echoed in the last script, where the girls attempt to raise the morale of a timorous and elderly author who is waiting in vain to sign copies of his work at Coro's bookshop (201).

There are thus clear discontinuities in the scripts that survive from this early series. Within what is a founding moment of the city girls genre, the textual strategies of plot, character development and narrative structure are unusually unstable. With no background in 'teleliteracy' to fall back on, producers and consumers are free to collaborate on narratives that intersect with specific and changing cultural contexts in unpredictable ways. However the 'woman's place' for these young singletons involves no caretaking of men, as traditional qualities of nurturance and emotional support are reserved for female friends. The celebration of emergent independence, participation in the workforce, individual freedom and self-control is, nonetheless, contradicted by the vestigial (or, indeed, socially dominant) ideology of the period of female superficiality and subservience, which makes its ghostly presence felt even here in the quintessentially modern medium. The show thus embodies an example of coexisting multiplicity that is inextricable from the placing of characters within a particular geographical location: the city of Madrid.

La mujer de tu vida ('The Woman of Your Life', 1990, 1994)

A production still of the youngish Carmen Maura and Antonio Banderas. She kneels by a large trunk, glossy-haired and clad in a bright red top. He peers out at her, quizzically, handsomely, from inside the trunk, his body hunched up, but incongruously clutching a paperback. Her hand is on the lid. Is she opening or closing the trunk? What has persuaded her male partner to submit to this confinement? (López Izquierdo)

The image could well have been lifted from Almodóvar's still recent *Mujeres al borde*, in which a glossy Maura also confronted an attractively timid Banderas. But it is in fact taken from the first episode of *La mujer de tu vida*, a series of TV movies executive-produced by feature director Fernando Trueba, best known for the Oscar-winning period picture *Belle epoque* (1992). These 60-minute romantic comedies were shot on 35mm and boast prestigious film professionals as members of both cast and crew. This is no accident. While *Chicas en la ciudad* represents the earliest days of the monopoly state broadcaster, the two seasons of *La mujer de tu vida* span TVE's decline when confronted with private competition. Feature film production values were thus an expensive and quixotic attempt to hold back inevitable changes in the industry. And if *Chicas en la ciudad* was exiled to the domesticated time slot of Sunday *sobremesa*, 30 years later *La mujer de tu vida* was promoted to Friday prime time.

In his short essay on the series, Javier López Izquierdo gives the budget as a hefty €600,000 for each episode. He also notes further cinematic references (to the film genre of romantic comedy) and the implications for gender politics of the series concept. As the title suggests, the programme is overtly aimed at a male audience and indeed serves as a parade of 'types' analogous to Armiñán's 'gallery of wives' so many years before. The first season thus began with Maura as the 'happy woman' (broadcast on mass channel TVE1 on 9 February 1990), and continued with the unfaithful, the lunatic, the oriental, the unexpected, the cold and the lost. Given its polished look and respectable audience results, it was no surprise that the first series was rerun and a second commissioned. Shot in 1992, the second series was not aired, however, until 1994, a sign perhaps that the state broadcaster's schedules were in flux. This second series treated the 'common' woman [*cualquiera*], the unpunctual, the vacant – appropriately played by Verónica Forqué, Almodóvar's empty-headed *Kika* (1992) – and the jinx. The last episode, much praised by López Izquierdo, broke the mould: veteran Fernando Fernán Gómez, who is dying in a whorehouse bed, sees his life flash before him in the form of female figures from his own films over the decades. There could be no clearer indication of the extent to which cinema is a storehouse of male memory and its women a vehicle for male self-realization.

Some aspects of *La mujer de tu vida* do indeed confirm this traditionalism. With the signal exception of Banderas, imprisoned by Maura just as he abducts Victoria Abril in ¡*Atame!* ('Tie Me Up! Tie Me Down!', 1990), the male protagonists are regular guys with average looks. Already known for their dependable filmic profile, here they are plausible identification characters for male viewers. Juan Echanove has bug eyes, Alex Angulo is bald, Pere Ponce skinny, and Antonio Resines (who plays the male lead in no fewer than three episodes) increasingly beefy. It is typical that when matinee idol José Coronado appears it is only as the best friend of a less sexy protagonist, schooling him in how to get a woman. Female stars are often insubstantial: Marta Fernández Muro, from Almodóvar's *Laberinto de pasiones* ('Labyrinth of Passion', 1982), is as whiny as Forqué, while Ana Obregón is just setting out on a long and undistinguished TV career as a shallow sexpot. Two of the eponymous women are ethnic stereotypes. The 'oriental', bought by Coronado's character for his lonely friend, is an expert housekeeper, cook and bedmate, who cannot speak Spanish.

Occasionally, however, strong sexy women (often stars for Almodóvar) make their presence felt. The happy Maura imprisons Banderas; Victoria Abril (as the 'lunatic') bewitches Santiago Ramos (much later a sleazy neighbour in the sitcom *Aquí no hay quien viva*, 'No-one Can Live Here', 2003–2006); and expert comedienne María Barranco (Candela in *Mujeres al borde*) lassoes distinguished veteran Francisco Rabal. The well plotted scripts (like those of *Chicas en la ciudad* long before) often have women come out on top: in the very first episode Maura tricks Banderas's character into sexually servicing her during his enforced confinement. And while all of the directors and screenwriters are men, and some, such as Emilio Martínez Lázaro, are specialists in the rom-com, they bring with them a varied history that transcends the genre's saccharine limits. Rafael Azcona, still best known for penning acid scripts for Berlanga, wrote his first teleplay for this series. Directors Ricardo Franco had made the brutally realist *Pascual Duarte* (1976), and Jaime Chávarri the queer psychological thriller *A un dios desconocido* ('To an Unknown God', 1977). If television is clearly a commodity here, its fiction now subject to a brutal battle for ratings, it remains an important ideological forum for the definition of femininity and female desire. Continuing social change is thus mediated, as it so often is, by the enforced coexistence of contradictory dominant and emergent depictions of a woman's place.

These representations of women, more varied than the male viewpoint of the series might have initially suggested, are inextricable from geographical place and space. The varied episodes make the most of location shooting enabled by movie-style budgets. And while some are set in anonymous small towns or picturesque villages (such as Navalcarnero on the outskirts of Madrid), most are based in the capital. But as we shall see, the metropolis, perfectly hermetic in the studio-bound *Chicas en la ciudad*, is now revealed to be open and interrelated with other places, and structured by power relations that bind it and those other places together.

One episode of the second series is exemplary of this newly dynamic spatial process. *La mujer duende* ('The Spirit Woman', 1992) was directed by Jaime Chávarri and scripted by El Gran Wyoming (José Miguel Monzón), who also stars with female lead Rosario Flores, scion of an illustrious flamenco dynasty. Diverging from the reliance on movie stars to enhance the series' brand, here producer Trueba cast an unprepossessing male lead who was (and remains) best known as the presenter of TV talk shows that have achieved patchy success. The mediocrity of the Madrid-born male is thus reconfirmed by his familiarity from the domestic medium of television, which contrasts with the highly coloured Andalusian exoticism of singing star Flores.

Although they are not by Almodóvar regular Juan Gatti, the credits to *La mujer de tu vida* are strikingly reminiscent of the then recent *Mujeres al borde*. Pink lips smile and pink eyelids wink. A black-gloved hand with a diamond bracelet (very *Breakfast at Tiffany's*) beckons the viewer forward, while a long svelte leg flexes in red high heels. To a lilting Caribbean beat, complete with steel drum, the male vocalist begins: '¿Quién es esa mujer que un buen día/ asaltó mis Palacios de Invierno en verano?' ['Who is that woman who one fine day/ stormed my Winter Palace in summertime?'] The woman who, we are told, 'changed the singer's destiny', thus represents both spatial and temporal disruption: assaulting the man's position at the most unexpected of times.

The opening sequence continues this theme of female agency and male passivity. In an odd scene reminiscent of TVE's battle of the sexes comedies of the 1960s, the male addresses the unseen audience, even acknowledging the camera: dressed in a casual blue shirt, frog-faced Gran Wyoming is shot against the sea. He tells us that as he's in close-up we can't see his situation, just as he did not have a broader perspective on the 'woman of his life' who would place that life 'on the verge of an abyss'. The Almodóvarian reference, albeit inverted (with the male now subject to the whims of a dominant female), is patent. While our point of view will coincide with that of main character Ricardo through the next hour, the fact that that perspective is ostentatiously limited and partial undermines its pretension to pre-eminence.

Director Chávarri cuts to the flashback in which the whole action will take place. In a large lecture theatre the soberly suited Ricardo is addressing an ecstatic academic audience on 'Chinese microsurgery'. His adoring fiancée takes a quick Polaroid of his triumph. We next see the couple with colleagues in a sterile shopping mall (white tiles, palms and ferns, elevator music playing in the background), which is presumably part of the suburban conference centre in which the lecture took place. The prissy fiancée, in a prim white suit, sneers at a gypsy beggar working the tables with her baby. Meanwhile, one level above this atrium, there is a pregnant gypsy: Rosario Flores' Paqui with flowing black hair and floral print dress. Her earrings as heavy as her accent, she loudly argues with a store detective who accuses her of shoplifting. As she apparently goes into labour, the physician Ricardo gallantly intervenes and they set off in a taxi for the hospital. Soon they are caught in the city traffic of an old, narrow street (wrought iron lanterns and balconies, cobbles on the pavement). Rapidly retrieving the shoplifted loot that padded out her false pregnancy, Paqui escapes her would-be saviour and hotfoots it out of the taxi and into the urban labyrinth. Ricardo is in turn pursued by the police for failing to pay the taxi fare.

It is clear from the beginning, then, that this emergent woman, at once ancient and modern, is equally at ease in the alienating sterility of the contemporary conference centre and shopping mall and the organic community of the old city centre. Ricardo, on the other hand, is at a loss in both places, repeatedly placed on the verge of an abyss by the female duende, who is the only one who can

4 Running from the city: *La mujer de tu vida*

save him from himself. Paqui next yanks him off the street into an old, anonymous building that proves to be a lively flamenco *tablao* in which, disguised in a green polka dot shirt and a kiss curl, Ricardo eludes the police. From the beginning, then, the textual strategies of genre (romantic comedy), plot (farcical coincidence), and character development work to define and renegotiate social issues of continuing importance, such as the battle of the sexes and the conflict between generic Spaniards or Castilians and ethnically marked others.

A third social issue is that of space and place. The suburbs and city centre give way to a third kind of urbanism: the shanty town that Paqui shares with innumerable aunts and cousins. This new location is revealed to us in a telltale technique: as the hung-over Ricardo emerges from a shack, wrapped in a sheet like some latter-day Roman senator, a crane shot slowly reveals that the desolation of the foreground is framed by a skyline of city towers in the distance. For all its geographical marginality (further from the centre even than the white-tiled mall), the shanty town is a dense and informal form of urbanism that facilitates, in traditional city style, intense and unexpected juxtaposition: professional Ricardo is forced into uncomfortable proximity with the criminal underclass and, indeed, will carry one of them in the boot of his car when Paqui persuades him to drive her back to her Andalusian pueblo.

As urban rom-com turns into road movie, familiar place gives way to unnerving displacement, and fixity (both social and spatial) cedes to mobility. We are treated to frequent landscape shots of the red car driving by roads and rivers, all to the sound of new flamenco pop on the radio. The noisy density of Madrid is exchanged for the parched emptiness of a southern desert, where only crickets are heard. This sense of spatial fluidity contrasts, however, with a narrative that is structured around the invention of obstacles to a male desire that fails to advance in its object. For example, when the odd couple stop at a (modern) motel, Paqui peels off her fire engine red miniskirt and knickers, but Ricardo (who keeps his boxers on) is forced to share a bed with her snoring male cousin, who has insinuated himself into their room. When, finally, they reach the pueblo with its tiny white houses and glistening sea (the location is Tarifa, the southernmost town in Europe), tall Ricardo is mobbed by a crowd of short, heavy women in fluorescent print shift dresses. Paqui's black-clad father, meanwhile (who has never been to Madrid and believes no city could be bigger than regional capital Jerez) pronounces that the couple must now marry to satisfy the family honour.

Here, television's role in mediating social change becomes apparent. An independent woman in the city, asserting her right to (albeit criminal) work and individual freedom, Paqui is transformed into a traditional caretaker in the pueblo, participating in gendered activities considered appropriate to her sex. Even when she sings, it is as other women wash her hair. Complicated by stereotypes of ethnicity, assumptions about women's proper roles are here (as in *Chicas en la ciudad*) unresolved and held in paradoxical suspension. The problem is not so much the character's as the programme's. *La mujer de tu vida* needs to appeal to and construct a subjectivity for women as a television audience, even as it attempts not to alienate the male viewers, encouraged as they are to identify with the hapless Wyoming character, repeatedly humiliated by a spirited female who sees and knows more than him (or us).

In this episode, then, a woman's place is structurally unstable. After another frustrated night of passion with Paqui on the beach (she actively initiates lovemaking that is interrupted once more, this time by the Guardia Civil, who come ashore in search of smugglers), Ricardo returns to the city. But now his old life is troubled by fantasies of the new: a squeaky clean nurse becomes a sexy Roma girl, a sterile scalpel morphs into a dangerously attractive gypsy dagger. The viewer is thus not surprised that Ricardo is soon heading south once more.

We are returned to the opening close-up as Ricardo tells the camera that he is now in possession of 'peace and tranquility'. The camera pulls back for the first time to show his crowded and chaotic surroundings: a seaside gypsy camp packed with caravans and children. Paqui holds the couple's small child by the hand as a horse gallops past. An unplumbed bath, inexplicably, takes pride of place amid the chaos. As Ricardo's final dialogue puts it: you may find the woman of your life where you least expect. The different human trajectories of the characters thus reveal that the city where they met is (like television) open, unfixed and multiple. The urban centre is now clearly interrelated to suburban, marginal and regional spaces that bind radically disparate locations together.

Moreover, the figure of the gypsy or the Andalusian, with its heavy burden of reminiscence to Lorca and even Carmen, is here modernized (urbanized) and definitively stripped of its trappings of tragedy. The femme fatale has become a city girl.

Con dos tacones ('On Two Heels', 2006)

Rarely can the relationship between TV production history and politics seem so self-evident as in the case of the latest example of the city girls genre, the female flat-share sitcom *Con dos tacones*, which aired on mass channel TVE1 for a bare 11 episodes in spring 2006. Manuel Palacio has cited this show in the context of 'public television in the age of [new President] José Luis Rodríguez Zapatero'. Although the PSOE came to power pledged to reduce government meddling in the media, it at once appointed its own Director of RTVE, Carmen Caffarel. As was noted in the previous chapter, she initiated a production slate that Palacio claims was 'unheard of' in the history of Spanish television: four new series with women as protagonists (76). Palacio relates this televisual trend to new political tendencies, at once general and particular: Spain was now proudly in the European vanguard for the participation of women in government; and the newly installed executives in TVE were actively soliciting female-centred projects within months of their arrival. He continues:

> En las series de TVE se refleja la vida social, laboral o amorosa de mujeres activas que son representadas con fuerza propia y en una posición de prevalencia con respecto a los hombres; de hecho el título de una de ellas (*Con dos tacones*) hace referencia a una frase del lenguaje común que tiene altos componentes sexistas como es 'con dos cojones'. (Palacio 76–77)

> [In TVE's series [under Zapatero] we can see reflected the social, work, and love lives of active women who are shown as being strong, independent, and dominant over men; in fact the title of one show ('On Two Heels') reworks the vulgar and highly sexist phrase 'with two balls'.]

The fact that the new show was scheduled in the most watched slot of the weekly schedule, Thursday prime time, and was coupled with *Desperate Housewives*, the prestigious import for which TVE had great hopes, reveals that, perhaps for the first time, production and consumption coincided in an attempt to construct a subjectivity for women as a television audience. Clearly, it was hoped that the 'heels' of these modern, progressive women (both on and off screen) would be more that a match for the 'balls' of traditionalist *machista* men. It is striking that one of the two 'creators' of the series (Marta González de la Vega) also took a script credit and even appeared in the show as a sarcastic secretary (a role reminiscent of the catty Karen in NBC's *Will and Grace*, 1998–2006). She thus stakes a claim to be the main author of the series, both in front and behind the camera.

The Spaniards who elected Zapatero's government, which Palacio describes as the most Leftist since the Republic, did not always seem to care for his and Caffarel's state-sponsored television, however. Although programmers toyed with the scheduling (using *Housewives* alternately to lead into and follow on from *Tacones*), ratings fell steadily over the season from 2,641,000 (19.2 per cent share) on the 23 March premiere to 1,356,000 (7.9 per cent share) on 13 June, the date of the last broadcast (formulatv). Indeed, as early as the day after the series took its bow, the mordant critic of the national daily *El Mundo* wrote that *Con dos tacones* was 'simply trash' [*sencilla bazofia*]. In a piece replete with macho double entendres (albeit ironically intended), El Descodificador ('The Decoder') uses the show as an example of how the public broadcaster cannot create quality programming equal to its imports (*Tacones* was produced for TVE by independent BocaBoca). Thus, *Tacones* is no more than a 'bargain basement' version of its nightly neighbour. It attempts the same caustic perspective on the world of women as *Housewives* and covers the same range of personalities, ages and professions in its female cast. But while the US import has an excellent cast and script, the Spanish imitator is 'lamentable'. He concludes:

> Cualquier intento por buscar posiciones feministas, teorías de rechazo al sometimiento de la mujer o referencias al discurso de la ideología diferente y complementaria de los sexos es una pérdida de tiempo. La serie la protagonizan mujeres, pero si la protagonizasen monaguillos, orangutanes o champiñones tendría el mismo interés. Cero.
>
> [Any attempt to find feminist arguments, resistance to women's oppression, or a commentary on the different but complementary nature of the sexes is just a waste of time. The series focuses on women, but if it focused on monks, monkeys, or mushrooms it would be just as interesting as it is now. That is, not at all.]

In spite of the overt motives of its creators and political paymasters, El Descodificador thus explicitly denies the show the role to which it lays claim: an ideological forum for public discourse about social issues and social change.

It is true that the premise of the first episode was not promising. Fifty-three-year-old housewife Carmen comes home to find Manolo, her politician husband, in bed with her psychologist, the much younger Cristina. Carmen holds the guilty couple hostage at gunpoint for two days. Smart blonde Mónica is Manolo's press agent; sexy airhead Laura is a TV journalist, avid for footage of the hostage; and daffy Malena a hairdresser who, having split with her boyfriend, turns up in search of her mother Carmen. Implausibly enough, the five women will finally get together in Cristina's flat. Here, four of them will begin a new life together, like their distant cousins in *Chicas en la ciudad* some forty years earlier. Mónica, the only city girl now with a partner, will move in with Carlos, a male press agent rival.

Rather than concentrate on the pilot, it seems fairer to analyse a later episode, where, free of the burden of exposition, the script is better able to exploit its relatively rare resource of five female protagonists. The official synopsis of Episode 4 (aired on 25 April to an audience of 1,691,000 and a share of 11.9 per cent) is unusually explicit on the question, so long debated on television, of the modern woman:

> El amor en tiempos de Internet
>
> Carmen, en su afán por convertirse en una mujer moderna, y alcanzar el orgasmo, decide, con la ayuda de Malena, meterse en un 'chat' de Internet para conocer a un hombre. En el último momento le da miedo dar el paso y le pide a Malena que corte la comunicación. Malena, sin embargo, queda con el internauta en nombre de su madre, y la obliga a aceptar la cita a hechos consumados. Lo que Malena no esperaba es que el internauta resultara ser el hombre perfecto. Malena, más desesperada por ligar que su propia madre intentará hacer fracasar la cita y seducir al internauta, para lo que se aliará con Manolo, bajo la excusa de mantener a la familia unida. Laura se siente mal pagada en su trabajo. Sus amigas la pican porque no la consideran capaz de conseguir un trabajo como periodista 'digna', ella se ofende tanto que decide demostrarles que es capaz de conseguirlo, aunque como es natural, el tiro le saldrá por la culata. Carlos, románticamente, planea celebrar el mes que lleva saliendo con Mónica. Decide hacerle un regalo muy emotivo y caro. Mónica, influida por Cristina, piensa regalar un detalle barato. Cuando ella se entera de lo que planeaba regalarle su novio, cambia el regalo por uno más caro y cuando él se entera de lo que planeaba regalarle su novia, cambia el regalo por uno más barato. Pero al intentar solucionarlo, se produce la 'tragedia'. Cristina tiene una mancha de humedad en el despacho y se entera por Lucas de que Eduardo se dedica a hacer chapuzas y solucionar ese tipo de cosas. Cristina le pide a Eduardo que le pinte la mancha. Eduardo lo hace, pero cuando Cristina sube a pagarle, se encuentra con una sorpresa. (formulatv)

> ['Love in the Time of the Internet'
>
> Carmen, who wants to become a modern woman and have an orgasm, decides, with Malena's help to go online in a chat room in order to meet a man. At the last moment she's too scared to go on and asks Malena to call it off. But Malena makes a date with the guy in her mother's name and forces her to acquiesce. What Malena didn't expect is that the internet guy turns out to be the perfect man. More desperate to hook up than her own mother, Malena will try to make the date a disaster and seduce the guy, so she joins up with Manolo, with the excuse that she's trying to keep the family together. Laura thinks she is badly paid at work. Her friends needle her because they don't think she can get a job as a 'serious' journalist. She gets so angry that she tries to show that she can, although of course it backfires on her. Carlos plans a romantic date to celebrate the month he's been dating Mónica. He plans to give her a heartwarming and expensive gift. Mónica, influenced by Cristina, plans to give him just a cheap token of her affection. When she finds out what her boyfriend was planning to give her, she changes her gift for a more expensive one, but when he finds out what she was

planning to give him, he changes his for a cheaper one. When he tries to solve the problem, tragedy ensues. Cristina has a patch of damp in her office and hears from Lucas that Eduardo does odd jobs of this kind. She asks Eduardo to paint over the patch. He does so, but when Cristina goes upstairs to pay him, she has a surprise in store.]

After the briefest of establishing shots (a woozy canted camera peers at night city traffic), we cut to the pre-credit 'hook' (intended to reel in reluctant viewers). The four girls sit round the table in Cristina's comfortable, 'modern' flat (the white decor is accentuated by a single red wall, a circular porthole pierced in the middle). The city skyline, as flagrantly artificial as in *Mujeres al borde*, is glimpsed through the terrace windows. Cristina has her friends taking a psychological test on their past partners. When they all discover, inevitably, that none comes near to the perfect mate, one complains that it's tougher for a woman to find a man than it is for a man to find a woman's G spot. Middle-aged Carmen laments that she's been living a new life for a month now, since her separation, and is not modern yet: she has never experienced orgasm or the Internet. The playful juxtaposition of woman's desire and screen media technology will be explored through the lengthy 75 minutes that follow.

We cut to credits. In what seems by now traditional in the genre, the women address the camera. Here they are lip-synching to the rock-themed title song which begins: 'Hoy voy a ser la mujer que quise ser' ['Today I'm gonna be the woman I always wanted to be']. Priding themselves on their self-asserted status as 'new women', each strides down the street in turn. But they are let down

5 Shoes in the city: *Con dos tacones*

by their footwear. Homely Carmen seems at first to be skating, but is in fact polishing her parquet floor, with cloths wrapped around her slippers. Professional Mónica's strappy sandals pitch into a pothole. Sexy Laura's heel comes off as she climbs city steps. Still the final shot sees them laughing as they pound the urban beat together, an image apparently modelled on US import *Sex and the City*. The retro logo of the series, however (a single, red high-heeled shoe on a geometric background) is more reminiscent of the graphic style of El Deseo.

What is new about the show, in comparison with the predecessors analysed above, is the stress on the interconnection of gender and consumerism. Displaying commodities and consumer lifestyles, *Con dos tacones* reveals women's many and incommensurable social and spatial places: Cristina's modern flat is countered by the traditional family home (dark wood and framed pictures) from which Carmen has escaped; or again, psychologist Cristina's consulting room (scholarly bookshelves are counterpointed by a large, bubbling water feature) is contrasted with actress Laura's garish TV studio (she auditions for a reality-news hybrid called *Información-Triunfo*, or 'News Idol'). The trendy bar-restaurant where Mónica and Carlos attempt to celebrate their one-month anniversary is far from the 'anything for one euro' shop where she buys him a joke present of a toilet cleaner, or the stuffy antique store where he buys her a rare teddy bear. Indeed, the theme of present-giving testifies to the awkwardness of love relations now predicated on equality: misled by their respective friends, the two partners (the only couple in the show) keep changing their gifts to match what they believe their partner has got them. When Carlos finds a gift that combines love and money (the teddy bear replaces one his girlfriend lost as a child) it meets a most unhappy end: accidentally flambéed at that too-fancy restaurant.

Even modern women can thus not take reciprocity in love for granted. But negotiating social issues (and confirming social change) the show confirms that women's place is no longer in the kitchen. Carmen may be lured briefly to her former marital home by her sleazy husband, who feigns illness in order to get her back in the obsessive domestic routine of ironing 'in alphabetical order'. But such housewifery is clearly presented as neurotic and she soon runs back to her more promising Internet boyfriend. Caretaking behaviour is rare indeed in this farcical comedy: even mothers and daughters compete bitterly for the same man.

This new femininity is intimately linked to television, here shown for the first time as not simply a representation of the world but rather an essential part of lived experience, including that of gender. TV journalist Laura tries to sell paparazzi pictures, only to discover that the breasts of a female minister are worth less than other celebrities' buttocks ('Who thought that tits were below bums?') The sleazy publisher is shocked, however, when Laura reveals her ambition to read the TV news: has she no scruples? Laura happily sleeps her way into the newsreading job, only to find her report on the stock market is reduced to one word: 'Subió' ('It went up': unfortunately it went down). Later, the girls gather to watch Laura's media misadventures at home, as if such an experience were perfectly natural.

As in so many sitcoms (in Spain as elsewhere), most characters seem to have media or creative jobs: Mónica works in public relations and even the hunky neighbour who Cristina takes for a house painter is actually a professional artist with a bent for abstraction. The Internet guy whom mother and daughter fight over is called Oscar, thus giving rise to inevitable cinematic gags (Carmen: 'Where's my Oscar?'; Malena: 'You're not even nominated'). Malena, played by daffy comedienne Mónica Cervera, is highly reminiscent, in this episode at least, of her character in the then recent feature *Crimen ferpecto* ('Ferpect Crime', Alex de la Iglesia, 2004). When she plots with her father on the phone to frustrate her mother's new love, the split screen mimics film thrillers.

Beyond this incorporation of various screen media (cinema, television, Internet), the formal hybridity of the show registers at a technical level also. The pre-credit sequence disorientates with a studio-style laugh track combined with musical prompts signalling the gags. The sitcom interiors are interrupted not just by the urban linking shots (streets and flats), familiar in sitcom, but by relatively frequent exterior scenes shot on Madrid's grand avenues (where the faithless husband lives), or the narrower streets of the old centre (where Malena pursues her plan). When the women breakfast on what looks very much like a real terrace (echoes of *How to Marry a Millionaire*), the city is reflected with apparent realism in the panes of the French windows behind them. Even in this farcical context, spatiality is taken relatively seriously, integrated (like television) with lived experience: Cristina repeatedly reminds her lodgers that their rent is due and they must pay their share to repair the damp coming in from the flat upstairs (the gags here revolve around another kind of moistness provoked by the sexy neighbour). In spite of its elements of caricature, there is thus some attempt to link the world of the diegesis to the world of social relations. Hence the stress on screen media that have transformed everyday life.

Con dos tacones does not, then, deserve such opprobrium from critics and audiences. Why did it fail? In the specific and changing cultural context of a new Socialist government, it voiced perhaps too clearly the superiority of the female (the men are foolish or dull), even as its urban women felt (after so many years of the genre) just too familiar to be compelling. The teleliteracy on which *Con dos tacones* relied, in its scripts and its audience, thus proved to be a mixed blessing, with real city girls now perhaps preferring, like the characters themselves, the immediacy of the Internet to the lumbering two-hour time slots still common for Spanish TV fiction.

Genealogy of a genre

In 2006 Amparó Baró, the spiky-haired 'steel butterfly' in *Chicas en la ciudad*, took part in a rare live episode of her then current and long-lasting sitcom, the trendy urban *7 vidas*. She noted in interview that unlike her young stars, she was perfectly used to this, being a veteran of countless live (and now lost) dramas broadcast in the early days of the medium from TVE's first studio in central Madrid's Paseo de la Habana (Rodríguez). There is a significant continuity of casting and character here: Baró's sarcastic, single Sole (emblematically short for 'Soledad'), a Communist retiree, is not so distant from her feisty young nurse Paula forty years earlier. There was also continuity in naming in the same TV season: one private network aired a reality show in which young women shared a flat. Its title? *Chicas en la ciudad*.

The influence of Almodóvar in so many shows of this kind (which I have dubbed the city girls genre) is so all-pervasive and long-lasting that it is invisible to domestic audiences. Foreign viewers, however, will be struck by the clear coincidence at the level of credits, graphics, and art design. El Deseo's local aesthetic, itself based on an idiosyncratic interpretation of Hollywood in the 1950s and 1960s, seems a more relevant reference than that of recent US television. When *Sex in the City* was aired on minority channel Canal +, the title was translated as *Sexo en Nueva York*, the show's claim to general significance thus particularized or localized. Foreign fare, however glossy, is not generally welcome to Spanish audiences: *Housewives* did not play on TVE, even when coupled with *Tacones*, with both shows competing for low ratings. There was thus no 'bandwagon effect' [*arrastre*] in scheduling a prime-time evening of viewing aimed at a female audience.

This question of local taste and global circulation of audiovisual commodities is clearly an important one. And it gives the lie to *El Mundo*'s claim that the female sitcom has no social significance, that it might as well be centred on monkeys or mushrooms. Clearly, the ill-named El Descodificador protests too much. It seems likely that such rare women-centred shows are pointers towards an intimate relationship to the affective life of the nation over decades. At the very least, the three programmes I have examined offer evidence for social change in the fields of gender, the city and politics. Thus, *Chicas* stages an explicit debate, pro and contra, on the rights of women; *La mujer* stages a holiday from domesticity in the figure of the spirited *duende* (at least until she returns to the traditionalist pueblo); and *Con dos tacones* reveals that conventional gender roles are now aberrant: women can only be trapped into domestic labour through their own pathology (the compulsion to iron in alphabetical order) or through a sleazy husband's transparent manipulation. Or again, *Chicas* celebrates urban spaces of encounter (the workplace, café and street); *La mujer* shows women at ease in the city street, the suburban mall, and the informal urbanism of the shanty town; and *Con dos tacones* combines female companionship in a shared space, female mobility in the street, and even the new technology of the Internet as a potential source of sociality (although the hunky neighbour upstairs remains a safer bet).

These sexual and spatial shifts coincide with political and institutional changes. *Chicas* actively anticipates the *aperturismo* that was soon to change Spaniards' lives, as the Dictatorship entered its final, technocratic and urbanized phase. *La mujer*, more reactionary, peddles stereotypes of the eternal feminine, even as it addresses the waning power of men and acknowledges the unevenly developed consumerization and globalization of a Socialist Spain in which shopping malls and Chinese microsurgery rub shoulders with flamenco and duelling gypsies. *Con dos tacones*, the most uneasy, perhaps, parodies women's right to sex and communication (to orgasm and Internet) even as it asserts in its very premise the need for a new life and a new active and autonomous woman outside marriage, an ideology openly preached by TVE's new paymasters and executives.

The three dramas inadvertently chart attitudes to television itself. In *Chicas*, the new medium is absent and cannot be assumed to be part of the everyday life of Spaniards: the girls' social life, both with boys and each other, centres around cinema-going in the city centre, which may involve chance encounters (say, with a tramp) in the street, or comforting rituals (the purchase of a 'bocadillo de calamares' to keep hunger at bay while waiting in the queue). In *La mujer duende* television is also absent, but here this seems more a function of the 'yuppie nightmare' premise, so common in its period: the encounter with the woman in the shopping mall leads to a forced escape from such safe, domesticated spaces, an escape that is at once exciting and threatening. By the time of *Con dos tacones*, the absence of television from the diegetic world would be just too implausible: here the medium is inextricable from women's domestic and professional lives. The girls watch in horror and fascination as Laura performs the news to a tropical beat, dressed as Carmen Miranda.

The theme of news broadcasting is vital here. As Palacio notes (75), although Zapatero's government was most exercised by the perceived degradation of news bulletins under the previous administration, viewers themselves are most engaged by drama: it is the fictional series ('tent poles' of the various networks) that lodge longest in their memories. Even today it is through scheduling that we feel closest to long-distant times and spaces: the lazy *sobremesa* (a uniquely Spanish time slot), when viewers first glimpsed city girls after a late Sunday lunch (no doubt prepared by a housewife); and the late prime-time Thursdays and Fridays (also distinctively Spanish), in which they consumed *La mujer* and *Con dos tacones* in two very different Socialist eras. Such female-centred narratives remain relatively rare, even as women openly constitute the majority of the

TV audience: at the start of the new decade, the Spanish association of authors and publishers reported that men watched 200 minutes of television a day, women 239, and 'housewives' a staggering 267 (435).

There is a certain generic continuity in these female-oriented shows, not just at the level of mise en scène (elegant costume and set design), but at that of cinematography (the persistence of that rare device of direct address to camera). Yet there are formal discontinuities also, most obviously at the level of length. Armiñán's 15-minute microdramas are replaced, in turn, by Trueba's 60-minute TV movies and González de la Vega's over-extended 75-minute dramedy (the now normal Spanish length for fiction), padded to a full 2 hours with wearisome commercial breaks. While common sense might suggest that audiences pay little attention during such lengthy time slots, or indeed zap from channel to channel, empirical research shows they can be surprisingly loyal to their favourite programmes, tuning in long in advance. This is what Spanish schedulers call, in a revealing spatial analogy, the *antesala*, or 'antechamber' effect. The model of distracted perception also fails to account for the intense emotion provoked by television. This is attested in Spain as early as 1961, when fans mobbed Marsillach in San Sebastián, confusing him with the televisual husband 'Bruno', who had recently invited himself into their homes with his gallery of wives. It is an affective charge based on a continued familiarity, which the one-off TV movies of *La mujer de tu vida*, nostalgic for cinematic production values and prestige, could not provide.

The formal questions of genre are thus inextricable from ideological questions of gender and space. Walking in the city (or, indeed, running, as Rosario Flores' *duende* does through much of her show) is a continuing trope and one whose significance is not to be taken lightly. After all, as the news magazine that preceded the rerun of *La mujer duende* noted, there are societies in which women are viciously punished if they dare to leave the limits of the home and take pleasure in the public space. But, celebrating the street, we should not neglect the home. In an essay on *Desperate Housewives*, Sherryl Wilson cites Raymond Williams on the room as a televisual space:

> The room is there, not as one scenic convention among all possible others, but because it is an actively shaping environment – the particular structure in which we live [...] the solid form, the conventional declaration, of how we are living and what we value. This room [...] [is] a set that defines us and can trap us: the alienated object that now presents us in the world. (Wilson 146)

In a different mode and register, Williams thus anticipates feminist geographer Doreen Massey when she writes that space is not simply an arena in which social relations happen but rather an active and dynamic producer of those relations.

My own microanalysis of three female-centred sitcoms would suggest that the room (which we watch, in which we watch) is not necessarily negative:

rather, it is a stage on which social questions and social change are actively and contradictorily explored and one in which the aesthetic, the ideological and, indeed, the financial are inextricably and unstably combined. We should, with Lynn Spigel and Denise Mann, reject 'big bang' theories of television as 'cultural wasteland' or, indeed, as 'global village', in favour of more culturally nuanced readings in which one girl's slacks or another's broken heel take on a special significance. But, as Massey suggests once more, we should not (like El Gran Wyoming) lose sight of the overall view, mesmerized by the extreme close-up of thick description. Even at a time in which the death of the sitcom is frequently predicted, the city girls genre, critically neglected or abused, remains a reliable index of female autonomy on Spanish television.

Chicas en la ciudad ('Girls in the City', TVE, 1961)
Production company   TVE
Creator and screenwriter   Jaime de Armiñán

Cast
Amparo Baró   Paula
Alicia Hermida   Ester
Irán Eory   Erika
Paula Martel   Coro
Rafaela Aparicio   Marcelina

La mujer de tu vida 2: La mujer duende
('The Woman of your Life 2: The Spirit Woman', TVE1, 1992)
Production company   Fernando Trueba Producciones, TVE
Director   Jaime Chávarri
Screenwriter   El Gran Wyoming

Cast
El Gran Wyoming   Ricardo
Rosario Flores   Paqui

Con dos tacones ('On Two Heels', TVE1, 2006)
Production company   BocaBoca
Senior screenwriters   Marta González de la Vega, Arturo González Campos
Senior director   Alberto Ruiz Rojo

Cast
Lorena Berdún   Cristina
Rosario Pardo   Carmen
Mónica Cervera   Malena
Raquel Meroño   Mónica
Raquel Infante   Laura

Works Cited

Armiñán, Jaime de. *Guiones de TV*. Colección 'Libros de cine', Cineclub Monterols, Barcelona. Madrid: Rialp, 1963.

—. 'Cinco años en TV'. *Guiones*. 13–23.

Buezo Armiñán, Catalina. 'Jaime de Armiñán y los medios de comunicación social como difusores de ideas reformistas'. *Espéculo: Revista de Estudios Literarios*. Universidad Complutense de Madrid, 2002. Accessed 10 Jan 2007. <http://www.ucm.es/info/especulo/numero20/arminan.html>

del Corral, Enrique ('Viriato'). 'En busca de lo televisivo'. Jaime de Armiñán. *Guiones de TV*. Colección 'Libros de cine', Cineclub Monterols, Barcelona. Madrid: Rialp, 1963. 26–31.

Dow, Bonnie J. *Prime-Time Feminism: Television, Media Culture, and the Women's Movement since 1970*. Philadelphia: U of Pennsylvania P, 1996.

El Descodificador. 'Con dos cojones'. *El Mundo*. 24 Mar. 2006. Accessed 10 Jan. 2007. <http://www.elmundo.es/elmundo/2006/03/24/descodificador/1143157616.html>

formulatv. 'Con dos tacones'. Accessed 10 Jan. 2007. <http://www.formulatv.com/series/87/con-dos-tacones/capitulos/2467.html>

IMDb. 'Entre nosotras'. Accessed 10 Jan. 2007. <http://www.imdb.com/title/tt0386931/">

López Izquierdo, Javier. 'La mujer de tu vida'. *Las cosas que hemos visto: 50 años y más de TVE*. Ed. Manuel Palacio. Madrid: RTVE, 2006:128.

Lury, Karen, and Doreen Massey. 'Making Connections'. *Screen* [Special Issue on 'Space/Place/City'] 40.3 (1999): 229–38.

Palacio, Manuel. 'La televisión pública española (TVE) en la era de José Luis Rodríguez Zapatero'. *Journal of Spanish Cultural Studies* 8.1 (2007): 71–83.

Rodríguez, Mercedes. '*7 vidas*, cumpleaños en directo'. 10 Mar. 2006. Accessed 10 Jan 2007. <http://www.hoy.es/pg060310/prensa/noticias/Television/200603/10/HOY-TEL-228.html>

Spigel, Lynn, and Denise Mann, eds. *Private Screenings: Television and the Female Consumer*. Minneapolis: U of Minnesota P, 1992.

Wilson, Sherryl. 'White Picket Fences, Domestic Containment, and Female Subjectivity: The Quest for Romantic Love'. *Reading* Desperate Housewives. Ed. Janet McCabe and Kim Akass. London and New York: I.B. Tauris, 2006: 144–55.

CHAPTER THREE

Crime Scenes: Police Drama on Television

Crime profile: reading a genre

There seems little doubt that crime fiction is one of the most important genres on television, serving both to work through vital social issues, such as gender and ethnicity, and to raise troubling questions about the relation between the television medium and everyday life. Articles in the British trade press have discussed how the *Police Review* can offer an 'insider view' of crime programming (Mason); how police and CCTV footage is facilitated (or prohibited) to broadcasters (Holmwood); and how a former detective chief inspector has worked as a consultant for TV crime drama (Marlow). The BBC was forced to defend itself when it paid a convicted burglar for his contribution to one programme (Matthews) and when one of its freelances on a crime show was himself convicted of murder (White). More, perhaps, than even reality programming, crime fiction presents or represents antisocial behaviour in ways that society may find disturbing. Moreover, while crime has waned as a theme in feature films it remains ubiquitous on television and thus seems intimately linked to the medium.

While there is a considerable body of research on English-language crime drama in the US and the UK, and in the social sciences and the humanities, there is to my knowledge almost no criticism on Spanish contributions to the genre. And, given the formulaic nature of crime drama, it seems likely that it will be relatively easy to discern distinctively Spanish components at work in local productions. This chapter thus studies the two most important crime dramas of the 1990s and 2000s: *Policías* (Antena 3, 2000–2003) and *El comisario* (Tele5, 1999–). It argues that they exemplify two different extremes of possibility within the current range of generic definitions. While the relatively short-lived *Policías* embraced feature-film production values and an apparently conservative perspective rooted in cognition and the preservation of the collective, the long-running *El comisario* embodies, at least on first viewing, a 'closer', more intimate televisual style, an implicitly progressive politics, and a sensibility based on affect and the dignity of the individual. In order to compare the two series I focus on parallel episodes that deal with two key social conflicts: the status of women and the integration of foreign immigrants. As a control I briefly examine at the end of the chapter a failed crime drama distributed as a feature film, which, I argue, is contaminated by TV production values. More generally, and following current trends in communication studies and criminology, I propose a return to Durkheim, functionalist father of French sociology, for a methodology that transcends current aporias in critical studies of the genre.

In the large literature on US and British crime drama there is a clear division between humanities scholars, who tend to focus on representation, and social scientists, who prefer to deal with relations of cause and effect. Thus Elayne Rapping, in her major book *Law and Justice As Seen on TV* (2003), argues of the influential *Law & Order* franchise that 'stylistic and generic choices [...] lend themselves to liberal or conservative readings' on 'major social issues' such as 'gender violence, juvenile delinquency, family dysfunction [and] the Victims' Rights movement' (Raney and Rapping 13, 15). She goes on to suggest that the proliferation of procedural shows points to the 'criminalization of American life [...] [the] tendency to define and approach all social issues and problems within the narrow confines of criminal law' (17). In the same year political scientist Timothy O. Lenz argued for the coexistence in US TV drama of the 1990s of conflicting liberal and conservative models of justice, the former characterized by due process, individual rights, and rehabilitation, and the latter by crime control, government powers, and punishment (31).

It is interesting to contrast Rapping's list of American social issues with Béatrice Cormier-Rodier's account of French social issues explored by a television drama that was also 'cop crazy' [*flicomanie*] in the 1990s: the suburbs [*banlieues*], immigration, unemployment, racism, petty crime (15). Meanwhile Charlotte Brunsdon suggested that the rise of crime-based fiction on British television in the 1980s and early 1990s spoke directly to concerns about a Britain in decline under a Tory government with a strong rhetoric of law and order. She writes: 'The police series in its various mutations [...] has been a privileged site for the staging of the trauma of the breakup of the postwar settlement' (223). While she cautions against 'too simple a correspondence between crime and unrest on the streets and crime on television' (224) she places the genre in the context of its conservative representations of varied social trends: punitive law and order rhetoric, the privatization of bodies, and equal opportunities policy (225–26).

Social scientists based in criminology or communication studies have attempted to establish more precise 'correspondences' between antisocial acts in programming and in real life (e.g. Potter). But results are once more inconclusive. One researcher finds that there is some positive correlation between social stress, as indexed by rising unemployment, and an increased preference for TV crime drama in the US and Canada, but not in Germany, where, paradoxically, unemployment is much higher than in North America (Reith 258). And if causes are unclear, then so are effects. 'Crime drama', writes Margaret Reith, 'channel[s] aggression in an authoritarian direction [...] [but] while its popularity may be an index of antisocial tendencies, its effect may be to reinforce aggression against such tendencies' (264). Another empirical scholar explores no fewer than three different 'causal explanations' for the relationship between television fiction and fear of crime (Van den Bulck).

Unsurprisingly, perhaps, humanities and social science scholars fight shy of exploring the dubious pleasures audiences find in crime fiction. One article in the *Journal of Communication* does call attention to this gap, aiming to provide an integrated theory of the enjoyment of crime drama. Arthur A. Raney and Jennings Bryant argue for an 'inextricable connection between affective and cognitive responses' in the 'enjoyment of media violence' (402). If 'affect' is a set of data corresponding to the experience of the characters, and 'cognition' a partially overlapping set corresponding to the operation of justice, then it is in the subset between the two (the common ground between affect and cognition, between individual character and collective law) that the audience's enjoyment is to be found (408). It is a theoretical analysis I will later use to explore the differences between the distinct pleasures of *Policías* and *El comisario*.

What is striking in this debate is the return of a wide variety of scholars to a formerly unfashionable figure, Emile Durkheim. One scholar gives a classical functionalist account of 'crime stories' in TV news magazines:

> [R]ituals of processing and punishing crime are functional in constructing a society's morality, teaching its members to abide by certain rules and promoting cohesion among members by making it public when individuals have violated shared moral values [...] Content analysis data support the Durkheimian notion that social systems ritualize crime events with functional implications for the maintenance of social order. (Grabe 155)

However, this conservative cognitive reading scarcely accounts for the pleasures audiences feel in such 'stories'. And Richard Sparks' excellent *Television and the Drama of Crime* argues for a different emphasis:

> [We should] reclaim that part of Durkheimian theory which recognizes punishment as an 'expressive' institution and thus takes seriously the proposition that 'passion' and social sentiment remain the 'soul of penality'. (Sparks 4)

This stress on 'expression' and 'passion' (like the earlier account of enjoyment as the crossover between affect and cognition) goes beyond positions often associated with Durkheim: the authoritarian demand for moral boundaries, which uses 'risks to uphold community' (Sparks 32) and the 'functionalist tradition of [...] heroes, villains, and victims [...] [and of] rituals of solidarity and norm-affirmation' (130).

John Sumser castigates US crime drama for being 'simplistic, boring, and repetitive' (ix) and, in an example of the logical fallacy known as *petitio principii*, duly finds evidence for 'social typing' (52) in the restricted corpus of programmes he set out to examine. But even he manages to find something in Durkheim beyond the functionalist slogan of 'crime creates the community' (6). He cites Durkheim's contrast between the violation of the rule of hygiene (which will lead inevitably to disease) and the violation of 'the rule that forbids me to kill', whose effects are less easy to anticipate:

> Analysis of the act [of murder] will tell me nothing. I shall not find inherent in it the subsequent blame or punishment. There is complete heterogeneity between the act and its consequence. It is impossible to discover *analytically* in the act of murder the slightest notion of blame. The link between act and consequence is here a *synthetic* one. (Sumser 14)

Durkheim's radical rejection of causality thus opens up a flexible space for the exploration of the social significance of crime stories, caught as they are between the affective and the cognitive, the individual and the collective. Moreover, it gives rise to a dynamic model of social change: crime does not simply reinforce current collective consciousness, it can also point the way to new forms of behaviour that will constitute future morality.

Sumser's quote on the chasm between a physical act (murder) and a social consequence (punishment) is taken from the translation of a collection of three essays by Durkheim, first published in French as *Sociologie et philosophie* (1924). The essays treat in more abstract, conceptual fashion than is common in Durkheim three related topics vital to an understanding of crime fiction and, I would argue, to police drama on television. They are individual and collective representations, the 'moral fact', and value judgements. Taken together they provide a framework for transcending current debates on such undecidable topics as the essentially conservative or liberal nature of images, or the relations of cause and effect between electronic media and social life.

In the first essay Durkheim posits an analogy between psychology and sociology (disciplines that he insists, nonetheless, are 'relatively independent') at the level of a common relation to their respective material 'bases' [*sustrats*] (2). Attacking the purely physiological accounts of memory current in his time, Durkheim argues that personal memories are things in themselves that persist in us beyond cerebral impulses. Similarly, on the public plane, collective 'social facts' are immanent in individuals, even as they remain exterior to them (34). Invoking 'synthesis' once more, Durkheim writes that

> private sentiments become social only by combining under the pressure of forces developed by association; through these combinations and the mutual alterations that result, they [private sentiments] become something else. (Durkheim 36, my translation)

Durkheim thus attacks both individualist sociology (which, deriving the complex from the simple, claims society is merely the sum total of personal feelings) and idealist metaphysics (which, deriving the part from the whole, claims the personal is merely a fragment of a theological totality) (41).

The second essay advances this dynamic model of the relation between the individual and the collective into the 'determination of moral facts'. Here Durkheim presents a curious characteristic of morality: that it is both obligation (imposed collectively from outside the individual) and desire (experienced by the individual as a good, albeit often an unpleasurable good) (50). Since this good cannot be reduced to the individual interest (all versions of morality exclude simple egotism), it must be located once more at the level of the collectivity or society: 'on the condition that society can be considered as a personality that is qualitatively different to the individual personalities that go to make it up' (52–53). Society is thus a good, desirable by citizens, but one that (like collective representations) goes beyond them, even as it is immanent in them: 'the individual cannot want and desire [morality] without doing some violence to its own nature as individual' (53). Durkheim goes on to refute the objection often made to him that such a theory is simply an apology for currently existing opinion. Reliant as it is on the material 'base', morality registers not how society appears to itself but how it truly is or is tending to become (54).

The final essay, which treats the tricky question of value judgements and reality judgements, concludes this attempt to situate social analysis in a dynamic space between empiricism and idealism. Thus Durkheim, arguing characteristically that ideals are profoundly social, denies that values can be reduced to reality (except in the special case of economics) and that they can be derived from man's relation to some transcendent faculty (137). And suggesting that (as in the case we saw earlier of murder) 'the value of things can be independent of their nature', Durkheim uncannily anticipates television as a mass medium of social representation:

> Collective ideals can only be constituted and take consciousness of themselves if they are fixed on things that can be seen by all, understood by all, represented to all people: figurative drawings, all kinds of emblems, written or spoken formulae, animate or inanimate beings [...] Collective thought transforms all it touches. It mixes up realms, confounds contraries, levels differences and differentiates similarities; in a word it substitutes for the world revealed to us by the senses a world which is none other than the shadow projected by the ideals it constructs. (137–38, my translation)

I will argue that Spanish police drama, broadcast to the flickering screens of millions of viewers, can have a similar heuristic capacity, based as it is on that fluctuating and inherently dramatic dynamic between obligation and desire

Crime figures: two series concepts

Policías, en el corazón de la calle
Una de las más prestigiosas series policíacas españolas de todos los tiempos. Interpretada por un plantel de actores de primer nivel, entre los que destacan José María Pou y Ana Fernández, *Policías* aborda de manera cruda y realista algunos de los más candentes temas relacionados con la delincuencia y la criminalidad: drogas, corrupción policial, asesinos psicópatas ... Una de las bazas de su éxito es la cercanía con la que se tratan todos los asuntos: los agentes, los delincuentes y las víctimas resultan mucho más próximos al espectador español que en el caso de las series americanas. (Calle 13, 'Nuestras series')

[*Police Officers, in the Heart of the Street*
One of the most prestigious Spanish police series of all time. With a cast of top notch actors, including the exceptional José María Pou and Ana Fernández, *Police Officers* tackles in a brutally realistic fashion some of the hottest topics in lawbreaking and crime: drugs, police corruption, psychopathic serial killers .... One of the secrets of its success is the closeness with which it treats all these themes: the officers, criminals, and victims feel much nearer to Spanish viewers than in American series.]

El comisario
Producido por Estudios Picasso y BocaBoca Televisión y dirigida por Jesús Font, *El comisario* recorre en cada uno de sus episodios muchos de los problemas relacionados con la inseguridad ciudadana que nos afectan a todos, desde el acoso sexual a las agresiones callejeras, pasando por el tráfico y consumo de drogas a la especulación urbanística, siempre desde una perspectiva realista y alejada de los estereotipos habituales. (Calle 13, 'Nuestras series')

[*The Police Commander*
Produced by Estudios Picasso and BocaBoca Televisión and directed by Jesús Font, every episode of *The Police Commander* tackles urban crime issues that affect all of us, from sexual harassment to mugging, by way of drug trafficking and abuse and property speculation, and always from a realistic perspective that couldn't be further from the conventional stereotypes.]

In 1999 respected TV commentator Ricardo Vaca Berdayes wrote that 'Spanish TV drama [*ficción*] [was] on the crest of wave' (78). While the common complaint remained that Spanish television was unoriginal and lacking in quality, Vaca notes that in fact the most popular programmes were now invariably innovative local dramas produced by and for the still new private networks. Such shows achieved higher rating and share than US imports or even football matches. Vaca has no hesitation in attributing this rise in quality to intensified competition since the end of the public TVE monopoly. While Antena 3 began the trend with its 'totem' *Farmacia de guardia*, Tele 5's *Periodistas* ('Journalists'), a pioneer workplace drama, had just received the record audience that its 'excellent' scripting, 'convincing' actors and 'efficient' production fully deserved (80). Such programming, writes Vaca, plays a vital role in the 'strengthening' of the Spanish audiovisual industry.

It is in this context that two private networks launched versions of a genre previously unsung in Spain: police dramas. Curiously, neither show coincided with the public image of its network. In 2000, Antena 3, known for family programming, fielded *Policías*, a dark and violent show focusing on the professional lives of a local force in Madrid. Meanwhile, in 1999 Tele 5, known for adult programming (in all senses of the word), replaced its now venerable

6 The ensemble cast of *Policías*

flagship series *Periodistas* with *El comisario*, a softer and brighter police drama, which paid close attention to the private lives of officers in another local station in the capital. While there is some crossover between the issues addressed by the two series (such as drug-dealing), more typical of *Policías* are themes such as police corruption and psychopaths, while *El comisario* tends towards topics such as sexual abuse and property scandals.

The difference in sensibility is also clear from the jackets of the DVDs on which the successive seasons were repackaged in box sets. The cast of *Policías* glower in their black and white uniforms, hands on hips, six on the front cover and no fewer than fourteen on the back. Behind them is a blurry image of endless skyscraper windows, which reads as 'cosmopolitan modernity' but

7 Pope (Marcial Alvarez, left) and Charlie (Juanjo Artero): *El comisario*

proves on closer inspection to be a photo of New York's Park Avenue. The warmer, kinder stars of *El comisario* are showcased in pairs on the box and individually on the front cover of each episode, smiling at the viewer and in civilian dress. The indistinct photo behind them is of a small-scale, traditional Spanish street, its familiar windows and balconies receding into the distance. While the series descriptions on Calle 13 (the subscription channel dedicated to the action and suspense genres on which both dramas were rerun in 2005) stress the 'closeness' of *Policías* and *El comisario* to the collective consciousness of domestic audiences, there is no doubt that it is *El comisario* that emphasizes cultural proximity to the Spanish viewer. Indeed, in the only extras included on the DVDs, sympathetic actors such as Margarita Lascoite, who plays romantically troubled administrative officer Lupe, attribute the lengthy run of their show to precisely this closeness to habitual viewers, who are unable to recognize themselves in US cop shows.

It is also no accident that Calle 13 should stress the 'prestige' of *Policías*. Publicity spots for the series, included on the first DVD in the pack, offer a blizzard of statistics: the area of the studio set is 2,000 square metres (2,400 square yards) and the show uses 135 locations, 16 permanent actors, 150 technicians, 400 supporting players, and 1,000 extras. The publicity also claims that this, the most expensive series on TV, shoots 200 hours of footage for each 60-minute episode and was rewarded with an audience of 3,500,000 for the final, cliffhanger episode of the second season. Much is also made of the action sequences: there are, it is claimed, 25 chases, 11 accidents, 10 explosions, and 5 'leaps into the void'. The theme music ('urban' drum and bass) and the credit sequence (action shots capped by a final view from on high of Madrid's grand Gran Vía) emphasize the series' ambitious bid for international distinction.

While the publicity and jacket confirm that *Policías* is clearly an ensemble piece, it still owes much to the central performance of José María Pou as troubled superintendent Ferrer. Pou was regularly nominated for best actor awards for the role. And while Pou is well known as a classical stage actor, Ana Fernández, the female lead of the first season, is a respected film veteran. Indeed, as the series began she had just starred in critically praised social realist feature *Solas* ('Alone', Benito Zambrano, 1999). The cinematic connection is characteristic of the series. The pilot episode of *Policías* began with an extraordinarily lavish action sequence twelve minutes long: when two cops spot a perp sniffing coke in his car, they pursue him down the pedestrian walkways of the Castellana in central Madrid before he is tracked by a helicopter down the length of the Gran Vía. The helicopter crashes into a high rise and balances precariously on the roof. A brave cop (the likeable Adolfo Fernández as Carlos) rescues the pilot after being precariously lowered on a fire hose. While there is some personal investment here (Carlos will not hear of a medal for his bravery: he was just helping a friend), in such spectacular sequences the emphasis is on the professional courage and proficiency of the ensemble cast. Indeed, three feature-length episodes in the DVD collection are named for the pairs of professional partners who are featured in them (the fourth is called simply 'Snuff'): it seems individuals only take on significance when alchemically absorbed into the collective or at least the classic dyad of police partners. Public morality, ambiguously immanent in the police officer, yet external to him, tends to triumph in *Policías*. Later in this episode Carlos could allow the criminal who shot his buddy to die, but instead calls for an ambulance. While the moral good is shown to be desirable, as well as obligatory, it clearly comes at the cost of individual affect.

El comisario feels very different. It is, however, anchored by a central performance by the respected Tito Valverde that is as emotionally repressed as Pou's in *Policías*. As the titular and emblematically named superintendent Gerardo Castilla, Valverde won ATV best actor awards in 2000 and 2001. *El comisario*'s credits are more ambiguous than those of *Policías*: the title music segues from a reggae beat to Caribbean brass and sultry sax (a more sensuous-sounding version of *Policías*' 'urban' theme) and the action shots (a mugging and a car chase) are qualified by images of reassuring order (police files and badges are superimposed). The production design is also more friendly than *Policías*', whose key colours are steel grey and gunmetal blue. The azure walls, crimson columns and magenta chairs of this police station set could almost have come out of Almodóvar. Likewise the lighting is higher key and the camerawork less busy than the gloomy mise en scène and jerky shooting style of its rival. Plot lines tend to focus on the private domestic sphere, especially insofar as it overlaps with the public operation of justice. For example, middle-aged married couple Laura and Pascual (Elena Irureta and Joaquín Climent) are based in the same station and in one episode (no. 14) their teenage son steals his father's gun from the family home. Or again, the lonely Lupe is caught up in the domestic abuse drama of her neighbours: a daughter who refuses to let her mother denounce her violent husband (Episode 19). It is no surprise to see Julio (Tristán Ulloa, soon to be the male lead in Medem's *Lucía y el sexo* ('Sex and Lucía', 2001)) impersonating a student in order to crack a drug ring in a university hall of residence (also Episode 19). Much of the young cast seem more at ease in civilian dress than in uniform. The most prominently featured partners, nicknames 'Pope' and 'Charlie' (Marcial Alvarez and Juan José Artero, a veteran child star from TVE's fondly remembered *Verano azul* ('Blue Summer', 1981)), wear conspicuously eccentric gear, including tartan trousers. Such popular characters have kept ratings high over seven years: the most recent season ended on 25 April 2006 with an audience of 4,680,000 and share of 26 per cent (Telecinco).

These distinct sensibilities are by no means invisible to audiences. Indeed, the bulletin boards of Calle 13 ('Foros de discusión'), home to connoisseurs of police drama, are vehement in their assertion of preferences. Interestingly, some postings focus on form, complaining about *Policías*' shooting style (shots that 'come and go') and score ('music even when they're in the toilet'). Too trendy (too distant), *Policías* is held to be an imitation of American models, while *El comisario* is 'more Spanish, more close'. It is a distinction that also maps on to oppositions we have seen earlier, such as that between cognition and affect.

We may now examine specimen episodes of the two series, both screened in the year 2000, to see how televisual form and ideological content intersect, with particular reference to the key issues of gender and immigration.

Crime scenes: specimen episodes

Ferrer y Ruso
Ferrer recibe un correo electrónico en el que a través de una cámara web ve a su hija Chus que ha sido secuestrada. Se trata claramente de una venganza, y sospecha de la banda de los iraníes que seis meses antes desmanteló. (*Policías* DVD jacket)

[Ferrer and Ruso
Ferrer receives an email in which he can see through a webcam that his daughter Chus has been kidnapped. It's clearly a case of revenge and he suspects the Iranian gang that he smashed six months earlier.]

En el límite
Lola debe infiltrarse en un psiquiátrico para esclarecer el asesinato de una joven embarazada. El asunto pondrá su vida en peligro. Mientras tanto, Laura y Pascual intentan convencer a su hijo, Totó, de que devuelva a su novia marroquí, Samira, a su padre, pues aún es menor de edad. (*El Comisario* DVD jacket)

[On the Edge
Lola has to go undercover in a mental hospital to investigate the murder of a young pregnant woman. This case will put her life in peril. Meanwhile Laura and Pascual try to convince their son to take his Moroccan girlfriend Samira back to her father, as she is still legally a minor.]

An article in the British professional magazine *Scriptwriter* gives advice on structuring successful TV crime dramas (Friday). Although it is entitled 'subverting the formula', it reveals, rather, how formulaic such narratives can be: from the opening 'hook' (intended to 'snare the audience's attention' (36) to the final 'catch' ('on which the audience [...] is encouraged to return') via a 'classic 3-act structure' from 'business as usual' (37), through 'obstacles' that cause the protagonists to 'struggle to reach [their] goals', to a resolution 'of the main story involving the key character' (38).

A Spanish manual on directing for television, published in the same year, recommends an identical structure, albeit with varied terminology, employing the English terms 'tease' and 'tag' instead of 'hook' and 'catch' (Barroso García 253). Here, the three acts are defined, in Aristotelian fashion once more, as presentation, complication and resolution of the main conflict. More stress is placed, however, on the subplot, which is said to be character-based, adding 'volume' and 'intimacy' to the action (254). There is also emphasis on the need for costly drama series to distance themselves from cheaper studio-shot soaps and sitcoms through a series of production practices: exotic and sophisticated plot lines, multiple locations, crowd scenes with extras, and special effects. Exteriors are also vital (294) and should constitute 35–40 per cent of all sequences (295). Significantly this Spanish manual charts the evolution of crime drama only through the successive renovations of the genre in the US: from the cross-cutting of multiple narrative threads in *Hill Street Blues* via the pop-video aesthetic of *Miami Vice* to the (oddly chosen) 'equilibrium' of *L.A. Law* (296–300). The author warns, however, that series whose stories are complete in one episode (such as current procedural shows) cannot develop rounded characters and risk 'banalization' (302).

The latter is clearly a problem for *Policías*, the most Americanized and action-based of Spanish shows, in that it consistently privileges the professional over the personal. The pre-credit 'tease' or 'hook' of the specimen episode I have chosen, however, has a personal dimension. The young woman abducted in broad daylight from the street is police inspector Ferrer's teenage daughter. But what is striking in this episode is the prominence of (impersonal or mechanical) visualizing technology, which undercuts (or perhaps, perversely, underlines) the affective charge of the premise. Thus the hostage victim, stripped to T-shirt and panties on a filthy mattress, is shown repeatedly through the blurry low-def image of a webcam. And when Ferrer meets his colleagues in the operations room (a Spanish flag and portrait of the King are prominent on the walls) the camera prowls around the actors in a restless 360-degree set-up. As we are plunged into a lengthy flashback (which takes up 1 hour of the feature-length, 100-minute episode), we are shown frequent shots of Ferrer, starkly reduced in size and clarity, in the viewfinder of his partner Ruso's digital movie camera (Ferrer is pretending to be corrupt in order to entrap the drug dealers who will later kidnap his daughter).

Policías' stylized *mise-en-scène* also suggests a stripped-down or degraded reality. When Ferrer first meets Abbas, an Iranian drug baron, it is in a murky underground car park, the gloom barely pierced by ominous blue spotlights. Post-industrial settings are also favoured for daytime exteriors: an abandoned paint storehouse or a graffiti-scarred urban playground studded with shivering junkies. Even a handsome and historic location named in the dialogue, the Plaza de las Descalzas (home to a famous convent), is transformed and degraded: the police officers pose as homeless people or street sweepers in a failed attempt to bust the gang. Shooting style reinforces this sense of urban stress. Conversation between the two partners, Ferrer and Ruso, is often shot in giddy swish pans rather than in conventional shot/reverse shot. The tour de force action sequences (multiple shoot-outs between the gangs and the police, culminating in that infernal garage) are shot with crash zooms, edited with jump cuts, and scored to fizzing electronic beats. The rare cinematic production values are thus used not just – as the scriptwriting manual recommended – to distance series drama from soap and sitcom, but also to suggest a criminalization of all social issues, including immigration, that is noticeably punitive in character. The Iranian drug baron Abbas will, by the end, be not only justly incarcerated but also badly beaten by Ferrer's prison buddies.

This conservative view of the operation of justice intersects with gender and 'race'. Women are largely excluded from the action in *Policías*: Ana Fernández's feisty Lucía, who leads the operational meetings, was written out in a spectacular death sequence that served as cliffhanging 'tag' for the first season and is included in the second DVD in the box set. In my specimen episode, Ferrer's young daughter Chus is the purest and blankest of victims, reduced to a heroin-pumped and semi-naked body on the computer monitor. Bald, paunchy, and perpetually preoccupied, Ferrer barely seems to notice when his wife comes to the station to break up with him. Once more shooting style also distances the viewer from the feminine, from affect: we glimpse one argument between the married couple from Ferrer's colleagues' point of view, way across the street. The father does offer the kidnappers his own life in exchange for that of his daughter. But it is clear that there is very little common ground between the operation of law and the experience of the characters who aim to enforce that law. Indeed, the two often seem incompatible. When Ferrer's partner Ruso is hospitalized, he claims to be 'at home'. There could be no clearer sign of the dereliction of domesticity and masculinity. As in so much buddy-style narrative, the true marriage is between the two male partners. While there is a subplot that adds 'volume' and 'psychology' (Ruso suffers from a gambling addiction), even this leads once more to spectacular violence (he is beaten with chains in another dark and rain-slicked parking structure).

Policías is thus classically functionalist in its conservatism, using the most blatantly emotional of risks (the loss of a child) to uphold community. And this social typing of heroes, villains and victims extends to 'race'. Gang boss Abbas is devilish indeed with his goatee, full-length black leather coat and jangling prayer beads. His overlord, an aged blind man, is yet more sinister. While good cop Ruso is himself an immigrant (as his nickname suggests), he has no accent or backstory. Abbas, meanwhile, speaks over-careful Castilian with a heavy, if unidentifiable, accent. And although the existence of Iranian drug gangs is presented as a fact of life, their nationality within the fiction is less clear: they are said to speak Arabic (a mistake by the characters or the scriptwriters?) and one typically exotic location is an oriental restaurant that is clearly Lebanese (a stained glass cedar tree, the national symbol of Lebanon, is prominent in the lobby window). Despite this unacknowledged confusion in the representation of the other, functionalist rituals of processing and punishing crime, of literally policing borders, could hardly be clearer than here.

It is striking that the main narrative, Ferrer's entrapment of the Iranians, is based on a feigning of criminality: while his colleagues fear Ferrer has indeed succumbed to corruption, he is simply miming crime in order more faithfully to promote the final cohesion of the collective and the maintenance of social order. Crime thus creates a sense of community, where previously that community was under terminal social stress: Ferrer will be, temporarily at least, reconciled with his wife when she agrees that only the kidnappers are responsible for their child's predicament. And if Ferrer breaks the rule of hygiene, by associating with the irredeemable Iranians, he will not be contaminated by them. As Lucía, the most reliable of witnesses, notes, her boss is 'crazy' but 'a good cop'.

It was perhaps with some relief that Spanish audiences turned in 2000 from the operatic *Policías* to the smaller-scale and more intimate tone of *El comisario*, which runs for a less-demanding 60 minutes. Yet here, too, the emphasis is on the policing of boundaries. The pre-credit tag shows a psychiatric hospital: the mother superior discovers a young female inmate dead on her bed (a crucifix hangs behind on a whitewashed wall). After the credits, the series' most popular partners, Pope and Charlie (dressed as normal in tartan trousers and lurid orange shirt), are briskly dispatched to the clinic, where they interview an unsympathetic doctor. The location, with its lush garden and roomy interior, is by no means unpleasant. The many conversations that follow will be shot in classic, even placid, style with little camera movement: establishing shots give way to leisurely shot/reverse shots. From the start, moreover, professional duties are cross-cut with personal issues. Charlie is hoping to further his brief affair with colleague Lola, who in turn confesses to a female colleague she is pregnant but doesn't know the father's identity. It is Lola who will go undercover in the clinic and end up (like Ferrer's daughter in *Policías*) drugged and bound to a bed. But she is clearly a major agent in the narrative and no passive victim of male rivalry. Indeed, the fact that the murder victim was herself pregnant means that the line between public and police is blurred in a common feminine vulnerability.

El comisario is thus more ambivalent than *Policías*, attempting to reconcile contradictory positions. Lola's authority is undermined by her chaotic personal life. But then so is Charlie's: when he presents his lover with a doormat inscribed with the slogan 'You and Me', she rejects his sentimental offer of domesticity in disgust. And the male officers of *El comisario* have relatively little opportunity to shine in action sequences. The fiercest fights in the specimen episode are between women: Lola battles with the nurse who, we discover in flashback, murdered the young patient with whom her husband was having an affair and now wishes to kill the undercover policewoman. It would seem that Spanish women can be as deadly, and as merciless, as *Policías*' Iranian males. The police inspector himself, a glum Tito Valverde, has little to do in this episode. While he clearly serves like his counterpart Ferrer as a patriarchal talisman (and is also equipped with national flag and royal portrait), he merely directs the action from the safety of his office. Like Ferrer, however, he is separated from his wife: collective cognition and individual affect remain irreconcilable.

One subplot does indeed serve in recommended style not just to add 'volume' but also to implicate the domestic in the criminal, the psychological in the social. The teenage son of husband-and-wife team Pascual and Laura asks if his girlfriend Samira, who in spite of her Western wardrobe and free-flowing locks is said to be 'Moroccan', can move in with the family. While the parents at first reluctantly agree (Pascual says they will be living 'like gypsies'), they are shocked when Samira's family subsequently reports her missing to the police. A central scene then follows in which the Spanish parents, in the presence of the teenage couple, confront the Moroccan father through an interpreter in a setting familiar to viewers: the bar where characters habitually work through personal problems. The father insists on the forced marriage of his daughter to a colleague in Morocco to whom he owes a favour. While the young people vigorously resist, the police officer-parents are forced to agree that the underage girl must return home. *El comisario*'s liberal ideology here thus reaches an impasse: the individual rights of the young woman are incompatible with the respect the show also suggests is due to the collective cultural traditions of others, not to mention the due process of law. Affect and cognition and gender and ethnicity are thus shown to intersect in uncontrollable or undecidable ways. When Shamira returns to take leave of Laura, her new hijab and modest dress cannot disguise the fact that she has been beaten into submission by her father. The comic tag at the episode's end, in which the departure of Tristán Ulloa's Julio is celebrated with a stripper in police uniform, barely covers this anomalous anomie.

Domestic violence is a repeated theme in *El comisario*, which takes the interests of its female characters (and viewers) very seriously. And, unlike *Policías*, *El comisario* takes care not to stereotype ethnic minorities: its drug dealers are just as likely to be fresh-faced Spanish college kids as saturnine Iranians. But staking out a broader overlap between emotion and judgement, the show does not generally use the risks it depicts to uphold pre-existing community. Rather, like Durkheim, it questions the link between act and consequence, attempting in its dramatic form a synthetic exploration of the meaning of crime. In *Policías*, the social becomes private (drug dealers wreak revenge on the family). In *El comisario*, conversely, the private becomes social (a son's girlfriend is transformed successively into a minor, an ethnic minority, and a victim of domestic abuse). Both shows reveal the pressure of forces (of combinations and alterations) through which the individual becomes something else in a collective representation that is ambiguously anchored at once inside and outside social actors. But the emphasis of each series is very different, as is its account of that violence which, for Durkheim, is a necessary part of the operation of morality and value judgement on the individual who both fears and desires the law.

Police lines: cinema and television

On 15 November 2001 Sony's Spanish distributing arm released Miguel Angel Vivas's feature film *Reflejos* ('Reflections'), part-funded by Antena 3, home of *Policías*. With female lead Ana Fernández only recently released from the series, it boasted a spectacular, even exotic premise that could have come from Spain's most cinematic TV drama: a serial killer of babies. In a stylish pre-credit sequence, the unseen villain murders a child in its crib in a comfortably furnished domestic nursery.

Casting, theme and even plot structure (the opening, clearly unnecessary in a feature film, makes sense only as a 'hook' to pull in the TV viewer) thus combine to prove the contamination of movie aesthetics by television. However, unlike *Policías* (which, we remember, regularly earned a rating of 3,500,000), *Reflejos* was not a commercial success, winning an audience of only 47,014 and grossing just €185,115 (Ministerio de Cultura). The reason for this failure was perhaps that, unlike on television and thus contrary to audience expectation, Fernández did not herself play a detective and thus spent much of the movie confined to the kitchen as her husband fought crime on his own. It is also the case that police drama, charting as it does the intimate and complex passage from the individual to the collective, is better suited to the regular domestic audience of television than to infrequent visitors to movie theatres. As Durkheim wrote, collective ideals can only be constituted and take consciousness of themselves 'if they are fixed on things that can be seen by all, understood by all, represented to all' (137). Cinema, a minority pursuit, has some difficulty in performing that socially transformative function. The quality of 'closeness', so valued by both producers and consumers of TV drama series, comes more naturally to the small screen.

The cliffhanger of *El comisario*'s ninth season (2005–2006) also used the heart-wrenching premise of stolen babies. In a spectacular finale the young kidnap victims risked incineration in a burning building. And later seasons of the show built and sustained healthy audience share by adding a procedural strand. In a clear reference to *CSI*, one of the few US shows to gain a mass audience in Spain, pathology acquired new prominence. As one of the longest-running series dramas in Spain (preceded only by *Hospital Central*) and the only police drama still on the air, *El comisario* could afford to be all things to all viewers and combine the psychological interest for which it was known with a stronger sense of the institutional operation of justice.

On final analysis, however, both of the shows I have examined prove more complex than expected. Though *Policías* prefers spectacle to psychology (who knows or cares why Ferrer neglects his wife?) it remains viscerally affective in its frequent focus on the body in peril (whether bound to a bed, beaten by chains, or suspended from a tall building). And if, cynically, *Policías* uses crime to confirm a sense of community, it shows in spite of itself that that community is always already wounded, with personal relationships almost beyond repair. Moreover, it is tough *Policías* that draws most heavily on the ambiguous emotional appeal of music. In a plot device unnervingly reminiscent of the fey *Ally McBeal* (Fox, 1997-2002), hardbitten cops retreat every week to a cosy nightclub, where they are treated to songs by carefully chosen performers (such as Uruguayan indie songwriter Jorge Drexler).

Fuzzy *El comisario*, on the other hand, normally favours domesticity, with many more scenes than *Policías* shot in officers' homes. But, as we saw in the case of Shamira, the unwilling, underage bride, the series sometimes demands of its viewers more subtle acts of cognition than those required by *Policías*. For if the operation of justice is already rooted in the home, the violence it does to individuals is all the more distressing. Thus, while *Policías* suggests that a good cop can be a bad person (Ferrer neglects his family until the kidnap), *El comisario* suggests that a good person can be a bad cop (well-meaning Laura and Pascual are only too willing to inadvertently abduct a minor). The stress in both plot lines on father-child relations is symptomatic of the social pressure on the traditional family: Totó begs his parents to 'stop being cops' and take pity on the young couple. Here, crime drama points beyond itself to new modes of morality and sociality in which, say, youth, gender and immigration will be conjugated in as yet unarticulated forms.

A functionalist approach to police drama that goes beyond the mere reinforcement of current community and convention would thus suggest that no TV series can be definitively classified as 'conservative' or 'liberal', as some critics have proposed. If the law is desirable as well as obligatory (and, in line with Durkheim, these dramas never suggest that egotism or compulsion can be good in themselves), then individual rights are inseparable from a collective social contract. We are in society and society is in us. Moreover there can be no clear causality in operation here. TV does not simply reflect or affect reality. Rather, its collective narratives are the 'projections' (Durkheim's word) that substitute for the world of the senses a world projected by the ideals the series themselves construct.

What these mass narratives show us, then, is how collective thought transforms all it touches: mixing the realms of public and private, confounding contraries of inside and outside, levelling differences of status, and differentiating similarities of groups, classes, and professions. Both series in their different ways dramatize the elusive 'expressive' or 'passionate' soul of 'penality', which was for Durkheim so difficult to analyse. But if value is independent of its object (that is to say, if it is profoundly social) this does not mean that we can, as viewers or as citizens, simply step outside its domain. This, then, is the 'police line', at once aesthetic and moral, that television cannot cross.

Policías, en el corazón de la calle
('Police Officer, in the Heart of the Street', Antena 3, 2000–2003)

Production company	Globo Media
Creators, executive producers and senior writers	Nacho Cabana, Manuel Valdivia, Chus Vallejo
Directors	Salvador Calvo, Jesús del Cerro, Guillermo Fernández Groizard, et al.
Art direction	Xabier Iriondo

Cast

José María Pou	Ferrer
Pedro Casablanc	'El Ruso'
Adolfo Fernández	Carlos
Ana Fernández	Lucía

El comisario, Tele 5, 1999–

Production companies	BocaBoca, Picasso Studios
Executive producers	César Benítez, Carlos Arias, Xabier Puerta, et al.
Directors	Alfonso Arandia, Jesús Font, Ignacio Mercero, et al.
Writers	Carlos Asorey, Joan Barbero, Verónica Fernández, et al.
Art direction	Carlos Dorremochea

Cast

Tito Valverde	Comisario Gerardo Castilla
Marcial Alvarez	'Pope'
Juan José Artero	'Charlie'
Elena Irureta	Laura

Joaquín Climent	Pascual
Margarita Lascoiti	Lupe
Mar Regueras	Lola
Tristán Ulloa	Julio

Works Cited

Barroso García, Juan. *Realización de los géneros televisivos*. Madrid: Síntesis, 2002.

Brunsdon, Charlotte. 'Structure of Anxiety: Recent British Television Crime Fiction'. *Screen* 39.3 (1998): 223-43.

Calle 13. 'Foros de discusión'. 20 Dec. 2005. <http://foros.calle13-es.com/viewtopic.php?t=3672>

—. 'Nuestras series'. 20 Dec. 2005. <http://www.calle13.com /series.php>

comisario, El. DVD Box Set (4 Disks: Episodes 14-26). Tele 5, BocaBoca, Picasso Studios, no date [2005].

Cormier-Rodier, Béatrice. *Policiers en séries: images de flics*. Nancy: Presses Universitaires de Nancy, 1994.

Durkheim, Emile. *Sociologie et philosophie*. Paris: Quadrige/PUF, 2004.

Friday, Matthew. 'Subverting the Formula – Part II: Pilot Episodes and Crime Dramas'. *Scriptwriter* 2 (2002): 36-39.

Grabe, Maria Elizabeth. 'Television News Magazine Crime Stories'. *Critical Studies in Mass Communication* 16.2 (June 1999): 155-71.

Holmwood, Leigh. 'Police Line Closes in on Footage'. *Broadcast* (7 Sep. 2001): 2-3.

Lenz, Timothy O. *Changing Images of Law in Film and Television Crime Stories*. New York: Peter Lang, 2003.

Marlow, Jane. 'Making Crime Pay'. *Broadcast* (25 April 2003): 17.

Mason, Gary. 'In My View: True Crime'. *Televisual* (July 1995): 12-13.

Matthews, Tony. 'BBC Stands by Decision to Pay'. *Ariel* (8 March 2005): 2.

Ministerio de Cultura. 6 June 2006. <www.mcu.es>

Policías. DVD Box Set (4 Disks with episodes re-edited as feature-length TV movies). Antena 3, Globomedia, no date [2005].

Potter, W. James, et al. 'Antisocial Acts in Reality Programming on Television'. *Journal of Broadcasting and Electronic Media* 41.1 (1997): 69-75.

Raney, Arthur A. and Bryant, Jennings. 'Moral Judgement and Crime Drama: An Integrated Theory of Enjoyment'. *Journal of Communication* 52.2 (2002): 402-15.

Raney, Arthur A., and Rapping, Elayne. *Law and Justice As Seen on TV*. New York: New York UP, 2003.

Reith, Margaret. 'The Relationship between Unemployment in Society and the Popularity of Crime Drama on TV'. *Journal of Broadcasting and Electronic Media* 40.2 (1996): 258-64.

Sparks, Richard. *Television and the Drama of Crime*. Bucks.: Open UP, 1992.

Sumser, John. *Morality and Social Order in Television Crime Drama*. Jefferson, NC: McFarland, 1996.

Telecinco 'Las audiencias de la serie'. 6 June 2006. <http://www.elcomisario.Telecinco.es/dn_19.htm>

Vaca Berdayes, Ricardo. *El ojo digital: Audiencias 1*. Madrid: Ex Libris, 2004.

Van den Bulck, Jan. 'Research Note – The Relationship between Television Fiction and Fear of Crime: an Empirical Comparison of Three Causal Explanations'. *European Journal of Communication* 19.2 (2004): 239–48.

White, Geoff. 'Shake-Up After BBC Employs Murderer'. *Broadcast* (24 Jun 2005): 3.

CHAPTER FOUR

Dramatic Professions: Workplace Fiction on Television

Medical and legal

It is no accident that workplace drama remains a staple on television in many countries. Social issues such as health and the law are increasingly intertwined with the television medium. The trade press has chronicled persistent crises and controversies in these fields. Recently in Britain there was a bitter debate over the protection of children, with one side arguing that 'kids TV should come with a health warning', producing as it does physical and psychological ill-effects through violent content, effects on the brain, and influence on diet and obesity (Lyford). Facing the prohibition of advertising for (ill-defined) 'junk food', the industry countered that the 'sweeping ad ban' (which extended beyond dedicated programming to all shows with a high percentage of viewers under 16) threatened production funding for children (Thompson and Rogers). 'Kids TV' was, we were told, 'caught in a perfect storm' of health issues (*Broadcast*).

A similar, but longer-running, battle in the legal field was over the much-delayed decision whether to allow cameras into British courts (Thompson, 'Court TV'). Meanwhile the Crown Persecution Service had finally improved media access, allowing journalists and filmmakers to screen video material used in building prosecutions (Thompson, 'CPS'), after broadcasters had fought a ban. These institutional struggles over the rights and responsibilities of television coincided with new and sometimes disturbing innovations in content, from 'shock docs' featuring extreme medical conditions to 'celebrity jury series' debating cases based on real-life trials for crimes such as rape (Thompson, 'BBC'). With dedicated cable channels for health and law now well established, images of the two professions were ubiquitous.

Social scientists have paid particular attention to the possible effects of such media images on audiences, with the *Journal of Broadcasting and Electronic Media* repeatedly returning to the topic in the US. An investigation of 'the influence of television viewing on public perception of physicians' in 1995 (Pfau, Mullen and Garrow) noted a cultural shift from early research, which found TV doctors to embody the traits of 'power, authority, and knowledge', to current images of medics 'as more likely to be female and young, and more imbued with interpersonal communication skill, physical attractiveness and power, but less imbued with the trait of character' (441). The authors' fear that such depictions 'may undermine public confidence' is taken up in 2001, when 'a content analysis [...]indicate[d] that television's physician portrayals are less positive than they were [even] in 1992' (Chory-Assad and Tamborini, 'Television Doctors'), thus leading to 'decreased [...] trust in physicians' (499).

This study acknowledges that fictional images may conflict with depictions of doctors found on non-fictional television and that such content is 'cognitively processed' in distinct ways by viewers ('heuristic' processing will lead them to hold negative beliefs, 'systematic' processing may lead them to discount such images as unrealistic (518)). But the implications of the findings are claimed to be wide-ranging: the television-related loss of confidence in real-life physicians could lead, we are told, to 'higher health care costs and noncompliance with [...] medical advice', or an increase in 'the anxiety associated with interacting with one's doctor' (517). Conversely, we are promised that television and other screen media are 'important sources of medical information that may be used to improve the health of individuals and the functioning of the medical industry' (519).

A later (2003) essay by the same authors confirmed the alleged 'negative relationships between exposure to prime-time doctor shows and perceptions' (Chory-Assad and Tamborini, 'Television Exposure' 197). These negative views are related to current controversies over health care, where 'decreased faith in physicians' is linked to 'a trend of medical consumerism in which the physician-patient interaction is viewed as a business transaction' (198). The analysis follows the theory of media 'cultivation' whereby

> recurrent patterns of television images are society's primary source of socialization and exposure to these recurrent images cultivates basic assumptions and common conceptions of societal facts, norms, and values in an otherwise heterogeneous population. (Chory-Assad and Tamborini, 'Television Exposure' 199)

However, the authors caution that 'total television exposure is not as strong or consistent a predictor of individuals' beliefs about real life as is exposure to specific programme types [e.g. news vs. drama]'. And social effects do not work only one way:

> [...] television and its viewers interact in a multidirectional process in the creation and distribution of television's messages that, in turn, impact the development, maintenance, or exploitation of society's needs, values, and beliefs. (199)

Scholars of legal drama go further, not only asking 'what [long-running franchise] *Law & Order* tells us about the American criminal justice system', but also positing that TV programmes can be studied as legal texts because they share a common feature with the 'normal legal trilogy of constitutions, codes, and cases [and are] cultural artifacts open to warring interpretations both on the descriptive and normative level'. (Sutton, Britts and Landman 5)

The newer and more critical hospital dramas of the 1990s spawned a major book, *Body Trauma TV*, in which Jason Jacobs argues that shows such as *ER* corresponded to 'the growing medicalization of everyday life [with its] body-centred fears and fascinations' (147). His conclusion is worth quoting at length:

> Hospital drama drew on these discursive contexts [of medicalization and the body] to combine the realization of the biological and melodramatic possibilities in visual and narrative terms. Harnessing this to a serial form that followed the development of workplace relations over time and linking these to the graphic nature of medical treatment secured the success of the medical drama as a hybrid genre in the mid-1990s. They borrowed and modified visual styles from reality television and action and horror film genres in order to present a distinctive mise en scène of interior-based action (interior in the sense of inside the building and inside the body). At the same time they explored the problems of a generation of doctors being trained and nurtured by another generation who were less confident than ever about their place in the world. The metaphor of the war zone extended beyond the treatment of professional and interpersonal relationships with groups and factions pitted against one another [...] and the prospect of 'playing God' – far from a privileged opportunity – was seen with trepidation. (Jacobs 147)

Jacobs' humanities-based approach is founded, unlike that of social scientists, on the qualitative approach of close textual analysis rather than the quantitative evidence of informant interview. He argues, however, that textual and social trends coincide: the 'nihilism, self-destruction, and despair' of medical dramas connect to 'the experience of authenticity in contemporary society [that] now seems to demand extreme measures' (148). Moreover, the new 'sophistication of television fiction' in the period recognized and nurtured an intelligent audience through 'generic innovation, multi-narrative, multi-character address [...] present[ing] complex moral, romantic, and ethical problems without resorting to [...] simple closure in their narratives' (148). The spectacular use of 'bodies as vehicles for dramatic material' thus comes up against 'the requirements of plausibility [that] are often in tension with the necessity for dramatic invention and the opportunities and constraints of genre and formula' (149).

Such pragmatic considerations of institution and genre contrast with Jacobs' main thesis: that hospital dramas embrace and promote 'the apocalyptic sensibility that pervades the contemporary western psyche' (149). However another major study of the genre (which also focuses on *ER*) has explicitly rejected the 'apocalyptic' trend of 'cartoonish postmodernism' (Bailey 59). Drawing on both humanities and scientific research, Steve Bailey argues convincingly for a new '(super)genre' of 'professional television', which permits a general analysis of specific workplace dramas, such as the medical and legal. He sketches out three essential characteristics:

> First the professional figure operates within a larger institution and must continually negotiate the demands of such institutions [...] in light of personal moral, financial, sexual, and physical needs [...] Second [...] there is a foregrounding of the professional's struggle between ethical demands and the ever-present capitalist imperative for profit [...] Finally, the professional always exists in the context of the nonprofessional other; this is not limited to the economically and socially disenfranchised but also includes the unethical yet successful administrator [...] and other one-dimensional figures who lack the moral complexity of the professional figure. (Bailey 47)

Crucially, professionalism is intrinsic to television itself as an institution. And it also serves as a link between dramatic content and other real-life contexts. Bailey examines a study published in the *New England Journal of Medicine*, which takes cardiopulmonary resuscitation (CPR) in *ER* as the object of its content analysis. This kind of article 'conjoin[s] real and fictional discursive fields in a classically institutional format: the quantitative research report' (58). This discursive fusion does not, however, point to what Bailey brands 'vulgar postmodernism', but rather to a newly critical engagement between two worlds:

> The ability to understand the media-saturated environment of the patient is critical to an ethical performance [by the physician] operating within a complex environment that includes both rigorous medical science and the fantastic mechanisms of popular entertainment, which draw on the very same science. (Bailey 59)

Media culture has thus not triumphed over reality. Rather, it must be inserted beyond the 'horizontal' context of, say, the evening schedule into a much deeper 'vertical axis', composed of 'a variety of discursive fields, many of which are far removed from the point of origin' (59). It is not just that television may influence public perceptions, as we saw in media effects research, but rather that television serves 'as a sort of hermeneutic apparatus for the understanding of public and private institutions'.

Surprisingly, Bailey sees a consensus between the central thematic premises of shows such as *L.A. Law* and *ER* and their Leftist cultural studies critics, a consensus based on what it means to be a professional: the mediation of 'ethical/financial/personal conflicts in the long-term interests of systemic maintenance by posing such conflicts as inevitable and as personally resolvable'. Finally, then, there is a 'homology between the symbolic construction of an individual/institutional relationship and the very skills that enable one to fully engage the texts that present this schema' (60). For Bailey, this parallelism explains the intensity of identification that audiences, including professionals themselves, feel for on-screen doctors and lawyers.

Interestingly, this sense of a two-way process between individuals and institutions recurs in some research on social science and medicine that is not related to television. One theoretical study appeals to Durkheim to suggest how social relationships and filiation have effects on physical and mental health, positing a 'cascading causal process' from the macrosocial to the psychobiological, in which different levels are dynamically linked. Where Bailey explored 'vertical' and 'horizontal' axes, Berkman, Glass, Brissette et al. posit movements 'upstream' and 'downstream'. The former embed social networks in larger sociocultural contexts, while the latter work through network structures to influence social and interpersonal behaviour. The authors identify four primary pathways through which networks operate at the behavioural level to affect health: the provision of social support; social influence; social engagement and attachment; and access to resources and material goods. We can now go on to examine how such pathways operate in two important and contrasting examples of professional drama on Spanish television.

Professional drama: two series concepts

There would seem to be no two series with less in common than private web Tele 5's *Hospital Central* (2000–) and public broadcaster TVE's *Al filo de la ley* (2005). While the former has been playing with great, indeed increasing, success since 2000 and is as I write approaching its 200th episode, the latter lasted just one season of 13 episodes in 2005. *Hospital Central* regularly won an audience of over 5,000,000 and a share of 30 per cent in 2006 (formulatv, 'Hospital'), but *Al filo de la ley* rapidly declined from its debut peak of almost 4,000,000 rating and 22 per cent share to 1,380,000 and 10.9 per cent at its close (formulatv, 'Al filo'). As we shall see, the production mentality of the two shows, which were scheduled against each other on Thursday prime time (10 pm) by their respective networks, is also very different, as is their audience address.

On the DVD covers, four of the modest stars of *Hospital Central*'s large and frequently changing ensemble cast look out in direct, smiling welcome at the viewer. Working-class nurses Rusti (Angel Pardo) and Esther (Fátima Baeza) seem especially approachable. Both have logged over 150 episodes in the series. Only the fifth figure, senior emergency medic Vilches, played by Jordi Rebellón, looks grumpy, a trait that faithful audiences now find reassuringly familiar. The series' official website helpfully cues us that, in spite of his habitual ill-humour, Vilches is 'greatly loved' by all in his workplace (Tele 5).

Of the four stellar protagonists of *Al filo de la ley* (familiar to viewers from their film roles), only one meets the spectator's gaze and even he, Emilio Gutiérrez Caba's senior partner Gonzalo, pinstripe-suited in a leather-backed chair, looks as if his tensely clasped hands are about to break a pencil in two.

8 Esther (Fátima Baeza, far left), Rusti (Angel Pardo, centre): *Hospital Central*

Of his colleagues, experienced and self-possessed Patricia (Fanny Gautier), pen in hand, gazes off into the distance from a similarly institutional chair, Natalia Verbeke's youthful and idealistic Elena appears to be absorbed in her brief, while Leonardo Sbaraglia's troubled Álex, in two-day stubble, leather jacket and impenetrable shades, looks more like a moody hit man than an earnest young lawyer. While the smiling medics pose against an abstract blue background (with workplace scenes relegated to the bottom of the box), the troubled but

9 The ensemble cast of *Al filo de la ley*

attractive lawyers are shot against the heavy furniture and loaded bookshelves that testify to their professional status.

What the two shows have in common is, of course, Bailey's (super) genre of 'professional television'. Moreover, both enact the different ways in which the social network of the workplace is caught between larger social contexts 'upstream' and interpersonal behaviour 'downstream'. We see this process in the press releases for successive seasons of *Hospital Central*, republished by specialist website www.formulatv.com. On 3 May 2005, the fifth anniversary of the show's debut and the end of the ninth season, the Director General of Tele 5 claimed that the secret of the show's success was a combination of the 'reality of its plot lines' and the 'recognizability of each doctor to the viewer'. For her part, the executive producer said that the motto of the now 'mature' show was: 'Closer than ever'. The audience's 'identification' with the characters was now fused with a greater engagement with 'life'. New plot lines will thus focus on organ transplants (with a regular character now moved to the new unit to ensure the audience's 'closeness' to the issue) and 'topics of social interest', such as the health problems of immigrants, domestic violence, anorexia, drug abuse and AIDS. All of these are again shown through the eyes of a familiar character, this time a trained social worker.

The launch of the tenth series (14 September 2005) stressed once more the series' 'adaptation' to the changing 'social reality' of everyday life, featuring as it did a major event hitherto impossible in Spain: the celebration of a lesbian wedding between regular characters Maca and Esther. Moreover, a plot line on Spanish NGOs saw two characters take a trip to Guatemala for a conference on tropical diseases. This provided an opportunity for the show to explore on-site and over several episodes the health conditions of Central American children and the role of education and preventive medicine in the developing world (the twelfth season would see a similar trip to India).

Beyond this stress on solidarity (which serves to legitimate the professionalism of the show's characters and its producers), Tele 5's CEO emphasized in his introduction to the eleventh season on 29 March 2006 what he called the 'pact of trust' between the audience and a series that was 'perfectly' written and directed and had, he claimed, been cited in a 'qualitative study' as the 'paradigm of quality drama'. The institution of medicine thus merges with that of television in their common appeal to professional standards that can be objectively and externally ratified.

But surely these global expeditions, however well-meaning and carefully focalized through familiar characters, would tend to distance faithful viewers from a show whose 'closeness' is all-important? And later seasons relied on stunt-casting for exceptional ratings: movie star Jorge Sainz featured in a live broadcast to mark the 100th episode (6 July 2004) and the show's biggest audience ever tuned in to see pop star David Bisbal entertain an audience of sick children, imperilled by a sudden fire (13 December 2006).

Moreover, this very domestic series had long and paradoxically prided itself (like *Periodistas*, Tele 5's first workplace drama) on spectacular exterior sequences of bloody accidents and dramatic rescues. As early as the first episode of Series 2 ('Panic in the stands') a high-school stadium had collapsed during a basketball match. While *Hospital Central* barely qualifies as 'body trauma TV' (and we will explore the 'interior' *mise-en-scène* when we come to examine specific episodes), there is clearly a tension between its intimate and familiar address to a local audience and its ambitious attempt to incorporate a dramatic world of much larger and perhaps threatening social and political issues. As Jacobs noted in the case of US medical dramas, the requirements of plausibility are thus in tension with the continued necessity for dramatic invention in Spain's longest-running series.

As a new show (and one scheduled against an established rival), *Al filo de la ley* did not survive to face such problems. Yet for all its movie-star protagonists it, too, stressed the closeness of its plot lines to the social reality of Spanish audiences. Indeed, the press release (accessible at formulatv) made much of the fact that all the fictional cases in the drama (there are just two in each episode) were based on real life. In an attempt at multidirectional cultivation, fledgling viewers were even encouraged to send in their own legal experiences as a basis for future episodes. The social topics given for *Al filo de la ley* often overlap with those dramatized in *Hospital Central*: drug use, immigration, domestic violence and gay couples. But TVE stresses above all the professionalism of the series, aided as it is by a team of experts who ensure that the legal procedures and technical language are strictly authentic.

In the traditional style of professional drama, these public questions are, of course, supplemented by personal plot lines, focusing in this case on a love triangle: Álex has to choose between current love interest Patricia and ex-lover Elena, with whom he unexpectedly finds himself working in the same office. Senior partner Gonzalo, on the other hand (described as 'shark-like' for his ruthless aggression) is going through a divorce and must reassess his relationship with a teenage daughter (a US drama with exactly the same premise would actually be called *Shark*, CBS, 2006–). Where the 'quality' of *Hospital Central* was said to lie in its scripting and direction, that of *Al filo de la ley* is also in its 'cinema look', which is in keeping with the high profile of its starry cast: TVE crows that this is the first national series in Spain to be shot on high definition, some time before it can be broadcast in that format (see also *El País*). The technical professionalism of the television institution thus validates both its product and, implicitly, its target audience, whose members are trusted to recognize such distinctive added value even if they cannot yet benefit from the full effect on their low-definition screens.

One aspect of the production process omitted by TVE is highlighted by www.muchatv.com. In its positive review, the specialist website notes that production company Plural Entertainment, a division of the massive PRISA conglomerate, had first developed the project for Univisión, the US Spanish-language channel. The format had then been adapted for the Spanish market by highlighting the professional plot lines and downplaying the personal stories, dismissed by this Spanish commentator as 'culebronescas' (i.e. reminiscent of the telenovelas treated in Chapter 6 of this book). It remains the case, however, that the director and the two junior stars (Verbeke and Sbaraglia are favourites of young filmgoers) are of Argentine extraction. Gutiérrez Caba, on the other hand, would be familiar to older audiences for a local film career stretching back to late Francoist classics such as *La caza* (Carlos Saura, 1966). Moreover, the executive producer of *Al filo de la ley* would go on to be the new Director General of TVE itself, thus suggesting that his show, transmitted in a prime slot on TVE1, fulfilled the values of Spanish public service broadcasting even as it drew on Latin American sources and stars.

Although both series lay claim to 'quality', then, *Hospital Central* and *Al filo* can be seen as embodying two different conceptions of professionalism, both on- and off-screen. But they also exemplify two different modes of integrating national address and international context in the production process. We can now examine single episodes of both series, which treat a topic that is crucial for social relationships and filiation: teenage suicide. As so often happens, the network structure (whether of medicine or law) serves to mediate dynamically (dramatically) between general sociocultural contexts and particular instances of interpersonal behaviour.

Bodies of evidence: specimen episodes

'Nunca sin ti' (*Hospital Central* 2.6)
Víctimas de odio de sus padres, una pareja de adolescentes intenta suicidarse; la chica muere y algunos de sus órganos son aptos para transplantes; el chico, muy grave, necesita la donación de un corazón. El Sámur recoge a una cantante de ópera y la intubación que deben practicarle puede dañar sus cuerdas vocales: las protestas del marido y representante de la artista les impiden hacerlo. [...] Javier parece haber perdido el norte con los juegos que le propone la mujer madura. Rusti sufre un accidente mientras atiende a un paciente con una enfermedad altamente contagiosa.

['Together Forever'
The victims of their parents' hatred, a couple of teenagers attempt suicide. The girl dies and some of her organs could be used for transplants. The boy is in critical condition and needs a heart donor. The Ambulance team pick up an opera singer and the tube they need to insert into her throat may damage her vocal chords: her husband, who is also her manager, prevents them from carrying out the procedure. [...] Javier seems to have lost direction because a mature woman is playing sex games with him. Rusti has an accident while he's dealing with a patient who is highly contagious.] (Ministerio de Cultura)

'Para los amigos ausentes' (*Al filo de la ley* 1.4)
Un adolescente se suicida tirándose desde un edificio en construcción. Los padres del muchacho deciden acusar a tres compañeros de clase que maltrataban física y verbalmente al chico fallecido. Álvarez y Asociados se encargarán de la acusación. Gonzalo, todavía ocupado con su divorcio y otros negocios con el extranjero, entrega el caso a Álex y Patricia [...] Elena ha aceptado por fin salir con el abogado Alfredo Molina y, sin buscarlo, ha despertado celos en Álex. En el terreno profesional, la joven letrada defenderá los intereses de Alicia, una mujer cuya pareja, María, ha muerto en accidente de tráfico. El padre de la fallecida, que nunca aceptó la homosexualidad de su hija, pretende quedarse con el piso de ambas. [...] Patricia parece haber convencido a Álex para irse a vivir juntos. El problema ahora radica en decidir a qué casa es mejor mudarse. El acuerdo no parece fácil.

['To absent friends'
A teenager commits suicide by jumping from a building that is still under construction. The youth's parents decide to bring charges against the three classmates who bullied the dead boy physically and verbally. Álvarez and Associates will take the case on. Gonzalo, who is still preoccupied with his divorce and foreign business, hands the case over to Álex and Patricia [...] Elena has finally agreed to go out with the lawyer Alfredo Molina and, inadvertently, has made Álex jealous. In the professional arena, the young lawyer [Elena] will defend the interests of Alicia, a woman whose partner, María, has died in a road accident. The dead woman's father, who never accepted that his daughter was gay, is trying to gain possession of the women's flat. [...] It looks like Patricia has convinced Álex that they should move in together. The problem now is deciding which home they should move into. It won't be easy to come to an agreement.] (Ministerio de Cultura)

The tagline of *Hospital Central*, shown before each episode, is 'Behind every doctor is a human being; behind every patient is a story'. It is a premise that clearly illuminates the tension between the public and the private and the form of narrative structure that are both characteristic of professional drama. The dozen characters named in the credit sequence (stylish blue monochrome and pounding music) would seem to bear out the content analyses of the *Journal of Broadcasting and Electronic Media*: Spanish TV medics, like their US equivalents, are likely to be young, female, skilful communicators, and more attractive than seems plausible in real life.

At first sight they also lack the trait of authoritative 'character'. Personal questions constantly intrude on the professional. Nurse Esther, concerned about her ex-boyfriend, is distracted from her work and accidentally pricks her amiable colleague Rusti with a needle that proves to be infected with HIV. Psychiatrist Cristina, a single mother, brings her disruptive small boy to work. Her unsympathetic male manager tells her she is inefficient and disordered, unable to write up proper case reports. Paediatrician Andrea, still in mourning for her recently deceased mother, treats colleagues brusquely. Young doctor

Javier, a strong defender of Spain's national health service, is led astray by an ex-patient, a sexually voracious mature woman who insists on kissing him in public. Esther even discusses her troubled love life as the nurses wheel an unconscious youth into the emergency room. Surely public perception of such figures must be damaged by the awareness that their power and knowledge are undermined by these unruly passions?

However, more is at stake than this, even for viewers who cognitively process this material in a heuristic way, naively taking it at face value. Esther shows maturity by apologizing to Rusti, even setting up a romantic date that she is forced to break (her ex- has emptied her bank account). As a psychologist, Cristina actively employs emotion as part of her professional repertoire, counselling a cancer patient who refuses invasive treatment in order to live life to the full. Andrea reveals her empathy with the working-class mother of the young female would-be suicide: her own mother was also a downtrodden caretaker, who bitterly resented her lot. Javier vigorously defends a singer patient with a breathing tube, whose husband-manager, fearing lost earnings if her voice is damaged, insists that she be discharged into private care. 'Systematic processing' of such dramatic material must surely lead audiences to the conclusion that figures of authority, newly humanized, are actively enriched in their interaction with the public by interpersonal skills such as empathy.

One feature here distinguishes the Spanish drama from the US models it clearly resembles in its complex multi-character, multi-narrative form, and shooting style (heavily reliant on steady cam for those trademark gurney shots). This is the explicit refusal of the trend of medical consumerism. When offered an HIV test, one patient jokingly welcomes this new 'free offer'. He is rebuked by the nurse who solemnly tells him that all treatment in the hospital is free. The husband-manager is punished for discharging his singer-wife into private care, which led to an unnecessary tracheotomy: senior doctor Vilches says he will sue his private rival for malpractice. The bourgeois father of the boy in the suicide pact, who also insists on private care, is told in no uncertain terms that 'you can't buy a heart [for transplant] in a store'. This recurrent pattern, even in a single episode, is thus a distinctive example of media cultivation: of television as a source of socialization (of basic assumptions and common conceptions concerning societal facts, norms and values) in an increasingly heterogeneous Spanish population. Several episodes deal with immigrants, who as characters (and, no doubt, viewers) are unlikely to be familiar with Spain's public health policies.

In spite of considerable stress on private problems, then, the episode makes space for social solidarity and even frank didacticism, as Tele 5's press releases and corporate mentality had suggested. Accidentally infected with HIV, rustic Rusti (who frequently invokes his village origins) is exhaustively informed of his prognosis and treatment. Indeed the final shot shows him profanely cursing his bad luck, but still conscientiously taking his cocktail of drugs in the restaurant where he has been stood up by colleague Esther. (Consistently unlucky in heterosexual love, she will not discover the lasting delights of lesbianism for another six seasons.)

Elsewhere we are shown not only the scenes in which the suicide's mother is asked for permission to harvest her daughter's organs but also the meetings in which the medics discuss policy and tactics in such cases. By the end of the episode viewers would thus have a working knowledge of Spanish transplant practices, a knowledge that would surely interact multidirectionally, impacting on the development of society's beliefs in the area. And there is a certain sobriety here, an acknowledgement of the limits of professional practice: unlike in *ER*, in *Hospital Central* CPR does not reanimate the boy on whom it is carried out. In spite of exhaustive counselling, the mother will refuse permission for organ donation and both teenage lovers (who had leapt from a photogenic location opposite Madrid's Palacio Real) will simply, disappointingly, die.

Hence, if everyday life is becoming medicalized, then this need not lead to apocalyptic trauma. Although the drama remains within the building (in the 65 minutes of the show there are only two brief final scenes shot outside the workplace), it rarely ventures within the body. While Madrid is in other episodes something of a war zone (with frequent shootings and gruesome accidents), here the only plot line to employ the spectacular use of bodies as vehicles for dramatic material is that of the teenage suicides. The youth's bloodied naked torso, often displayed to the camera, is finally opened to reveal his fatally damaged heart. Teenage suicide is thus presented as a particularly, even melodramatically, charged motif for social conflict: the boy's wealthy father blames the girl's impoverished mother for his child's fate. Finally, however, there is a modest and qualified resolution: the boy's distraught mother embraces her counterpart, returning the First Communion medal that the girl had given to her young lover.

Even in extremis, then, the social network of the medical profession mediates between larger sociocultural contexts (such as class), working to influence conflictive interpersonal behaviour. As Bailey suggests of US 'professional television', such conflicts are presented as personally resolvable in the long-term interests of systemic maintenance of both the medical and the televisual institution. It is striking, however, that the ethical and financial question of public vs. private medicine receives an authoritative, definitive diagnosis from the lugubrious Vilches. The manager will be punished for his greed both legally and poetically: with his wife's singing voice now ruined he will now receive '20 per cent of nothing'. Vilches does not play God. But he clearly stands for (and stands up for) the ethics of a universal national health service.

Hospital Central's professional figures thus clearly fulfil Bailey's three criteria: they negotiate institutional demands with personal needs, fight economics with ethics, and contrast with non-professional others (the hard-hearted bureaucrat, the exploitative manager). But still they are coloured by a specifically Spanish commitment to collective solidarity in health care as in social networks. We can now see if this diagnosis of a much-loved and long-lasting medical show holds true for short-lived legal drama *Al filo de la ley*. The episode chosen also focuses on teenage suicide.

As elsewhere, legal dramas have had less success on Spanish television than medical shows: Antena 3's equally starry *Lobos* ('Wolves', 2005) was also pulled from the schedule after just five episodes. Yet, given the viewer's presumed lack of sympathy with the setting, *Al filo*'s aesthetic is daringly austere. In a near silent pre-credit sequence, shot with jittery hand-held camera and edited with jump cuts, we see an unprepossessing youth climb a half-built structure on the edge of the city: shot from below he is a tiny, pathetic figure. Back in the building, the camera pans left to take in a passing train before a vertiginous shot down to earth. We see the boy's body already spreadeagled on the ground below.

Hence, where *Hospital Central* showed us the spectacular leap of their doomed teens (and placed them in an unusually picturesque setting), *Al filo* typically denies us the visual pleasure of graphic action and dramatic mise en scène, suggesting perhaps through its relative austerity that the show is to be viewed as a legal text, a cultural artefact whose presentation of constitutions, codes and cases is open to warring interpretations. More than the specific events depicted, these conflicting interpretations form the substance of the drama.

Much more explicit than *Hospital Central* about its Madrid location, *Al filo de la ley* uses credits that juxtapose urban blight (dawn or dusk behind electricity pylons) with big-city sophistication (the Gran Vía and business district of Azca, even a glimpse of the Opera). Portrait shots of the attractive stars are digitally overlaid with scratches and stains that signal urban distress. The *mise-en-scène* is similarly restrained. The morning meeting, setting out the cases for lawyers and viewers (a staple of the legal genre), takes place in a discreet wood-panelled office. Patricia is professional in a grey tweed suit with a modest neckline; Elena arrives late in bright green, flashing a little more flesh. But the high-def photography is muted throughout, with trendily washed-out colours.

The two cases for today are briefly sketched: the parents of a teenage suicide are suing his alleged aggressors; the partner of a deceased lesbian is being sued as a squatter by the latter's relations, who are anxious to take hold of the flat that is the legal property of the 'natural family'. The personal plot lines, equally restricted in number, are also economically established at the start: senior partner Gonzalo claims to be adapting to single life after his separation;

Patricia and Álex are planning on moving in together. Beyond the fact that this is a workplace romance, it is not clear, however, how the demands of the legal institution dramatically intersect with the personal moral, financial, sexual and physical needs of the characters.

Nor is there much sign of that other characteristic of professional drama, the struggle between ethical demands and the capitalist imperative for profit. Gonzalo breaks a lunch date with his teenage daughter because of the unexpected arrival of senior colleagues from Amsterdam (cosmopolitan sophistication is taken for granted) and takes phone calls when they finally have lunch in a fine restaurant together (the series boasts many such attractive exteriors). But if the parents of the bullied boy and the widowed lesbian have trouble paying their legal bills, we are not privy to that problem: when Elena loses the impoverished lesbian's case she is apparently rewarded with only a warm hug.

Both cases do, however, feature Bailey's third trait of professional drama: the interaction with a non-professional other who is economically and socially disenfranchised. The bullied boy's parents are isolated by a school system that fails to protect their interests; the lesbian lover appeals to the legal institution to defend her against her girlfriend's father and brother, who harm and exclude her. *Al filo de la ley* is surprisingly explicit about such questions of natural justice and does not fail to guide the viewer. When the homophobic brother claims it is unjust that a 'dyke' [*bollera*] should hold on to a roomy flat when he and his family have to share a cramped apartment with his father, then there is no doubt where the audience's sympathies lie. Indeed, the elderly judge himself rebukes witnesses in the court for sniggering when there is a reference to the women displaying public affection. If television is indeed a hermeneutic apparatus for the understanding of public and private institutions, then the process of interpretation seems excessively one-sided here.

But there are some ambivalences, nonetheless. One of the school bullies was in fact a friend of the suicide (they bonded over *The Lord of the Rings*) and, torn between telling the truth and tribal loyalty to his gang, finally, tearfully, gives testimony. The dead lesbian's father, whose moustache has him stereotyped to Spanish viewers as an unsympathetic reactionary, is shown to be moved by a last letter from his daughter, given to him by sympathetic lawyer Elena. But where in *Hospital Central* emotional responses, initially disruptive, finally reinforce professional performance, here their effects are unclear. Placing the blame 'upstream' on the macrosocial level, Álex claims in his powerful closing speech that it is not the teenage bullies but the education system as a whole that should be in the dock. Shifting emphasis 'downstream' onto interpersonal relations (and in an eerie echo of *Hospital Central*), the lesbian lover shows the grieving father the medal her girlfriend gave her. She says: 'My only vice was to love your daughter'.

The result of the twin cases is decidedly undramatic, no doubt conditioned by the Spanish inquisitorial system of justice, less intrinsically dramatic than the Anglo-Saxon adversarial tradition that underwrites long-running shows such as *Law & Order*. The bullies are not sentenced: the parents will accuse the school of negligence. The lesbian simply loses the home to which she has no legal title and the apparent reconciliation with the father comes to nothing. Unlike in the US shows studied by Bailey, institutional conflicts are thus not shown to be personally resolvable. The Spanish show's bias towards the collective overriding the individual is also reminiscent of *Hospital Central*.

Finally in *Al filo de la ley* the lack of dynamic links or 'cascading' connections between the professional and the personal (emotional empathy is untried or useless) is fatally debilitating. This failure is inadvertently emphasized by the clunky closing dialogue that hinges on the word 'case'. When the insinuating senior partner Gonzalo asks his younger colleagues Álex and Patricia how things are going, they reply with reference to their legal duties. But he claims he was asking whether the pair of (lukewarm) lovers will move in together. As the show has failed in the symbolic construction of the all-important individual/institutional relationship, there can be no homology between this on-screen negotiation and the off-screen skills that enable viewers to fully engage with its televisual text. Lacking both the social didacticism and the affective urgency of *Hospital Central*, *Al filo de la ley* is thus unable to create the intensity of identification with its professional characters that might have ensured its continuing success.

Quality and consciousness

In 2003 the feature film *Planta cuarta* ('The 4th Floor'), a hospital drama about a children's cancer ward, gained over one million admissions. It was directed by Antonio Mercero, a veteran creator of classic TV series over three decades (whom I examine in Chapter 7), and produced in association with TVE and Canal + by BocaBoca, a company known for television franchises such as *El comisario* (examined in Chapter 3). This rare example of a cinematic success with a medical theme, which even here focused more on patients than professionals, was thus dependent on talent and expertise more associated with television than film.

Media consultant Ricardo Vaca Berdayes reminds us just how popular professional drama can be on television. Writing also in 2003, when *Hospital Central* was gaining 4.4 million ratings and 30 per cent share, he notes that the best performances in the then current TV schedule come from good-quality returning series that, if supported by their networks, achieve high levels of 'complicity' from their regular audience (208). Moreover, *Hospital Central*'s demographics show that that audience is not just large and profitable, but also qualitatively diverse, leading in such varied segments as 'women', 'young adults' (25-44), 'housewives with children', and (surprisingly for a drama set in Madrid) Basques.

Far from the 'shock docs' and celebrity rape trials that have made the trade press, the two series I have studied here are clear examples of 'quality', although that is defined in different ways in each case. And while Leftist commentators may be hostile to such professional dramas (as they were to *L.A. Law* and *ER*), it is worth remembering that Raymond Williams, the grandfather of British cultural studies, looked more kindly on television drama. In his pioneering *Television: Technology and Cultural Form*, Williams was sceptical of social science 'effects research' (9). And though he was wary of the unprecedented explosion in the consumption of drama, especially in the medical and criminal genres, he saw it as an antidote to what he called 'the widespread withdrawal from general social experience' manifested by other, more traditional media (61). This social engagement is self-evident in Tele 5's official website for *Hospital Central*. As I write (17 March 2007), the headline news is that the whole cast has donated blood in an attempt to 'raise the viewer's awareness'. A recent trip by cast and crew to India is also intended to increase 'social consciousness' of child health in the Third World through 'messages of solidarity'. 'Their' problems have thus been brought close to 'our' homes and 'our' desire to help has been made reality (Tele 5).

Social participation in the present is, however, linked to nostalgia for the televisual past. If you remember the beginnings of the show with affection, asks the website, why not buy the first two seasons on DVD? Viewers are also encouraged to chat with fellow fans, post messages on the show's bulletin board, or find their other half: 'thousands of boys and girls [*chic@s*] are waiting for you!' The informational, the economic and the emotional thus flow freely, even indiscriminately, together in the hermeneutic machine made jointly by professional dramas, their producers and their audiences. It seems likely that *Hospital Central* provides some of its loyal viewers with at least a facsimile of those relationships that affect physical and mental health: social support, social influence, social engagement and attachment, and access to resources and material goods. Certainly these forms of filiation are dramatized, in a cascading causal process from the macrosocial to the psychobiological, within the plots of the show itself, focusing as they do on the socially mediating role of the medical institution.

As we saw, teen suicide seems especially important here as an issue, suggesting as it does (like the neglect of the elderly, another issue covered by both series) that family filiation has broken down. Both shows feature some risky plot lines in this context. A grieving mother who has lost two children is revealed to have killed them herself, as a sufferer of Münchhausen syndrome by proxy (*Hospital Central* 2.8); another mother who killed her husband, alleging domestic violence, is in fact covering for her small son, who suffered sexual abuse from his father (*Al filo de la ley* 1.2). While the de jure family is clearly in crisis, the de facto family is shown to thrive. No one doubts the happiness of the lesbian couple in *Al filo*, before the accident that kills one partner and makes the other homeless. In *Hospital Central* the love affair between nurse Esther and doctor Maca has run successfully over four seasons, charting initial antipathy, flirtation, wedding and parenthood, interrupted only by the inevitable bloody car accident. Scenes from this gay marriage are lovingly preserved and edited together by fans on YouTube.

Tellingly, the DVDs of *Hospital Central* include 'introductions' to each character in which at least one actor speaks of the 'didactic' role they play in educating the audience on health issues. Clearly, the personal and professional are linked at the level of audience address, as well as that of the diegesis. Beyond skilful script editing, which runs 'arcs' over several seasons, familiarity with actors plays a vital role here. Movie star Leonardo Sbaraglia made major films on a yearly basis in Argentina and Spain (*Plata quemada* ('Burning Money', 2000); *Intacto* (2001), *En la ciudad sin límites* ('The City of No Limits', 2002)), before trying his hand at long-form television. A jobbing actor like Angel Pardo, on the other hand, had supporting roles in controversial films by Eloy de la Iglesia in the 1970s and took part in Lluís Pasqual's famous stage production of Lorca's *El público* ('The Public') in 1988, before enjoying a six-year stretch in *Hospital Central* from 2000 as the much-loved Rusti (the male nurse returned to his native village in 2006). Although Sbaraglia has a far higher and more consistent media profile, there can be little doubt that he has played a smaller role in the affective life of the nation.

Spanish professional drama clearly has its generic origins in the US. But I have tried to show that there are indeed specific differences here, especially in the relative absence of conflict between the ethical and the economic. *Hospital Central* certainly boasts less body trauma and apocalyptic rhetoric than later seasons of *ER*. However, Spanish dramas are also different from their Latin American cousins. To those familiar with the low-key Spanish show, the Univisión version of *Al filo de la ley* is almost unrecognizable with its bombastic announcer and melodramatic performance style. It is perhaps the case, however, that Spanish public broadcasters, too restrictive in their notion of quality, reduced the emotional charge of *Al filo* too much, draining it of dramatic intensity and opportunities for identification as they sought to distance it from its Latin American origins.

As Bailey noted, the final and only slightly concealed professional drama at stake here is that of television itself. *Hospital Central* and *Al filo de la ley* not only stage the 'vertical' processes by which the social networks of the workplace are embedded in wider sociocultural contexts. They also dramatize the conflicting notions of quality proposed by two models of the TV profession: a prolific private broadcaster, assured of a mass market for a tried and tested product, and an ailing public service provider, targeting a smaller audience with a relatively risky show that failed to attract the Spanish public either socially or emotionally. But whether they proved to be a success or a failure, these professional dramas succeeded in conjoining real and fictional discursive fields in a newly critical engagement between the two worlds.

Hospital Central ('Central Hospital', Tele 5, 2000–)

Production company	Estudios Picasso
Screenwriters	Alberto Grondona, Carmen Llanos, et al.
Directors	Javier Pizarro, et al.
Executive Producers	Santiago G. Lillo, Cristina Castilla, Mireia Acosta

Cast

Fátima Baeza	Esther
Angel Pardo	Rusti
Jordi Rebellón	Vilches
Antonio Zabálburu	Javier

Al filo de la ley ('On the Edge of the Law', TVE1, 2005)

Production company	TVE
Screenwriters	David Pastor, Elvin Rivera
Directors	Rafael Lara, Javier Olivera

Cast

Emilio Gutiérrez Caba	Gonzalo
Fanny Gautier	Patricia
Leonardo Sbaraglia	Álex
Natalia Verbeke	Elena

Works Cited

Bailey, Steve. '"Professional Television": Three (Super)texts and a (Super)genre'. *The Velvet Light Trap* 47 (1 April 2001): 45–61.

Berkman, Lisa F., Thomas Glass, Ian Brissette et al. 'From Social Integration to Health: Durkheim in the New Millennium'. *Social Science and Medicine* 51.6 (15 Sept. 2000): 843–57.

Broadcast. 'Kids TV: Caught in a Perfect Storm'. 29 Sept. 2006: 22–23; 25.

Chory-Assad, Rebecca M., and Ron Tamborini. 'Television Doctors: An Analysis of Physicians in Fiction and Non-Fictional Programs'. *Journal of Broadcasting and Electronic Media* 45.3 (1 July 2001): 499–521.

—. 'Television Exposure and the Public's Perceptions of Physicians'. *Journal of Broadcasting and Electronic Media* 47.2 (1 June 2003): 197–215.

Jacobs, Jason. *Body Trauma TV: The New Hospital Dramas*. London: BFI, 2003.

formulatv. '*Al filo de la ley*: ficha'. Accessed 27 March 2007. <http://www.formulatv.com/series/39/al-filo-de-la-ley/ficha/index.html>

—. '*Hospital Central*: ficha'. Accessed 27 March 2007. <http://www.formulatv.com/series/8/hospital-central/ficha/index.html>

Lyford, Joanna. 'Should Kids TV Come with a Health Warning?' *Television Business International* (1 Apr. 2006): Kids Supplement: 22–24.

Ministero de Cultura. Accessed 3 November 2007. <http://www.mcu.es>

muchatv. '*Al filo de la ley*: reparto de lujo en despachos de lujo'. Accessed 27 March 2007. <http://www.muchatv.com/serie/138/Al_filo_de_la_ley>

País, El. 'TVE comienza el rodaje de la serie de abogados *Al filo de la ley*'. 12 Feb. 2005: 69.

Pfau, Michael, Lawrence J. Mullen and Kirsten Garrow. 'The Influence of Television Viewing on Public Perceptions of Physicians'. *Journal of Broadcasting and Electronic Media* 39.4 (1 Oct. 1995): 441–58.

Sutton, David L., Melissa Britts and Margaret Landman. 'Television Programmes as Legal Texts: What *Law & Order* Tells Us About the American Criminal Justice System'. *Kinema* 14 (1 Oct. 2000): 5–20.

Tele 5. Official website for *Hospital Central*. Accessed 27 Mar. 2007. <http://www.hospital-central.telecinco.es/>

Thompson, Susan. 'BBC Nets Huge Response from The Verdict'. *Broadcast* (23 Feb. 2007): 6.

—. 'Court TV Group Criticizes Delay'. *Broadcast* (11 Aug. 2006): 4.

—. 'CPS Improves Media Access'. *Broadcast* (21 Oct. 2005): 3.

Thompson, Susan, and Jon Rogers. 'Sweeping Ad Ban Rocks TV Industry'. *Broadcast* 24 Nov. 2006): 1.

Vaca Berdayes, Ricardo. *El ojo digital: Audiencias 1*. Madrid: Ex Libris, 2004.

Williams, Raymond. *Television: Technology and Cultural Form*. London: Routledge, 1990.

CHAPTER FIVE

Two Suicides and a Funeral: The Euthanasia Debate on Film and Television

Synergy and suicide

In an unpublished lecture given in Cambridge in 2005, Vicente Benet charted the professionalization of the Spanish cultural industry over the previous decade. Long dependent on direct subsidy from the state, the audiovisual sector was consolidated in the 1990s by private conglomerates, which understood leisure and entertainment as a single unit and integrated television, cinema, and new media. Exemplary here is Prisa, the holding company that embraced newspaper *El País*, radio chain SER, and TV pay channel Canal +. Prisa's vertical integration extended into the three sectors of the film business through its producer Sogecine, distributor Sogepaq (allied with Warner), and exhibitor Sogecable, which opened new multiplexes in shopping malls.

For Benet the most representative Spanish feature film of this new regime or era is a Sogecine product: Alejandro Amenábar's *Mar adentro* ('The Sea Inside', 2004). This Goya- and Oscar-winning film, based on the real-life assisted suicide of quadriplegic Ramón Sampedro, combines the stunning technical effects and visual spectacle of cinema (in which perception is stretched to it limits) with the smaller-scale and more conservative style of TV melodrama, based as this genre is on private emotion. For Benet, this expert synthesis of the cinematic roller coaster and televisual weepie is clearly negative in effect, for all its commercial success, based as it is on a series of fabricated impacts that fail to provide viewers with the unique testimony and privileged experience the self-consciously important film claims to offer.

Benet notes that one aspect of *Mar adentro*'s 'synergy', or media convergence, is the prominence in it of an actress previously known only for her television work. Belén Rueda plays Julia, a composite character who here serves as Sampedro's lawyer and publisher, even as she herself suffers from a degenerative disease. In this chapter I further examine the complex interplay between the two media, film and television. I do so first by examining *Mar adentro* – which is widely held (in Spain, at least) to be a cinematic masterpiece – in the light of its depiction of and relation to television. And second, I compare this well known feature to the now forgotten first audiovisual depiction of Sampedro's story, which was aired simultaneously with the real-life narrative and six years before the prizewinning film – that is, the eighth episode of Tele 5 's quality workplace drama *Periodistas* ('Journalists', 1998–2002), which was the prototype for the professional series examined in the previous chapter. It is perhaps no accident that Belén Rueda, the female protagonist of *Mar adentro*, also played a prominent part in *Periodistas*, receiving third billing. As we shall see, just as *Mar adentro* is ambiguously reliant on television, so *Periodistas* drew on cinematic aesthetics and production processes. But I will argue that it is the televisual specificity of the drama series, more modest and less spectacular than the film version, that enables audiences to engage more directly and productively with Sampedro's individual legacy by integrating his testimony and experience into the collective sociability of everyday life.

Sampedro's history remains well known in Spain and his moving last will and testament is still posted on a Spanish right-to-die website (Asociación) as I write (September 2006). Born in 1943, the Galician seaman was paralysed at age 25, after diving into shallow water at the beach. An accomplished author (Amenábar takes his title from a poem by Sampedro that is recited over the Spanish trailer), Sampedro took his argument for euthanasia to the local court in A Coruña without success in 1994, arousing great media interest as he did so. Leaving the local village where he had been cared for by his sister-in-law in 1998, he committed suicide, assisted by a group of well-wishers, including Ramona Maneiro, with whom he was romantically linked. Sampedro's final statement and death from cyanide were filmed and the videotape (which had been sent to a pro-euthanasia society) was broadcast on Spanish television. In 2005, now protected by a statute of limitations, Maneiro confessed on a television talk show that she had handed the cyanide to Sampedro and had videotaped his death. She subsequently published her own, ghostwritten, version of events (Maneiro and Blanco).

Like other crimes (the act remains illegal in Spain), euthanasia thus raises general questions explored by criminologists such as Durkheim and addressed in Chapter 3 of this book: the relationship between individual and collective representations; the question of morality; and the problem of value judgement. As Robert Alun Jones notes, Durkheim himself considered suicide to be socially symptomatic, devoting a major book to the theme in which he distinguishes three 'social types'. The 'egoistic' suicide suffers from excessive individuation and places his or her individual rights over those of the collectivity. The 'altruistic' suicide suffers from the opposite tendency: insufficient individuation that leads to the renunciation (heroic or pathetic) of a life held to be subservient to the social needs of the group. Finally the 'anomic' suicide testifies rather to a lack of fit between individual and new social conditions, whether economic or domestic. Durkheim writes that 'every disturbance of equilibrium [...] is an impulse to voluntary death' (Jones).

Now it is not my aim to make value judgements on Sampedro's act. And he himself argued for euthanasia somewhat contradictorily on the basis of both 'death with dignity' and 'the respect for private property' (i.e. the right to do as one wishes with one's own body). But it is clear that his act can be read within the context of all three of Durkheim's social types: egotistically, Sampedro wished to abandon a life that held no pleasure for him; altruistically, he presented his struggle for euthanasia as one that would be invaluable for others in a similar predicament; anomically, his desire could be seen as testifying in part to radical disturbances in the social equilibrium of twentieth-century Spain. Durkheim might well have cited the decline of traditional forms of social cohesion, such as the Church and the patriarchal family, which once enveloped Spaniards and tended to inhibit egotism, anomie, and (perhaps) suicide. While these conflicting viewpoints are allotted somewhat schematically to Amenábar's characters in the unique, individualist melodrama *Mar adentro*, I argue that they are explored more subtly through their integration into the continuing and collective drama of what Durkheim calls the 'occupational group' in *Periodistas*.

Mar adentro ('The Sea Inside', 2004): The trace of televisuality

Galicia, the present. Lawyers Julia and Marc visit Ramón, a quadriplegic since a diving accident 26 years ago, to prepare a court case to grant him the right to die, assisted by Right to Die representative Gené. After seeing Ramón on television, Rosa, a single mother with a factory job, visits him to dissuade him. Marc and Gené begin a relationship. On a return visit to the house Ramón shares with his father, brother, nephew sister-in-law and chief carer Manuela, Julia questions Ramón about his life and his feelings. Ramón fantasizes about kissing her. Julia collapses and in hospital expresses the desire to die to avoid the consequences of CADASIL, a degenerative condition that leads to strokes and dementia. Ramón loses his court case. After losing her job, Rosa interferes with Manuela's care of Ramón. Julia arrives in a wheelchair and offers to help Ramón to publish his writings. As the two become closer she promises to bring him a copy of the book and then to kill both him and herself. Ramón travels to A Coruña to appear in court, but is denied the right to speak. When Rosa continues to refuse to support his wishes he explains to her that anyone who really loves him will help him die. Julia sends a copy of the book with a letter reneging on the agreement. Rosa offers to help Ramón and he moves into a flat with her. Assisted by anonymous friends, Ramón dies. Gené, Marc and their child visit Julia to give her a letter from Ramón, but she can no longer remember who he is. (Wilson, slightly corrected)

A typical Spanish review of *Mar adentro* (Mirito Torreiro in *Fotogramas*) stresses its cinematic credentials. Amenábar has extended his 'mastery' of the medium beyond direction into scriptwriting and composing and is now at the peak of the Spanish film profession. With each film, he has, we are told, taken on greater risks. After *The Others*, the biggest success in the history of Spanish cinema, now he faces a new challenge: the depiction of a Galician family and of a 'public figure' such as Sampedro. The critic's only quibble is that the director 'plays' with the viewer's emotions, using his 'facility' to please the audience at any cost.

It is instructive to compare this with the film's reception in English-language countries. In the British *Guardian*, a broadsheet normally sympathetic to foreign-language films, *Mar adentro* is denounced as an 'extraordinary shallow [...] weepie': its score is 'sucrose' and it looks like 'a classy TV movie'. Even the Oscar nomination is dismissed: this is the kind of 'unchallenging issue movie' likely to please the Academy (Bradshaw). The *New York Times* also decried the film's sentimentality. The famous sequence (later much parodied) in which Sampedro apparently leaves his bed and flies to the beach for a tryst with lawyer Julia is 'milked for the last drop of heartbreaking impossibility'; the scene in which Rueda's character collapses and Bardem's is unable to help her is an 'arm-twisting emotional ploy'. The *New York Times*' review opens precisely with the conflict between cinematic technique and televisual theme: 'As the camera restlessly circles the sky and the ocean [...] *The Sea Inside* [...] struggles to escape the disease-of-the-week genre to which it belongs [but] is defined by its theme' (Holden). The supposed mediocrity of the film is thus identified with its failure to distance itself from the all-too-commonplace medium of television. This judgement is somewhat ironic, given that English-language critics were as unfamiliar with the role and function of television in the true story of Sampedro as they were with the televisual antecedents of Amenábar's cinematic version of that story.

Unsurprisingly, Amenábar went to great lengths to protect and promote the cinematic prestige of his project. In his introduction to the lavish two-disk Spanish version of the DVD, he declared that *Mar adentro* was consistent with his first three features in focusing on the common theme of death. Even his appeal against video piracy is couched in lofty ethical terms. He claims that it is immoral to betray creators who have done their best to create a quality product and that intellectual property may seem intangible but is in fact 'as real as bread'. The two hour-long documentaries on the second disk make a convincing bid for artistic (or filmic) distinction. The first opens with the auteur brooding by the Galician sea where a memorial to Sampedro's 'dignity' is incised in the rocks. The lengthy 'making of' that follows relates in exhaustive detail the story of the film from pre- to post-production, focusing on how cinematic resources were used to open up a potentially 'claustrophobic' narrative. We are shown the scouting of locations in Galicia and Barcelona, and Javier Bardem's rigorous training for the role, including visits to a specialized hospital in Toledo. Amenábar's minute planning of the shoot is illustrated with the spectacular dream-flight sequence (elsewhere, storyboards are included on the disk); and the scene in which Sampedro takes leave of his family is compared, in an unexpected film reference, to *ET*. Much attention is paid to the laborious process of makeup (transforming Bardem into an invalid 20 years older than his real age) and to the meticulously authentic art design. In spite of such minute preparation, the relatively lengthy shoot allowed actors the freedom to essay improvisation on set. The composition of the score and its recording in London and Galicia are also treated at length.

The international dimension of this local tale is stressed in the second documentary, a minute account of the film's US promotional campaign, in which Amenábar and Bardem put themselves at the mercy of distributor Fine Line. In spite of what we are told is an 'unprecedented' push that culminates with victories at the Golden Globes and Oscars, it is clear that not all is well here. Modest and stubbornly uncharismatic, Amenábar compares himself in New York and Los Angeles to Paco Martínez Soria: the archetypal *paleto* of Francoist comedy, a country bumpkin stranded in the big city with his battered suitcases. Elsewhere, box office figures confirm the film's failure in the US. While *Mar adentro* gained an audience of 4 million (10 per cent of the entire population) and a box office of €20 million in Spain (twice its nearest rival in 2004 and three times Almodóvar's *La mala educación*, 'Bad Education'), in the US final figures barely reached $2 million, even after the huge boost of the Oscar for foreign-language film. Clearly, the 'disease of the week' reviews had damaged its prospects.

If we return to the film itself, however, we see that virtuoso cinematic resources and techniques, heavily stressed by the promotional materials, are much in evidence. Apparently citing Amenábar's own oeuvre, *Mar adentro* begins (like his second feature *Abre los ojos*, 'Open Your Eyes', 1997) with a female voice over a black screen. She speaks of the 'screen' or 'window' of the imagination, one of the visual leitmotifs that Amenábar sought to base his film on. The opening sequences exploit the expensive resources allowed by Amenábar's relatively high budget (estimated by IMDb at €10 million): the saccharine score (recorded by a full orchestra in London) comes in over Sampedro's first speech (on 'life without dignity'), while secondary characters are established against a variety of exterior locations (Sampedro's boorish brother by the cowshed, his bewildered father by the sea, his future love interest, Rosa, in the fish cannery where she works). When Belén Rueda's Julia (the lawyer) asks Ramón to recount 'the day that changed his life', we cut to a sun-drenched beach where the handsome young seaman casts his shadow on the rocks (another metaphor for film?). All too soon, neck broken and backlit by the sun, he floats, Christlike with extended arms, on the luminous surface of the sea. The fantasy-flight sequence, set to an ecstatic 'Nessun Dorma', is still more virtuoso, seamlessly flowing in a single shot from domestic interior to rollercoaster exteriors, as the aerial camera hugs the green hills and rocky coast of Galicia, and climaxing with the sensual embrace (willed by both character and audience) between twin stars Bardem and Rueda. Amenábar exploits here the vertiginous confusion of fantasy and reality familiar from his earlier films, effortlessly wrong-footing the audience: when we are treated later to a second fantasized embrace, he cuts back to reveal that the would-be lovers are this time indeed kissing in Sampedro's all-too-real bedroom.

Subsequent aerial shoots seem less motivated, even self-defeating. As Sampedro is driven to court in A Coruña, escaping for once the confinement of his house, the camera soars over the green fields as it follows his van. Quick cut montage shows the diversity and density of life in this verdant setting: farmers and cyclists, lovers and children. Sampedro's refusal of mobility in the rest of the film (he rejects even a wheelchair) here seems perverse, an egotistic self-separation from the possible pleasures of the world. Likewise, Sampedro's final evening in a rented apartment by the sea is shot against a glorious sunset, the spectacular cinematic form curiously contradicting the sobriety of the content. The very last shot of the film shows young couple Marc and Gené (the too-good-to-be-true euthanasia activists) frolicking on the beach with their baby in a transparent hymn to life, love, and hope. Risking cliché, Amenábar's camera once more spirals up into the air and out over the waves.

As I mentioned earlier, even some Spanish critics found such virtuoso cinematic moments emotionally exploitative. And if we look back at *Mar adentro* we find a smaller-scale televisual rhetoric, which both undercuts and supplements Amenábar's all-too-transparent filmic ambitions. This TV subtext is even present in the promotional material. Amenábar may see this fourth film as all of a piece with his earlier cinematic oeuvre, death-obsessed as it is, but the original motive for *Mar adentro* was more simple: he saw Ramón Sampedro on television and was struck by how plainly he spoke on such a dramatic subject. In the 'making of' documentary, the director complains of how Hollywood 'blinds' viewers to the local view, while his producer, Fernando Bovaira, claims the film is anchored in verisimilitude and realism. The expansive exteriors are countered by the studio sets, which remain claustrophobic spaces in which to shoot. The distinguished DP Javier Aguirresarobe talks of his desire for a colourless, 'cold' palette, far from the fiery sunset of the late sequence. Bardem may have benefited from a lengthy period of rehearsal, possible only in a well funded film production, but he trained for the role by scrutinizing a video screen, inspired by the responsibility of reproducing a real person. Most telling is the account of the casting of Belén Rueda as Julia. The producer Bovaira has no compunction in revealing that he was hostile to the use of a TV star in a major motion picture. Rueda herself claims, with no apparent false modesty, that she could not believe Amenábar would cast her, a novice in cinema, as

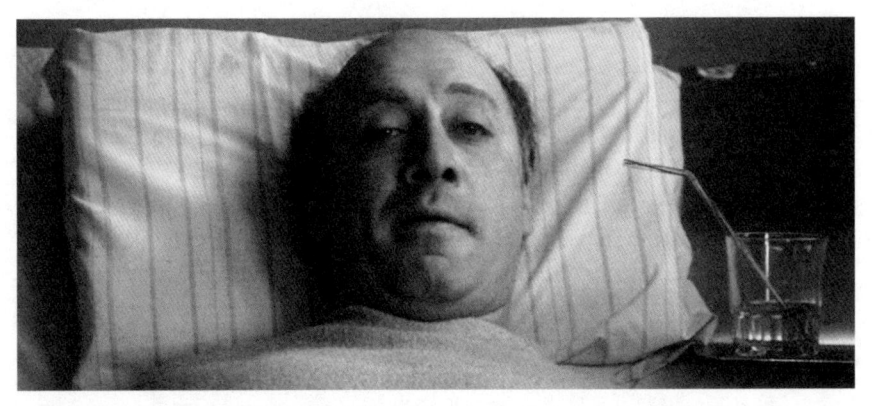

10 Ramón Sampedro (Javier Bardem) faces the camera: *Mar adentro*

the female lead in his film. Her misgivings were later confirmed: at the Goya ceremony Lola Dueñas, whose work in films such as Almodóvar's *Hable con ella* ('Talk to Her', 2002) eclipsed the fact that she had had a featured role on TV's *Policías* (see Chapter 3), won the award for Best Actress, even though Dueñas's part as rural Rosa was clearly smaller than that of big city lawyer Julia. In spite of innumerable TV appearances, Rueda had to be content with 'Best New Actress'.

If television inspired *Mar adentro*'s production (both its narrative and casting), it is also ubiquitous in the film itself. When lawyer Julia (Rueda) first visits the Sampedro family home, she is told 'tomorrow the TV people will come'. Dueñas's Rosa ingenuously tells Ramón on first meeting him: 'I saw you on telly'. Other forms of electronic communication intrude in the face-to-face narrative of an immobilized man and his visitors: Julia replays Ramón's account of his accident as he has told it to a tape recorder; Rosa, the fish cannery worker and downtrodden single mother, is even a somewhat unlikely radio DJ (she dedicates a song to the listening Ramón). Many scenes focus on telephone communication or are played over a television, which receives varying degrees of attention. Sometimes the family bicker against the background of TV sport and weather. But television is not always innocuous. Ramón's sister-in-law is bitterly offended by a television interview with a priest (José María Pou, recently the star of Antena 3's *Policías*), who claims that Ramón wishes to die only because his family does not love him enough. And, of course, Ramón's final monologue, as he takes the fatal cyanide, is addressed direct to the video camera. It is a static frontal set up far from the dizzying mobility of the earlier aerial shots and one inextricable from the television medium that broadcast the original tape. The final credits, which show brief shots of each actor, are also reminiscent of opening credits of ensemble TV dramas.

This hidden televisual connection is also implicit in the highlighting of Julia, played by TV star Rueda, a figure whose possible models in real life were eclipsed by Ramona (the film's Rosa). Rueda is not only second-billed, after Bardem and before Dueñas, but her character is also intimately and consistently connected with the protagonist Ramón. Julia is seen and heard before Ramón and her first words are: 'I understand him very well'. An early montage sequence shows couples eating or making love, but ends with Julia reclining on a plane. Amenábar cuts to Ramón in the same position on his pillow, the graphic match clearly implying that the two characters are to be identified with each other. Julia is even granted the film's final close-up. After Ramón's death, activist Gené visits her at her house by the sea (the location rhymes with Ramón's last home) but, pathetically, Julia's degenerative disease now means she no longer remembers him. Ramón's romantic partner (she is granted a kiss Rosa is not awarded on-screen), Julia is also his other self, his equal in condemnation to living death.

What is the reason for the unusual prominence of this character in Amenábar's screenplay, which must surely have proved disconcerting to Spaniards familiar with Sampedro's story? I would suggest that Belén's Julia is a vital component of that unacknowledged televisual subtext, invisible to foreign audiences, that underwrites *Mar adentro*'s cinematic virtuosity and helped facilitate the film's massive popularity in Spain. We can now go on to explore the first, televisual version of the Sampedro story, one in which Rueda herself also participated in a perhaps unexpected fashion.

Periodistas ('Journalists', 1998–2002): Television 'del tiempo'

Ramón Sampedro died on 12 January 1998. The next day, as the press carried reports of the death, Tele 5 broadcast the first episode of its innovative workplace drama, *Periodistas*, set in a fictional Madrid newspaper. Publicity for the series stressed three aspects that contributed to its 'quality' status (Smith 20–22). The first was its generous production values, which for the first time approached those of cinema. Boasting a large and prestigious cast (including veteran film actor José Coronado as head of the local section), *Periodistas* prided itself on its expensive location shooting, which took up an average of two days for each episode. The second aspect was its modernity. While previous Spanish television had focused on the traditional family home (Globomedia's own *Médico de familia* ('Family Doctor') had been the most successful example), *Periodistas* concentrated on a large number of professionals who, testifying to recent social changes in Spain, were all single, separated, or childless. Finally came contemporaneity. *Periodistas*, journalists were told, would dramatize the social issues that most engaged Spaniards at the present time. Executive producer Mikel Lejarza even said that there was no good or bad television, only television that was up to date ('del tiempo') or out of date (Smith 23). Shamelessly cross-promoting its new show (co-produced with Globomedia) and confusing real and fictional immediacy, Tele 5 even made *Periodistas*' first episode an item on the news bulletin that preceded it. This 'present-ness' of television made the show well placed to explore a developing drama such as that of Ramón Sampedro as it unfolded to the Spanish public. While Amenábar was to take two years over the production of *Mar adentro*, each feature-length episode of *Periodistas* was shot in just one week.

In the opening pilot the main characters and conflicts are economically established with a minimum of exposition. Luis (Coronado) has returned from a spell in New York to take over the local section, only to discover that his wife wants a divorce. His boss and the deputy editor of *Crónica* is Laura (Amparo Arrañaga), an unmarried career woman, romantically drawn in spite of herself to her new subordinate. Third-billed is Belén Rueda's Clara, a single mother and photographer who shares a flat with female colleague Ana (Alicia Borrachero). Significantly, the character of Rueda (then partner of the series' co-creator and director Daniel Écija) was the only one already familiar to Spanish audiences, thus directing sympathy and attention towards her from the outset. Clara had appeared in the final seasons of the huge success *Médico de familia*. Readers of gossip magazines would also have been aware that one of the daughters of Rueda and Écija had died tragically young.

The 'issue' of the opening episode is softer than others in the first season: the journalists investigate the mysterious death of a famous writer in a hotel, finally discovering that his widow, fearful for her late husband's estate, had attempted to bribe the young lover who was with him when he died to abort the great man's adulterously conceived child. The ethical conflict here (is the story an exploitative intrusion on private grief or a legitimate subject of public interest?) is explored, with Luis and Laura taking opposing positions pro and contra. Clara, meanwhile, struggles to combine personal and professional life. In her very first sequence, she is obliged to leave the newsroom and abandon her duties to pick up her bedraggled daughter waiting in the rain outside school. The episode title ('Where the Action Is') is thus ironically undercut by the action of the show itself: public spectacle (the dramatic demise of a celebrity) is always interwoven with private intimacy (the everyday problems of women and their workmates, single parents and their children).

By Episode 8 (entitled 'A Love Story') *Periodistas* had swiftly established itself as the most popular and critically acclaimed drama on television. The pre-credit sequence here shows the ensemble cast having breakfast in a bar. Two plot strands are established. Clara is worried about her daughter's new teacher, who has taught the class to call everyone 'comrades'. Meanwhile, sexy photographer Willy (Joel Joan) has quarrelled with homely intern José Antonio

(Pepón Nieto), who had briefly moved in with him, cramping his love life. After the now familiar credits (shots of the ensemble cast in Madrid exteriors and the large newsroom set), the opening sequence is the jocular morning meeting, reminiscent of similar expository scenes in avowed 'quality' antecedents of *Periodistas*, Steven Bochco's *Hill Street Blues* (1981–87) and *L.A. Law* (1986–94). Suddenly the festive tone changes. Laura, the deputy editor, enters to announce that 'Marta Cuesta' has died. As Luis informs his colleagues (informs us), Cuesta was a euthanasia activist suffering from multiple sclerosis who had inspired him to write editorials in favour of changing the law. Laura speaks out against euthanasia: if Cuesta's suicide has been assisted, as seems likely (cyanide has been found), the paper cannot condone lawbreaking. She tells Luis he is 'too close' to the story, while he retorts that from her 'distance' everything looks the same. The continuing exploration of these conflicting objective and subjective viewpoints is ensured by the editor's decision: in spite of their bitter disagreement on the topic, Luis and Laura will collaborate on researching and writing up the story for next morning's edition.

Unlike Amenábar, *Periodistas*' screenwriters thus changed the name, sex, and condition of their paraplegic from the real-life original. But, given the immediacy of the theme (Sampedro's suicide took place just weeks before the

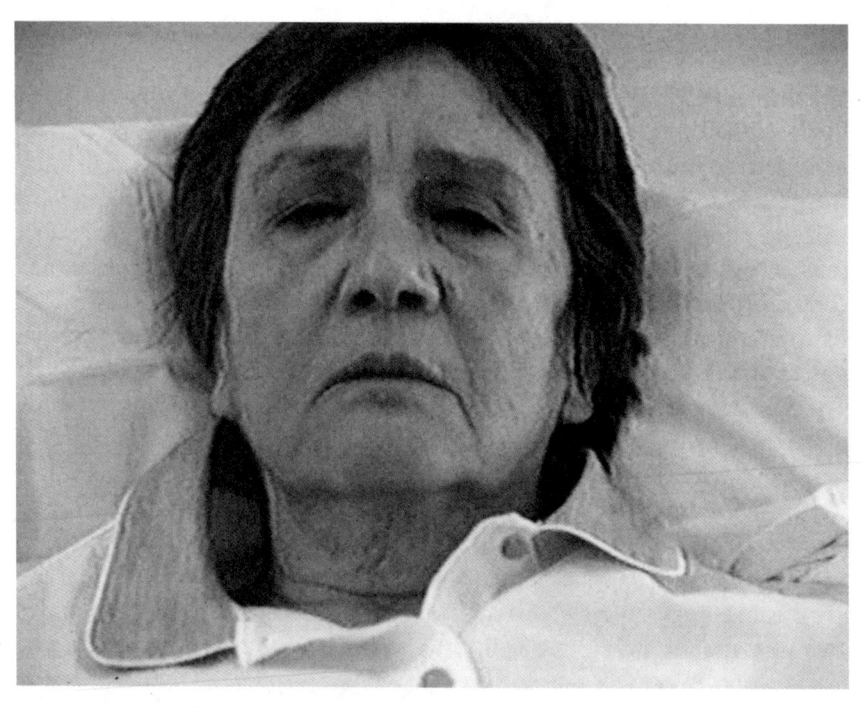

11 Marta Cuesta (Amparo Valle) faces the camera: *Periodistas*

broadcast and the police investigation was still in progress), there can be no doubt to whom the show is referring (Sampedro even gets a brief name check in this opening sequence). But what is striking is that the euthanasia debate is both taken seriously in its political and moral dimension and fully integrated into the private and affective relations of characters with whom viewers are already familiar. Thus, Luis and Laura voice arguments that will be echoed by Amenábar's characters six years later: that life under such conditions has no 'dignity' and that, conversely, no one has the right to terminate a life, whatever the circumstances in which it is lived. But these ethical arguments (on egotism, altruism and anomie) are cross-cut with personal investments, such as the long-running sexual tension between them. As the two colleagues heatedly debate the issue, one workmate remarks wryly that love and hate are not so far apart.

Over the 80 minutes of this episode, then, the euthanasia plot strand is intertwined with the two domestic conflicts, as Clara and the new teacher argue over her daughter's education and Willy and José Antonio bicker about their living arrangements. While the euthanasia strand occupies only some 20 minutes of running time, it is granted expansive (and expensive) exterior shots, which signal its importance. Thus Luis and Laura, seeking leads, attend the funeral of the fictional assisted suicide in a distant suburb far from their metropolitan

12 Luis (José Coronado) and Laura (Amparo Larrañaga) watch the screen: *Periodistas*

office block. The bereaved son attacks Luis as the journalist who 'put ideas into [his] mother's head'. Laura's more maternal approach, resting the young man's head on her breast, proves more productive than Luis's hard news agenda. Soon a videotape arrives at the office. It contains the farewell of Marta Cuesta (played by veteran Amparo Valle), which is closely modelled on Sampedro's statements (at the time of broadcast Sampedro's will had been made public, but not his final video). After 25 years of illness, Cuesta says, she seeks death with dignity: 'life is a right not a duty'. Plangent music plays over the monologue, delivered, of course, straight to the viewer (straight to Luis and Laura), as the camera moves in for a closer look. The director Écija cuts to a muted but moved reaction shot of the couple, but he also inserts an exterior of the newspaper building's facade. Even here, then, the individual representation (the dying farewell) is opened out, located quite precisely in the collective context of a working relationship and a professional institution.

The everyday nature of an extraordinary event (a public assisted suicide) is continually underscored. When Luis and Laura note a fleeting reflection in a mirror in the video, they ask a technician to blow up and clarify the image. He exclaims: 'I thought this kind of thing only happened in films'. Television, more intimate and less spectacular than cinema, is clearly on the side of real life, not fantasy. The senior journalists' sleuthing, often shown in close-up, is bracketed by group shots of their (mainly female) junior colleagues working through everyday problems with warmth and humour: for example, Clara and her friend conspire with a friendly real estate agent to ensure Willy and José Antonio are finally reunited in a new flat together. The moral is quite literally one of co-existence, the sharing of scarce living conditions in an often unpropitious city.

Urban density and intensity are next contrasted with rural reflection. Following up the ghostly image in the mirror, Luis and Laura visit a village said to be 300 kilometres (about 190 miles) from Madrid: the picturesque exteriors are of steep cobbled streets and ancient stone houses, clearly reminiscent of Sampedro's Galicia. They track down Mario, a kindly old man equipped with cap and fishing rod. As they follow him to a quietly lapping cistern and mossy ancient walls, the stage is set for a second confession: Mario, Marta's first love, admits he is the one who facilitated her suicide and sent the videotape. As he breaks down, the plangent piano theme merges with birdsong on the soundtrack. Deftly orchestrating changes in tone, the episode now shifts from pathos to humour. The city slickers are forced to share a room in a country inn, a stock situation of the comedy of sexual tension since at least *It Happened One Night* (1934). But even here when the lights are out they talk over their interview with Mario, working through a public issue in the most private of settings.

Back in Madrid, it is no surprise that a compromise has been reached. Laura now believes that to tell Mario's story (anonymously) will serve altruistic purposes, helping others to deal with the same problem. The videotape will be forwarded to the authorities, but only after the shot revealing Mario's identity is edited out. Luis and Laura are thus temporarily reconciled over their dispute (the sexual tension remains unresolved to feed future episodes), just as Willi and José Antonio are resigned to their continuing flat share. In the final comic 'tag' of the end credits, the whole cast help the male couple move to their new home, but miss out when the 'dinner' they have been promised in return for the favour turns out to be just crisps and olives. Clara, meanwhile, reassured that the new teacher is not indoctrinating her daughter, now sees him as a possible romantic partner.

It becomes clear, then, that the 'love story' of the episode title has multiple applications: to Marta and Mario, suicide and helper; to Laura and Luis, combative colleagues; to Willy and José Antonio, unwilling cohabitees; and, mixing parental and romantic roles, to Clara and her beloved daughter and the child's attractive teacher. The euthanasia plot strand, successfully explored and resolved in one episode, is thus structurally and thematically integrated into continuing private narratives that will engage audiences over seasons, even years, to come.

Occupational ethics

Periodistas' assisted suicide episode is sandwiched between two very different themes: Episode 7 had treated police corruption and Episode 9 would address the more humdrum problem of city traffic and parking. Yet these narratives also charted the interpenetration of public and private: the bent copper exposed by Luis threatens the journalist's daughter, and during the traffic investigation a petrol station explodes (one the most spectacular pseudo-cinematic sequences of the first season) and Luis is badly burned. But there is no doubt that the euthanasia theme achieved the highest profile for the series, subsequently cited as it was by the proud producers as not just coinciding with, but 'anticipating' the news. While the show did not, in fact, predict Sampedro's suicide, it did antedate the broadcasting of his final video, which took place three days after the *Periodistas*' episode, by Tele 5's rival Antena 3. Tele 5 responded by repeating their prescient version of events just three days later. Investigation into the source of the video (the main narrative drive of the fictional version) continued in the real world well after Luis and Laura had solved their fictional mystery. Spanish viewers could be forgiven for being confused between real and televisual narratives, given the extent to which the first was reliant on the second.

Print narratives of Sampedro's predicament had relied more on his literary culture. On 1 October 1994 *El Mundo* had published a lengthy piece on the

Galician, interspersed with quotes from his favourite poet, Neruda, on the weariness of being a man and the burden of residence on earth (Malvar). Conversely, the televisual element in Sampedro's drama was downplayed by the press or delegitimized, the screening of the final video branded a 'controversy' and placed in the polemical context of *telebasura* [trash TV]. It is striking also that Amenábar, cinematic auteur, makes no reference in the DVD extras to a TV movie on Sampedro made in 2001, Roberto Bodegas's *Condenado a vivir* ('Condemned to Live'). *Mar adentro* remains a film phenomenon: with five million tickets sold, more than one-fifth of admissions to Spanish films in 2004 were to that single feature. *Periodistas*, however, effortlessly won audiences of some five million per episode over its four-year run (1998–2002). Significantly, it is through video that *Mar adentro*'s legacy has been explored. As I write, a search for the Spanish title on YouTube gives links to parodic amateur clips such as *Birra adentro* (a paralytic drunk flies magically on his bed to the nearest bar) and *Sierra adentro* (giggling Andalusians recreate the deathbed scene among their native hills). Sketch comedy clips, also available through YouTube, also replayed now classic scenes: in one, defeated President Aznar (propped up in bed) is encouraged by his colleagues to do the decent thing; in another, a Basque lover of Rioja wine tragically commits suicide by drinking a glass of *mosto* (grape juice). Such replays point to one of the most refreshing aspects of Amenábar's feature: its effortless incorporation of the various historic nationalities and languages of the Spanish state, a subject more often addressed on television than in cinema.

Film thus finds it easy to converge with television and video. Indeed *Mar adentro* had been part funded by TVE (the state broadcaster), Canal + (then a private subscription service), and TVG (the autonomous Galician channel). Movement the other way was more difficult. Belén Rueda, whose role as Clara (the professional woman struggling to fulfil her domestic commitments) had clearly paved the way for her Julia (a character also caught between public and private roles) has found it hard to build a movie career. The televisual trace in *Mar adentro* was thus unusually volatile and ambivalent: in Spain it helped create a mass market for a blockbuster movie; abroad it damaged the prospects of a 'foreign' film with a 'niche' target demographic that looked down on television.

Yet I would argue that the TV version of Sampedro's story (re-released as part of *Periodistas*' first season on DVD in 2006) was the one that most productively engaged with his legacy and voiced his testimony to Spaniards, even as they were still confronting the real-life events and the moral dilemmas of egotism and altruism they raised. Yet even *Mar adentro*, an assured cinematic spectacle, alludes tangentially to those disturbances of social equilibrium that Durkheim called 'anomie': Rosa faces unemployment and single motherhood, Sampedro's brother rages impotently that he is the head of the (patriarchal) household; the conservative priest played by José María Pou has clearly lost authority even among the faithful. Amenábar's Galicia, however aestheticized, resists being reduced to a series of picturesque locations.

But there remains one bulwark against anomie: the occupational group (see also Chapter 4). Durkheim's description of its operation is eerily appropriate for both the workplace drama of *Periodistas* and the ubiquitous medium of television:

> The occupational group is always in contact with [individuals] by the constant exercise of the function of which it is the organ and in which they collaborate. It follows the workers wherever they go [...] Wherever they are, they find it enveloping them, recalling them to their duties, supporting them at need. Finally corporate action makes itself felt in every detail of our occupations, which are thus given a collective orientation. (Cited by Jones)

For Durkheim this collectivity is not simply social but also moral, protecting the individual from corrosive egotism and anomie. If the question of suicide is indeed socially symptomatic, the case of Sampedro clearly inspired intense corporate action: some 20,000 Spaniards claimed responsibility for his death, taking on collective blame for an individual act they judged should not be a crime (G. C.). It seems likely that television, so often blamed for moral disintegration, served here as a potent force for ethical cohesion. And it is telling that while both film and television versions show the suicide, only the latter recreates a funeral: the communal ceremony that commemorates an individual's life. Certainly *Periodistas*, in constant weekly contact with a mass audience, provided a very visible model for the working through and commemoration of a newly prominent political issue, both recalling viewers to their democratic duties and supporting them in a time of disturbed social equilibrium. It was a televisual example whose memory Amenábar could later build on to produce the cinematic phenomenon that remains most characteristic of the newly converged Spanish audiovisual sector.

Mar adentro ('The Sea Inside', 2004)

Director and original music	Alejandro Amenábar
Screenwriters	Alejandro Amenábar and Mateo Gil
Production companies	Sogepaq, with Sogecine, Himenóptero, and TVE, Canal +, TVG.
Executive producers	Alejandro Amenábar and Fernando Bovaira
Cinematographer	Javier Aguirresarobe
Art direction	Benjamín Fernández
Special make up	Jo Allen

Cast

Javier Bardem	Ramón Sampedro
Belén Rueda	Julia

Lola Dueñas	Rosa
Clara Segura	Gené
Francesc Garrido	Marc
José María Pou	Padre Francisco

Periodistas ('Journalists', Tele 5)
1.8 'Una historia de amor'
('A Love Story', 3 March 1998)

Production company	Estudios Picasso
Screenwriters	Salvador Perpiñá, Ignasi Rubio, et al.
Director	Daniel Écija
Original music	Emilio Aragón

Cast

José Coronado	Luis
Amparo Larrañaga	Laura
Belén Rueda	Clara
Joel Joan	Willy
Pepón Nieto	José Antonio

Works Cited

Amenábar, Alejandro. Introduction. *Mar adentro*. Spanish DVD: *edición de lujo*. Sogepaq, 2005.

Asociación Derecho a Morir Dignamente. 'Testamento de Ramón Sampedro'. Accessed 10 Sept. 2006. <http://www.eutanasia.ws/ramtest.html>

Benet, Vicente J. 'Observations on the Spanish Cinema Industry'. Unpublished paper read in Cambridge 2005.

Bradshaw, Peter. Review of *Mar adentro* ('The Sea Inside'). *The Guardian* 11 Feb. 2005. Accessed 10 Sept. 2006. <http://film.guardian.co.uk/News_Story/Critic_Review/Guardian_review/0,4267,1409960,00.html>

G. C. 'Más de 2.000 autoinculpados por la muerte de Sampedro'. *El País* 27 Feb. 1998. Accessed 10 Sept. 2006:
<http://www.elpais.com/articulo/sociedad/SAMPEDRO/_RAMON/EUTANASIA/2000/autoinculpados/muerte/Sampedro/elpepisoc/19980227elpepisoc_2/Tes>.

Holden, Stephen. Review of *Mar adentro* ('The Sea Inside'). *New York Times* 17 Dec. 2004. Accessed 10 Sept. 2006. <http://movies.nytimes.com/2004/12/17/movies/17thes.html>

Jones, Robert Alun. 'Suicide (1897)'. Excerpt from *Emile Durkheim: An Introduction to Four Major Works*. 1986. Accessed 10 Sept. 2006. <http://lecerveau.mcgill.ca/flash/capsules/articles_pdf/suicide.pdf>

Malvar, Aníbal C. 'Cansado de ser hombre: el derecho a la eutanasia'. *El Mundo* 1 Oct. 1994. Accessed 10 Sept. 2006. <http://www.elmundo.es/elmundolibro/2004/10/01/protagonistas/1096632791.html>

Maneiro, Ramona, and Xavier R. Blanco. *Querido Ramón: un testimonio de amor*. Madrid: Temas de Hoy, 2005.

Smith, Paul Julian. 'Quality TV? The *Periodistas* Notebook'. *Contemporary Spanish Culture*:

TV, Fashion, Art, and Film. Oxford and Cambridge: Polity, 2003: 9–33.
Torreiro, Mirito. Review of *Mar adentro* ('The Sea Inside'). *Fotogramas* 2004. Accessed 10 Sept. 2006. <http://www.fotogramas.orange.es/fotogramas/CRITICAS/9850@CRITICAS@0.htm>
Wilson, Vicky. Review of *Mar adentro* ('The Sea Inside'). *Sight & Sound* 15 (March 2005): 71–72.

CHAPTER SIX

Transnational Telenovela: From Mexico to Madrid, via Barcelona

Methodology and melodrama

For any viewer or critic of Spanish-language television, telenovela is inescapable, yet indefinable. Industrial and academic studies both chart the complex career of a genre that changes in time, space and form as the decades roll on, as it is exported around the world from its home base in Latin America, and as it splits into multiple sub-genres. As early as 1998 at the first 'summit' of Latin American telenovela producers, Caracas's *Encuadre* reported on the 'controversy' between the 'romantic' original version [*rosa*] and the 'realistic' break [*ruptura*] with the original model (Kaiser).

By 2002 a special report in Spain's *Cineinforme* (Michelin, 'Informe') claimed that the 'continent was in movement', citing executives on the key points of the genre: that it was a tool to maximize audience loyalty, carefully calibrated to distinct ages and social classes (36); that the main goal was continued expansion into Spain (38); that current experimental innovations were a 'new realism' and the introduction of humour (39); that telenovela was the lowest-cost way of securing the highest rating, albeit with the addition of more contemporary and 'sophisticated' plot lines, such as artificial insemination (44); and, finally, that the genre was holding up under the pressure of reality shows, as local fiction was 'closer to the hearts' of local viewers (45).

Just one year later, to coincide with what was called the 'First World Summit of Telenovelas' (held, significantly, in Miami), *Cineinforme* gave another round-up of what it claimed was the 'engine' of an audiovisual sector hitherto dependent on US product (Michelin, 'Telenovelas'). Here Latin American executives stress, rather, the role of the genre as the 'backbone' of weekday prime-time scheduling in their territories (44) and reject the European accusation of 'low quality' made of their product (45), citing the growth of distribution in Spanish autonomic and local stations (46) and the genre's new hybridization with comedy and reality formats (47). Gerardo Michelin writes that the 'internationalization' of the telenovela, beyond its main 'factories' in Mexico, Venezuela, Brazil, Argentina and Colombia, is now matched by its 'diversification', away from the 'hardcore' drama [*puro y duro*] of the 'classic' towards novelties such as children and teen soaps, period, erotic and even animated versions. The 'versatility' of the genre thus enables it to 'camouflage' itself with new formats (39).

For all its persistence and inescapability, the telenovela has met a mixed reception in Spain. Jesús Sánchez Tena, of Madrid's media consultancy GECA, traces several stages in its development. After TVE lost its monopoly in broadcasting in the early 1990s, telenovelas led the ratings in prime time, before falling behind reality shows, Hollywood films, Spanish series drama and football in the second half of the decade (40). Exiled to daytime by the millennium, telenovelas also suffered at the hands of 'docu-shows' (the Spanish equivalents of *American Idol*), with only the breakout Colombian *Betty la Fea* ('Ugly Betty') airing briefly in the evening on private Antena 3 in 2001. Meanwhile, locally produced telenovelas hesitantly began to catch on, especially in the regions: Canal Sur's home-produced, prime-time soap *Arrayán* ('Myrtle') topped the ratings in Andalusia in the 2002–2003 season.

Telenovela thus only briefly jumped the scheduling 'fence', which had held it captive on TVE1's afternoon [*sobremesa*] slot from its first arrival in Spain. In spite of its longevity, the genre's profitability is less in Spain than it is in Latin America, Portugal, or even eastern Europe (41). Beyond this, there is a fundamental difference in programming. The Latin American networks use telenovelas as 'tent poles' of their grids, stripped across weekday prime time; the European equivalent of this 'foundation' is, Sánchez Tena believes, the news bulletins, which are less successful in ensuring viewer loyalty. Yet Spain's own serials now seek to imitate the scheduling efficacy of their Latin American models, following an 'eclectic pattern' by mixing stylistic, thematic and structural elements from three sources: US daytime soaps; European serials; and (still despised) Latin American *culebrones* [soap operas] (42). One particular link between Spain and Latin America is the 'closed structure', through which – unlike, say, the unending British soaps – Spanish-language serials build to a classic climax (43). It remains the case, however, that Spanish telenovelas in the Latin American mould are, properly speaking, few in number (*El secreto*, 'The Secret', a co-production with Mexican Televisa, is cited as the first in 2001), and the genre's audience remains restricted with its time slot to an undesirable demographic of women over 45.

Recent academic commentators, more focused on reception than production, have coincided with these industrial consultants in stressing both the inescapability and the elusiveness of telenovela. One study of Mexico (Beard) calls the genre 'the most vital cultural product that Latin American countries export to the world and share among themselves' (73), and notes a 'break with generic traditions' in, for example, the introduction of positive gay characters (87). Another study of reception by Mexican American girls (Mayer) argues that these viewers have 'extended the boundaries of the narrative to cope with problems they faced as young women of colour in the US' (493). A third study of the Ecuadorian adaptation of a feminist novel (Ávila-Saavedra) examines how the 'radical discourse' of the source is 'maintained, transformed, or eliminated' on television (383), arguing (once more) that 'classic formulations of the genre are no longer commercially viable' (397).

The 'contra-flow' argument of telenovela as a critique of the US cultural imperialism thesis has itself been critiqued (Biltereyst and Meers), albeit with the acknowledgement that there were in the millennium 'striking parallels between US and major Latin American corporations' strategies to conquer overseas markets' (410). The 'internationalization' of strong domestic monopolies such as Televisa thus means that they, not the US networks, now 'play the predominant role' (Fox 52). But while transnationalization within Latin America may lead to a loss of particularity (Argentine productions abandon their characteristic locations and language (Mazziotti 139)), it may also establish newly particularized connections (one Argentine and Spanish co-production was shot in the emblematically named Estudios Pampa and in the Galician countryside (Mazziotti 133)). Meanwhile, relatively rare and little-studied subgenres such as the historical soap opera engage in their own kind of fluidity and hybridization, 'blend[ing] historical characters with common people and historical events with scenes of everyday community life'. to produce what one critic has called a 'kinetic mural' (Rodríquez Cadena 49).

The most exhaustive and authoritative study of a single country (in this case Colombia) remains Martín Barbero and Sonia Muñoz's *Televisión y melodrama* of 1992. The couple's methodology is impeccable, embracing as it does production, reception and textual analysis. The 'structure and dynamic of production' covers areas such as industrial and communicative competition, decision-making processes, professional mentalities, work routines and commercialization strategies (30). 'Social uses and ways of seeing' is divided into habits of consumption and family routines (31), spaces of circulation (such as the home, neighbourhood and workplace) (32), and 'cultural competency and collective imaginaries' (the experience, memory and retelling of narratives) (33). Finally, 'textual composition' comprises the material represented (social actors, conflicts and places), the structure of images (spaces, times and symbolic oppositions), forms of narration (how the story is told and articulated), and media language (what kind of TV syntax is used) (35–36). The authors claim in conclusion that their aim here is to study not contents or codes but rather 'cultural moulds' or 'matrices'. They specify:

> Hablar de matrices no es evocar lo arcaico, es hacer explícito lo que carga el hoy, para indagar no lo que sobrevive del tiempo aquel en que los relatos o los gestos populares eran auténticos sino lo que hace que ciertas matrices narrativas

o escenográficas sigan vivas, esto es, conectando secretamente con la vida, los miedos y las esperanzas de la gente. (Martín Barbero and Muñoz 36)

[Speaking of 'matrices' means not invoking the archaic, but rather making explicit the burden of the present. It means investigating not what survives from a distant time when popular narratives and gestures were authentic, but what causes certain narrative and dramatic matrices to remain alive, that is, to connect secretly with people's lives, fears, and hopes.]

As we shall see, the historical telenovela has a particular role to play in this interpenetration of past and present. But one British scholar has expanded this critical focus on a single nation to address transnational telenovela in the special case of Spain, offering an alternative methodology as he does so.

In his pioneering study of what he calls 'the domestic Spanish television serial' Hugh O'Donnell avoids both the stress on Latin American-US relations favoured by academics and the Latin American-Spanish dimension studied by industry commentators, focusing rather on the pioneering imitators of British soaps (broadly realist) in the *autonomías* and the less successful imitators of (broadly melodramatic) Latin American moulds or models in Madrid. O'Donnell's brief history of the genre in the Peninsula lays much greater stress than do industry reports on early prime-time shows such as the Catalan *Poble nou* ('New Town', 1994) and *El cor de la ciutat* ('Heart of the City', 2000), Andalusia's *Arrayán* ('Myrtle', 2001), and Galicia's *Rías Baixas* ('Down River', 2000) (41). And he draws out no fewer than fourteen differences in storytelling and visual style (Martín Barbero's 'textual composition') between what we might call the Anglo-Catalan tradition and the Latin American. In the former, all filming is in colour; there is consistent colour tone; everything is shot at eye level; there is no privileged point of view; no 'inner vision' shots; no 'impossible shots' (e.g. from ceilings); no 'symbolic' shots (e.g. through railings that symbolize imprisonment); relatively static camera; speaker always in focus; medium duration takes; predominance of medium close-ups; no addressing the camera; no interior monologues; linear narrative time (i.e. no flashbacks); 'real' narrative time (i.e. no slow or fast motion); no self-conscious intertextuality; and no non-diegetic music (42–44).

The Latin American melodramatic model (adopted for the most part in the few Madrid-made daytime soaps) is opposite to all these realist characteristics. But beyond textual analysis, O'Donnell's contention is that 'differing visual styles [...] work to locate the viewer differently in relation to the source of the drama' (47), with the British (or Catalan) 'work[ing] to locate the viewer as a plausible participant in the drama', while the Latin American 'positions the viewer [...] as a spectator', however 'thrilled, moved, horrified, or anguished' (48). O'Donnell rejects gender and underdevelopment as causes for this stylistic and spectatorial divergence (after all, Madrid is no less developed than Barcelona), arguing, rather, for a difference in the conception of the 'popular public sphere' (51), a term he takes from Milly Buonanno. Mundane local engagement is thus contrasted with a more transcendental perspective in which conflict is resolved at a symbolic level (52).

O'Donnell may not be comparing like with like here. As we have seen, television serials may be prime-time national narratives in Mexico City and Barcelona, but in Madrid they are relegated to the minority afternoon audience. Series drama, shown once a week and with an annual season of only 20 plus episodes, is the dominant form for both audiences and producers in Castile and the US (which also lacks daily prime-time soaps). Each national audiovisual field thus distributes its narrative load across different formats and time slots in a different way.

It remains the case, however, that the relative absence or failure of the long-running television serial, whether local or foreign, on Spanish national broadcasting, when compared with the cases of Latin America, Britain, and the *autonomías*, is a distinctive feature that deserves further investigation. As we shall see, only one series has bucked the trend in recent years, and that is anomalous: *Amar en tiempos revueltos* ('Loving in Troubled Times') is a historical soap based on a Catalan model. But first we must examine the inescapable Latin American models with which it shares the *sobremesa* slot.

Amarte así and *Los Plateados*

Amarte así ('Loving You This Way', 2005)
Margarita es una joven que trabaja en un restaurante como cantante de mariachi e Ignacio es un joven médico. En el pasado, ellos tuvieron una relación fugaz de la que Ignacio no tiene memoria pero que le dejó a Margarita un pequeño 'regalo': 'Frijolito'. Éste, sin saberlo, conocerá a su padre y se volverá su gran amigo. Es más… hará de Cupido para reunir a Margarita e Ignacio. (Iaguia, Amarte)

[Margarita is a young woman who works in a restaurant as a mariachi singer and Ignacio is a young doctor. Some time in the past they had a brief fling which Ignacio doesn't remember but which left Margarita a small souvenir: 'Frijolito' ('Little Bean'). Unaware that Ignacio is his father, Frijolito will get to know his father and become his great friend. What's more … he'll play Cupid to bring Margarita and Ignacio back together again.]

Los Plateados ('Silver Plated', 2005)
La joven Camila Castañeda se dirige en tren con su familia a la mansión de su prometido, Emilio Gallardo, un maduro hacendado violento y mujeriego. El tren es asaltado por unos forajidos a quienes llaman *Los Plateados*. Las miradas del jefe del grupo y Camila se cruzan por un momento. Ésta queda prendada del gallardo individuo. Al día siguiente se celebra la boda entre Camila y Emilio. (Iaguia, Los Plateados)

[Young Camila Castañeda is travelling with her family by train to the mansion of her fiancé, Emilio Gallardo, a mature landowner who is a violent womanizer. The train is attacked by some outlaws, known as Los Plateados ('The Silver-Plated Ones'). The leader of the band and Camila exchange a brief glance. She is smitten with the dashing young man. The next day Camila and Emilio's wedding takes place.]

Two shows aired on TVE in the 2005–2006 season give an example of the versatility of the telenovela genre as it is distributed in Spain. *Amarte así* is a traditional 'hardcore' romance set in small-town Mexico. Round-faced, good-hearted brunette Margarita (singing star Litzy) is a single mother who cleans house at the mansion of young doctor Ignacio (cute, unthreatening Mauricio Ochmann) and his disciplinarian widowed brother Francisco by day, and plays in a mariachi band in a restaurant by night. Engaged to brittle blonde Chantal, little does Ignacio know that Margarita's impish young son, Frijolito, is his own child. It will take 110 episodes of 45 minutes each before the predictable climax: the fairy-tale wedding at a perfect whitewashed chapel of the young couple in the presence of the grinning child.

Los Plateados (produced by Telemundo in the same year) is a historical romance, also a standard sub-genre in Mexico. The central figures here are three brothers and a sister who, after the unjust murder of their father, become Robin Hood-style bandits, stealing from the landed rich and giving to the poor peasantry. Romantic, virginal Camila (Spanish-born Tamara Montserrat) is due to be married to caddish older landowner Emilio (Humberto Zurita), who is

13 Margarita (Litzy) and Ignacio (Maurico Ochmann): *Amarte así*

sleeping both with her sister and his servant). Kidnapped on her wedding day by the chief bandit, the brooding Gabriel (Mauricio Islas), she will wait 148 lavish episodes to conclude her longed-for romance. *Los Plateados*, much more erotically charged than the domestic and contemporary *Amarte así*, has a credit sequence that dwells on the swelling bosoms, tightly corseted waists, and lacy garter belts of its nineteenth-century heroines.

Let us examine two specimen episodes broadcast by TVE on the afternoon of 9 January 2006. Although *Amarte así* and *Los Plateados* are both produced by Telemundo (the second-ranking US Spanish-language network, which has its studios in Miami), they could not be more different. As the smiling faces of its protagonists in the credit sequence suggest (not to mention the saccharine lyrics of the theme tune sung by the amiable Litzy herself), *Amarte* clings to the 'romantic' original template, apparently unaware of the realist 'rupture' that took place at the start of the decade. But scheduled as it was in the US (and Mexico) as part of Telemundo and Azteca's 'backbone' block of primetime novela programming, the show shows some sign of appealing beyond the middle-aged female target addressed in Spain's *sobremesa* slot.

There is thus in the opening sequence a taster of the more contemporary and sophisticated themes that had recently been introduced. The MacGuffin of this episode is an anonymous letter sent to the rich family's mansion, alerting protagonist Ignacio to the fact that he has a secret and still unidentified love child. When the moralizing Francisco accuses his brother of thoughtless promiscuity, Ignacio attacks him in turn for hypocrisy: he has merely feigned Catholic chastity after the death of his wife. (Later, Chantal's bitch goddess mother will even suggest Margarita get rid of the child she erroneously believes she is carrying.)

Gesturing timidly towards sophisticated themes, *Amarte* is more obviously hybridized with comedy. Ironically echoing the 'primacy of marriage' plot (alerted to her fiancé's love child, steely Chantal replies only 'The wedding, above all'), Margarita's comic co-worker aims to marry two women at once, cycling crazily between the simultaneous ceremonies. While this is hardly a break with generic traditions, the parody of matrimony does perhaps suggest an extension of the ostensible boundaries of the main narrative: female viewers are presented with a number of independent single women, beginning with Margarita and her own mother, who cares for child Frijolito.

This hybridization of romance and comedy (the farcical subplot takes up a good deal of screen time and is heavily signalled by musical prompts) is echoed by a second pervasive trend in telenovela production: internationalization. *Amarte* carries a credit for 'neutral dialogue coach': the Mexican stars have thus been actively trained to adopt a vernacular that will prove inoffensive around the Spanish-speaking world. And the attractive locations (the glamorous mansion of the rich family and surprisingly comfortable, colourful homes of the poor) are studiously non-specific. Alarmed by the letter and fearing Frijolito will be taken from her, Margarita tells her mother they must move to 'another town' (without specifying which or where). Yet *Amarte* does permit particularizing elements, just so long as they are universally recognizable: hence Margarita's somewhat unlikely twin career as daytime maid and night-time songbird. The least attentive Madrid housewife would no doubt recognize (and take pleasure in) our heroine's mariachi costume.

The fact that the older female demographic is the show's target audience in Spain (if not in the US and Mexico) is reconfirmed not only by *Amarte*'s failure to jump the scheduling 'fence' that restricts it with its fellow novelas to the *sobremesa* slot, but also by Frijolito's guest appearance on *Cine de barrio*, a film-themed talk show that has long played on Saturday afternoons on TVE1. Older Spaniards would no doubt make a connection between the Mexican urchin and the Spanish child stars frequently showcased on *Cine de barrio*'s Francoist features.

If the structure and dynamic of production of Miami-based Telemundo favours transnational blandness, social uses and ways of seeing remain differentiated. For example, consumers in the US, posting on a dedicated discussion forum, praised *Amarte* for its restraint, especially in the context of the trashy talk shows they deemed inappropriate for Latinas, which were carried by some Telemundo affiliates in the traditional novela time slot (telemundodallas). And, indeed, if we look at the textual composition of the show (Martín Barbero's third broad category, after production and consumption) we find that shooting style does not coincide with the melodramatic mould that O'Donnell claims is typical of Latin America (and Madrid).

This episode of *Amarte* features not one of the visual trademarks O'Donnell lists: colour, camera height and perspective are consistent and unremarkable and there are no subjective or fantasy shots, flashbacks, slow-motion shots, or inner voices. The camera cuts calmly between medium close-ups, however melodramatic the dialogue. Even Margarita's appeal to the Virgin to protect her child is not visually reinforced by some special technique. Inescapable, however, is the non-diegetic music (wholly absent in British and Catalan soaps), which ranges from swelling strings (Ignacio steals a kiss from Margarita in her maid's uniform) to electronic dissonance (Chantal's criminal accomplices plan to murder Ignacio), via *Benny Hill*-style comic brass (the reluctant bridegroom pedals his cycle between the two weddings). The diverse target audience may no longer respond to visual prompts, but are clearly assumed to need auditory cues to negotiate abrupt tonal shifts in the show.

The shooting style thus suggests that the viewer (situated on the same level as Ignacio, Margarita and, indeed, Frijolito, when he appears at the dinner

14 Camila on the train (Tamar Monserrat): *Los Plateados*

table) is a plausible participant in the drama. The plot, nonetheless, tells us something else. We may be engaged in the fictional world, but it is one in which the characters themselves have no control over their fates. Class conflict is an unbridgeable chasm (good-hearted Margarita is repeatedly reminded she is only a servant, even as she is romantically involved with both rich brothers). The problem can be resolved only by an accident of birth (Ignacio will learn that Frijolito is his own flesh and blood). Moreover, when Margarita's mother tells her that her child cannot be taken from her, she replies that money is more powerful than the law of the land. There is thus no sense of a popular public sphere with recognizable rules to which all of the characters can contribute, albeit in different ways.

As we shall see, *Los Plateados*, a luxury period piece, echoes this fundamental theme. But what is striking is that its textual composition is so different. In keeping with the cinematic sweep and production values (it was promoted as Telemundo's most expensive show), *Los Plateados* exploits almost all of O'Donnell's melodramatic motifs. It breaks into black and white for flashbacks (the bandit children play with their father, who is now deceased), gives flashy high and low angles as horses thunder through forests, or the bandits prepare their raid on the rich man's wedding, and offers giddy travelling shots from horseback, handsome carriages, or even from the top of a speeding steam train. As patriarch Emilio pursues his sex-starved sister-in-law on his wedding day, the camera breaks into a shaky, 'subjective' POV. There is even a heavy dose of self-conscious intertextuality: inexperienced Camila reads aloud repeatedly from a romantic novel on the train. Soon she will meet the dashing bandit who will interrupt her journey and win her heart with a single ardent look over his bandanna.

The broad canvas and restless movement of *Los Plateados* thus mean that it can indeed serve, as one critic suggested of the historical subgenre, as a 'kinetic mural'. But in spite of the particularity of muralism in a Mexican context, the show is carefully transnationalized. Foreign audiences need no familiarity with Mexican history to recognize the conflict between traditionalist landowners and progressive redistributors of wealth. Ideological emphasis is helpfully underlined in the dialogue: characters comment unfavourably on how cruelly don Emilio treats his workers. One young man is even training as a lawyer to defend the underprivileged. After a seductively bare-chested dip in a local lake, he tells his strait-laced girlfriend that there are 'two worlds' in Mexico City: the rich and the poor. The wealthy may wear the finest costumes but our sympathy is never directed towards them.

Los Plateados likewise dips its elegantly shod feet in 'sophisticated' themes. Heroine Camila may begin as a blushing bride, but she gallops off with the bandits given half a chance. Her sister dons riding breeches to renew her affair with the bridegroom, grappling with him on a tabletop. The female bandit shoots a policeman's pistol straight out of his hand. Even Camila's widowed mother, as poisonous as Chantal's in *Amarte*, shows steely determination in negotiating the arranged marriage. It is not difficult to see how female viewers could extend the boundaries of the bodice-ripping narrative to emphasize the opportunities for female autonomy even in a patriarchal age.

Action set pieces, absent, of course, in the domesticated *Amarte*, stake a claim to a male audience also. This episode boasts both the assault on the steam train and the attack on the wedding party. With its lush locations (shot in picturesque Vera Cruz) and exquisitely detailed costumes, *Los Plateados* lays claim to distinction, setting itself apart from the everydayness of most telenovelas and distancing itself from domestic routines even as it invokes collective imaginaries. Familiar symbolic oppositions (of rich and poor, conservative and progressive) are supplemented by new, less expected conflicts: the son of an exotic family (alternately identified as 'Arab' and 'Turk') is rejected when he asks a local girl for a dance at the wedding. *Los Plateados* thus gestures towards the contemporary question of racism, even as it revels in the visual pleasures of the past (lacy lingerie and vintage locomotives).

Contemporary viewers are not, however, located as plausible participants in the fiction, whether they choose to identify with browbeaten indigenous servants or haughty aristocrats. Rather, as spectators, we are thrilled at the action sequences, moved at the passionate romance, and horrified at the intermittent violence. In a curious echo of *Amarte*, it is explicitly stated once more that it is the rich who make the laws: heedless of police and army, patriarch Emilio vows to hunt down and execute the bandits himself.

Moreover, romantic love (which in *Amarte* is integrated, albeit unrecognized, into the everyday life of domestic labour) is in *Los Plateados* reduced to an uncontrollable urge or a stroke of fate (legend has it that a single look from a bandit will bewitch an innocent girl). Flesh and blood or love at first sight: these are the symbolic drivers in these Latin American telenovelas, which serve to resolve conflict at a transcendental level far from the mundane local engagement of European soaps.

Amar en tiempos revueltos ('Loving in Troubled Times', 2005)

Madrid, febrero de 1936; mientras Antonio y muchos compañeros, de clases populares, celebran el triunfo del Frente Popular en una verbena improvisada en la calle, Andrea regresa a casa en compañía de su amiga Consuelo. Llegan noticias del alzamiento militar y mientras los partidarios de la República salen a la calle dispuestos a defenderla, Rodrigo, hermano de Andrea, prepara con los suyos la neutralización de los rojos. En esta escaramuza estúpida se produce un trágico suceso que favorece el acercamiento entre Andrea y Antonio, obrero e hijo del encargado del almacén de la empresa de don Fabián, que ha sido despedido de la fábrica por agitador. Entre ellos surgirá un amor apasionado, que se ha mantenido latente desde la adolescencia. (laguia, Amar)

[Madrid, February 1936. While Antonio and his working class comrades celebrate the triumph of the Popular Front in an improvised street party, Andrea walks home with her friend Consuelo. News arrives of the military uprising and as the supporters of the Republic take to the streets ready to defend it, Rodrigo, Andrea's brother, is getting ready with his friends to kill some Reds. In this stupid skirmish a tragedy takes place which draws Andrea closer to the working class Antonio. The son of the foreman in the factory of Don Fabián [Andrea's father], Antonio has been sacked for being a labour activist. Antonio and Andrea will experience a passionate love affair, which has been on the cards since they were teenagers.]

As Elena Galán writes in her excellent account of the 'traces of time' in *Amar en tiempos revueltos*, this serial is unprecedented in its setting: the Civil War and its immediate aftermath. While literary adaptations frequently explored the past in the TVE of the Transition, no such dramas had been made in the 1990s, a time in which contemporary local production flourished. Only *Cuéntame* (premiered in 2001) addressed Francoist issues, but even that successful weekly series was set in the more accessible and less traumatic 1960s and 1970s and leavened past repressions with humour and nostalgia.

The production structure and dynamic of *Amar en tiempos revueltos* is equally unusual. Broadly based on a Catalan-language series, 'Temps de silenci' (which embraced the whole of twentieth-century history in Barcelona), *Amar en tiempos revueltos* remained a Catalan project even when shooting and setting transferred to Madrid: the most illustrious name on the team is respected playwright Josep Maria Benet i Jornet, who served as chief writer. *Amar en tiempos revueltos* is produced by Diagonal, named for a famous boulevard in Barcelona. Part of a cluster of Catalan media producers who aim to rival Madrid, Diagonal is also a division of Endemol, the Dutch-based multinational that created Spanish-language versions of reality franchises such as *Big Brother*. Sister company Gestmusic-Endemol was also notorious for *Crónicas marcianas*, a scandalous late-night talk show broadcast live from Barcelona. Thus there was no industrial precedent for a Madrid-based, Catalan-produced show. Thematically and stylistically *Amar en tiempos revueltos* raised the possibility of an innovative link between two modes or (in Martín Barbero's word) 'matrices' of telenovela that had previously been quite separate: the more melodramatic Latin American-Castilian and the broadly realistic Anglo-Catalan.

From the start, press coverage and public response were positive. An account in *El Imparcial* (2 September 2005), followed by lengthy and diverse posts by viewers, places the unsettlingly new production in the familiar context of telenovela scheduling and consumption. *Amar en tiempos revueltos* on public broadcaster TVE1 is programmed Monday to Friday at 4pm against a new serial-reality hybrid on a private network (a competition-romance in which one contestant pretends to be gay), itself based on a Latin American original. TVE's 'tent pole', which ran for 45 minutes, led into import *Amarte así*, which achieved similar ratings and share: respectively 21.1 per cent and 2,418,000 viewers against 26.1 per cent and 2,638,000 viewers (the feature-length premiere of *Amar en tiempos revueltos* had 'leapt the fence' to air in prime time on 26 September 2005 to a respectable 23.3 per cent share). Clearly, there was an audience for both innovation and tradition in the neglected *sobremesa* demographic. *El Imparcial*, giving the pros and cons of the new format, stresses both continuity and change within the genre: *Amar en tiempos revueltos* will benefit from a newly urgent interest in the period and its unusually 'serious' tone, but will also pull in viewers with its cute young stars and predictable plot lines. The extended length of the series (given here as 130 episodes, finally drawn out to 200), will encourage that holy grail of the scheduler: viewer loyalty.

Amar en tiempos revueltos remains controversial from the start, however. *El Imparcial* notes that it has already been criticized by the conservative People's Party for digging up episodes in Spanish history that should remain buried. In its interviews with producers and actors, specialist website vertele.com actively stresses this engagement with the past: shooting began, we are told, on 18 July, the same day as Franco's rebellion. The star here is given as Pilar Bardem, a veteran actress from a theatrical dynasty known for its radical politics (her role as Elpidia, leading man Antonio's mother, is, in fact, quite small in the opening episodes) (see also vertele). The executive producers admit that their show may indeed 'offend the sensibilities' of some viewers, but assert that it should not be neutral in its depiction of the past: different characters are, however, apportioned different perspectives on the tumultuous time in which they live, a period that has a 'dramatic potential' that is absent in the present. An interview with formulatv.com also stresses the producers' and actors' 'fidelity' to the past, although this does not aim for exhaustive reconstruction or analysis. In interviews for the launch of the second season (with plot lines parallel to but distinct from the first, and the introduction of some 24 new characters) a new and suggesting phrasing emerges: 'the truth of feelings'.

Elena Galán has minutely examined this relationship between the present time of production and the past time of representation in her essay, the first rigorous academic study of the serial. She establishes five precise parallels between the periods 2000–2006 and 1939–45. Thus the much-debated proposal for a Law of Historical Memory is paralleled by the show's depiction of the unjust repression of the losing side after the Civil War; the reform of the Civil Code permitting 'express divorce' on 28 November 2004 counters the prohibition of divorce after the defeat of the Republic (protagonist Andrea's civil marriage to Antonio will, in fact, be declared null); Law 39/1999, promoting work/life balance for women and men, is shadowed by the prohibition of female participation in the labour force after Franco's victory (Andrea will be forbidden even to attend university); the Law of Protection from Domestic Violence of 28 December 2004 is contrasted with the acceptance of wife-beating and forced prostitution in the postwar period; and finally, the law extending marriage rights to same-sex couples (1 July 2005) is countered by the prohibition and rejection of prominent gay and lesbian characters in the period depicted in *Amar en tiempos revueltos*. Far from promoting a generalized nostalgic fantasy in the manner of *Los Plateados*, then, *Amar en tiempos revueltos* is working through quite precise political questions that were actively debated at the time of its production process. These 'traces of time' may not be immediately visible to the show's target audience but, as we have seen, they did not pass unnoticed by contemporary politicians.

In spite of its sociopolitical focus, *Amar en tiempos revueltos* does not, then, neglect the essential elements of the romantic drama, even melodrama, that seem to predate the new realism of telenovela and are still prominent in its similarly titled *sobremesa* stablemate, *Amarte así*. Thus, *Amar en tiempos revueltos* is structured around the Romeo and Juliet motif of star-crossed lovers divided (as in Latin American telenovela) by unbridgeable class conflict. Crucially here, however, the gender division is inverted, with Andrea the daughter of the wealthy capitalist in whose factory poor Antonio works. The fact that both actors (Ana Turpin and Rodolfo Sancho) were relatively unknown before starring in the series makes them easier to identify with as romantic leads. Over its lengthy arc, the serial will also exploit the classic motif of the lost child (as in Frijolito) who will finally, tearfully, bring together his parents: Andrea's son, the emblematically named Liberto, will be taken from her when she is imprisoned as a Republican sympathizer and the family will be reunited only at the end. Arranged marriage is also a familiar, deep-level structuring device: after her civil wedding to Antonio (Episode 3) is annulled and he disappears into prison, Andrea will be obliged to marry the Francoist Mario.

In the first three weeks of the serial, melodramatic crises are exploited between a wide variety of family members: Andrea defies her patriarchal father Fabián and leaves home (1); she is tearfully separated from her mother, remaining in Madrid as her family leaves for the Nationalist zone (4), and from her husband when he leaves for the front and she tells him she is pregnant (6). When they return at the war's end and Andrea is arrested (10), her father disowns her and her Falangist brother Rodrigo disobeys him, using his influence to have her transferred to a convent (11). Andrea's child Liberto is taken from her (she weeps bitterly behind the bars) and Antonio's mother Elpidia (played by the dignified Bardem) visits his sick father in prison, selling her wedding ring to bribe the guard (13). Rebelling against a tyrannical mother superior and grieving for her lost son, Andrea is confined to a punishment cell in the convent (also 13).

There are pointed parallels throughout between the fate of the rich family and the poor: Andrea's mother gives thanks that her Falangist son has returned safely from war, while Antonio's mother waits in vain for her own Republican son to return (14). When they discover that Andrea has a child, her mother embraces Antonio's mother, Elpidia, saying they can now both be grandmothers; but her father tells Elpidia that the ill-fated marriage and child 'did not take place' and that she 'is not family, is nothing' to him.

Yet when the Falangist son and capitalist father argue bitterly over the future of the factory (14), the former says 'Let's not be dramatic'. And, as *El Imparcial* noted, the tone throughout is 'serious'. There are almost no comic subplots here, except perhaps where a priest and a nun in hiding are schooled in how to pretend to be an old married couple (they should argue bitterly) (3). Moreover, the melodramatic motifs are disposed of at an indecently fast pace. Heedless of the endless postponements in the traditional telenovela and seeing no need to wait for marriage, Andrea and Antonio have consummated their love by the second episode (their tender dialogue is, as I write, memorialized by a fan on YouTube).

Realistic motifs or sophisticated themes, typical of the new wave of telenovelas, abound. Arguably the main plot strand is not Andrea's tragic love for

Antonio, but her quest for independence (she is first shown as a talented artist, frustrated at her father's refusal to let her train for her vocation). Rodrigo, the smooth-shaven, sharp-suited Falangist (latterly in a flattering uniform, sewn by Antonio's mother) is a disturbing foil to Antonio's bearded, cloth-capped worker (often shown in sexy singlet). Rodrigo will much later decline into rape, sickness and tragic death.

The first episode also reveals a remarkable pragmatism around sex, which is held in tension with the romantic 'childhood sweethearts' motif. Antonio, first shown flirting with Andrea in the street as his comrades celebrate the Popular Front's election victory, is soon making love with Paloma, the feisty owner of the local grocers, his naked back glistening attractively with sweat (Paloma, who notes that some women have only one thing to sell, will later open an upmarket brothel). One very deep plot line is also planted in the very first episode: Andrea's little brother Sito, who likes to play with pistols, exclaims that he would like a boyfriend like his sister has. Only in Episode 14 will he literally bump into the impoverished Angel, thus preparing the way for an unrequited gay love story, which parallels the rags and riches story of Andrea and Antonio. Clearly we are a long way from the grinning, gurning Frijolito.

Politics, like sex, is shown to be more complex than the stark dichotomies of telenovela tend to suggest. Divisions arise not only between victors and vanquished but also within the two bands: Andrea's capitalist father argues not only with his Republican daughter but also with his Falangist son; bitch goddess Eulalia, mother of Andrea's second husband Mario, plays a monarchist landowner who despises Franco almost as much as she hates Communism; Antonio's working-class father (unlike his revolutionary son) wants only to put in a good day's work for his boss (7).

Moreover, in spite of its historical setting and broad canvas (the Civil War is skipped over in just a few episodes), *Amar en tiempos revueltos* does not exploit the big-budget, kinetic-mural properties of *Los Plateados*. Antonio's battle in the Casa de Campo is reduced to urgent dialogue with comrades in the bushes (7). Further location shots are limited to brief excursions to the Retiro, or the steps of the Prado, where Andrea works during the war. The convent confinement plot strand (reminiscent of the Las Micaelas episode in *Fortunata y Jacinta*, faithfully recreated in TVE's version of 1980), gives a rare opportunity for a handsome historical location, even as it stresses the cruelty of the hypocritical nuns, who require 'humility' of the mothers whose children they have stolen. The modest main set is focused on a small square (with bar and grocer's) and the single building in which Antonio's family are lodged in the spare caretaker's basement, while Andrea's family enjoy a comfortable apartment above.

Large-scale historical events are depicted only in No-Do newsreel, a vital resource lodged in TVE's archives and also exploited by *Amar en tiempos revueltos*'s

15 Andrea (Ana Turpin) and Antonio (Rodolfo Sancho) on the roof: *Amar en tiempos revueltos*

fellow family period piece, *Cuéntame*. As in *Cuéntame*, black and white actuality footage is made to fade into colour fictional sequences, thus suggesting a certain bracketing of the past, even within a period drama. It is significant that the only images shown in the credits (accompanied by a newly written song on the 'hunger and scarcity' of the time) are documentary shots of streets and trams, orphans and war veterans, and markets selling the skinniest of chickens (the black market is a frequent theme in the show itself). This flickering footage is, however, framed by a black, empty edge on all four sides, insisting on the distance between past and present, even as that past leaves traces to be explored by modern viewers.

Certainly *Amar en tiempos revueltos*, for all its domestic focus, pays more attention than normal in a telenovela to the workplace. Beyond family business conflict (a staple even in *Amarte así*), industrial relations between bosses and employees are prominent as a theme, with the threat of expropriation made in the first episode. The most radical of the workers is not depicted in a positive light (Andrea's family is protected by Antonio when an angry proletarian mob visit their comfortable home, even though he has just been dismissed by their father). And, on closer inspection, the purist 'romantic' elements of *Amar en tiempos revueltos* are consistently embedded in historical or political commentary, or vice versa. In the first episode, when Andrea complains that 'social differences' of class are paramount, her hunky art teacher tells her to follow her desires. Conversely, when she tells best friend Consuelo of her love for a lower-class man, she replies that 'laws may change [under the Republic], but people never do'. The personal and political are frankly juxtaposed at the episode's climax, when Andrea and Antonio embrace on their building's rooftop. She says: 'I'll never let anyone tell me what to do', and he replies 'There's a freer world struggling to be born'.

While these broadbrush conflicts are hardly inaccessible to audiences, elsewhere *Amar en tiempos revueltos* is notably local in its historical and geographical reference, especially in an era of transnational telenovela production. Viewers are assumed to be familiar with the Popular Front and Manuel Azaña. The young couple make love, quite precisely, in Dehesa de la Villa (a park in the north-west of Madrid), while Andrea's family claim they will summer in El Escorial, while actually setting off across the battle lines to Salamanca. The (briefly) happy Antonio is described as looking like 'a priest enjoying chocolate and churros' (a local delicacy), while a much-admired turkey, bought on the black market, is said to be 'bigger than Cibeles' (a local landmark). Such exclusive references clearly produce a reality effect on Spanish audiences and substitute for epochal conflicts impossible to represent on a small-screen budget. It is clear, then, that unlike Telemundo's fictions, Diagonal's dialogue has not been 'neutralized' and rendered accessible to wider audiences. Indeed, the particularity of time, place and language has been faithfully preserved.

This localization points to the unique success of *Amar en tiempos revueltos* in a Spanish context. Why was it that a period setting and a Catalan production, both elements that might be thought to limit the show's reach, proved so attractive? I would argue that it was only in this period setting that *Amar en tiempos revueltos* could reproduce those elements of Latin American romance that still attract some Spanish afternoon viewers. We remember that O'Donnell distinguished between the spectator of melodrama, transcendentally distanced from a conflict resolved only symbolically, and the participant of Anglo-Catalan soaps, engaged by local and mundane concerns. While the existence of a popular public sphere of contemporary Spain makes the melodramatic imagination difficult to pull off in a modern setting, the absence of such a sphere in the cruelly repressive early Franco era makes melodrama fully appropriate for *Amar en tiempos revueltos*.

Indeed, the melodramatic and historical elements are mutually reinforcing: the star-crossed lovers and missing child motifs are all too convincing, even commonplace, in the tragic 1930s and 1940s. It is striking, then, that *Amar en tiempos revueltos* repeats dialogue on the powerlessness of individuals over their fate that we have seen in the Latin American shows, both modern dress and period. Even Falangist Rodrigo has little faith in the new Spain he extols so frequently. Pleading for his sister's freedom, his superior tells him he should 'trust in justice'; he replies: 'No, I trust in you'. (11) As banned books pile up for burning in the little plaza (one literate character recognizes the poems of Antonio Machado among them), the melodramatic imagination does not seem inappropriate or exaggerated.

If *Amar en tiempos revueltos* combines thematically, then, melodrama and social realism (Latin America and Catalonia), it does the same stylistically in what Martín Barbero calls its 'textual composition'. Musical tags are relatively discreet, as is the shooting style, which generally employs few of the showy effects described by O'Donnell. Moreover, the extended working-class scenes are reminiscent of the British soaps that served as an acknowledged model for the Catalan and Basque versions, especially in the recurring use of two emblematic locations: the neighbourhood bar and the grocery. But extreme moments permit extreme measures. When Andrea is interrogated, after her child has been taken, a blinding white light floods into the bare room and the camera restlessly circles her (11). Or again, when she is thrown by the truly terrifying Mother Superior into a bleak punishment cell, the hand-held camera shakes in sympathy with her (13). In the convent once more she sees (we see) in a kind of fantasy flashback her beloved missing Antonio return from the war: on a cut we see she is passionately hugging not her husband but a fellow female inmate (14). It seems likely that such techniques (and comic relief plot lines) increased as the first series went on.

What remains the case, however, is that in an unforgiving landscape of transnationalized telenovelas, *Amar en tiempos revueltos* managed the twin, singular achievement of investigating the particularity of Spanish history in a way accessible and relevant to local audiences, and expressing that investigation in an attractive hybrid form, which drew on both Latin American and Anglo-Catalan expressive matrices. Viewing figures showed that such a strategy clearly, if secretly, connected with the lives, fears and hopes of modern Spaniards.

Endless Love

Hubo que aprender
a llevar y a tener
el corazón y el alma heridos.
Días de avidez,
de hambre y escasez,
de vencedores y vencidos.

Tuvo que aprender
a ganar y a perder
a fuerza de amor y coraje.

Días de un ayer
marcado para ser
vivido sin equipaje.

Amar en tiempos revueltos,
tiempos de ruina y lamento,
Amar en tiempos revueltos
por vientos que trajo un mar
de batallas por contar.

Tuve que aprender
que el odio y el querer
no tienen patria ni bandera.
Tuve que vivir
sin tu presencia, y
pagar el precio de la espera.

Amar en tiempos revueltos ...

You had to learn how to carry on with wounds in your heart and soul. They were days of eagerness, of hunger, and scarcity, days of victors and vanquished.

She had to learn how to win and lose with love and courage. They were days of yesteryear which had to be lived in destitution.

Loving in troubled times, times of ruins and weeping; loving in times that were troubled by winds whipped by an ocean of untold battles.

I had to learn that love and hate have no country or flag. I had to live without you and pay the price of waiting.

Loving in troubled times ...]

With its stress on wounds, hunger, ruins and tears, the theme tune of *Amar en tiempos revueltos* is decidedly downbeat. Even the (little-used) third stanza, with its promise that emotions transcend politics (homelands and flags) is qualified by the irreparable cost of lost time (the price of waiting for an absent loved one). It is perhaps no surprise that, for all its critical and popular acclaim, *Amar en tiempos revueltos* lost out to the more upbeat *Yo soy Bea* (the Spanish version of the Colombian *Betty la Fea*) in the telenovela category at the annual TP awards.

I have argued, however, that *Amar en tiempos revueltos* staged (like *Betty* but more covertly) a transnational process by fusing what I have called the Anglo-Catalan realist model with the Latin American romance. To this should be added elements of the prime-time Spanish dramas with which local audiences were also familiar. In spite of the limited budget permitted to a daily telenovela relative to weekly evening shows, *Amar en tiempos revueltos* is clearly a quality product, with excellent costumes and art design. At a Madrid seminar on 50 years of TVE in Spain, producer Eugeni Margalló also called attention to the factor he thought rarest in the *sobremesa* slot: convincing and rounded characters (Margalló). While some of these characters were familiar from Latin American melodrama (the stern father and monstrous mother), others embodied challenging new types: aristocratic and self-possessed lesbian Beatriz, introduced as a potential love match for lawyer Mario (21), means what she says when she tells him she 'does not believe in love between men and women' (he, of course, fails to understand her true meaning).

Some viewers were disappointed by the tragic fate of such queer characters: one fan argues that Sito, forced into a disastrous marriage, should find happiness reunited with his childhood love Angel (although their love would remain hidden from Franco, of course!) (Iaguia, 'Comentarios'). As in the case of Latin American telenovela, viewers thus chose to extend the limits of the narrative in ways that contradict the screenwriters' rigid arcs.

But the viewer's qualification of his wish-fulfilment (the acknowledgement that the period could not allow openly happy homosexuality) reveals that the show does not use history simply as an alibi or picturesque window-dressing for romance, whether gay or straight. One excellent episode (number 21, some five weeks into the run of the first season) is set quite precisely on 19 May 1939, the day of the military parade named variously, and ironically, for both 'Victory' and 'Peace'. All of the main characters dress in their finest, some more reluctantly than others, to participate in a historic event shown in extended documentary clips. Even troubled little Sito wears a miniature blue Falange uniform. But there is conflict among the 'winners': Andrea's capitalist father refuses to attend until an official promises his factory a profitable contract on the stone needed to construct Franco's war memorial, El Valle de los Caídos. The Republican barman is only persuaded to attend by sexy shopkeeper Paloma, who puts on her finery and warns him, with suspiciously accurate foresight 'This regime could last forty years'.

In hiding at a friend's house in Madrid, Andrea, who has escaped from the convent, opens the door when she hears a knock. The camera tilts slowly (scarily) up from the boots to the blue uniform and red cap of a Falangist. But it is her beloved Antonio, who, having himself fled prison has been secretly concealed in the bar's cellar and has borrowed the uniform to be reunited with his civil wife. With their fierce and passionate looks, they make a handsome couple. But what is striking is that through the episode, even as the two star-crossed lovers murmur to each other in bed, we hear the strident announcements and martial music of the parade from omnipresent radios. This expert and affecting romance is thus quite clearly embedded in history and politics. Indeed, the pathos and intensity of the couple's brief happiness comes from the viewer's awareness of those very precise pressures. Historical pedagogy is inextricable from what the producers called 'the truth of feelings' and is thus in no way in conflict with it.

The contrast with *Amar en tiempos revueltos*'s Mexican stablemates of the *sobremesa* is clear. *Amarte así*'s contemporary cross-class romance is placed in a vague no-man's-land, purged of local referents and accents; *Los Plateados*' lush costume drama is likewise sufficiently generalized to allow access to any Spanish-speaking viewer. *Amar en tiempos revueltos*, on the other hand, makes little sense without a working knowledge of the Republic, the Civil War and the privations of early Francoism and, indeed, it invites its viewers to meditate on the effects of such huge events on the small-scale narratives of everyday life. This may be a big burden for the studio set of the little plaza to bear, even assisted by the rich archive of documentary footage to which TVE has unique access.

But, finally, *Amar en tiempos revueltos* succeeds in reconciling that last division to which O'Donnell called attention: the transcendental (Latin American) perspective and the mundane (Anglo-Catalan) point of view. It achieves this partly, as I mentioned earlier, through the period setting, in which melodramatic motifs are all too convincingly everyday. But it also does so by employing an unshowy technique (or 'textual composition') that signals to us that modern viewers are plausible participants in the show, even as it reveals that period protagonists of that same show are mere spectators of their own lives, unable to participate in (indeed, brutally excluded from) a popular public sphere that has ceased to exist. This is the true moral for an anxious modern age that has gained democracy but remains troubled by disturbingly similar social problems to those depicted some seventy years before.

Amar en tiempos revueltos ('Loving in Troubled Times', TVE1, 2005)

Production company	Diagonal TV
Executive producers	Jaume Banacolocha, Eugeni Margalló
Directors	Eduardo Casanova, Carlos Pérez, Diego Lesmes, et al.
Chief writer	Josep Maria Benet i Jornet
Original music	Noel Molina

Cast

Ana Turpin	Andrea
Rodolfo Sancho	Antonio
Pilar Bardem	Elpidia
Félix Gómez	Rodrigo
Héctor Colomé	Fabián
Ana Otero	Paloma

Amarte así ('Loving You this Way', TVE1, 2005)
Production companies	Promofilm, Telemundo
Executive producers	Arnaldo Limansky, Cristina Palacios
Directors	Heriberto López de Anda, Alejandro Hugo Moser
Chief writer	Enrique Torres

Cast
Maurico Ochmann	Ignacio
Litzy	Margarita
Alejandro Felipe	Frijolito

Los Plateados ('The Silver-Plated', TVE1, 2005)
Production companies	Argos, Telemundo
Executive producer	Epigmenio Ibarra
Director	Walter Doehner
Writers	Richard García, Leticia López

Cast
Maurico Islas	Gabriel
Tamara Montserrat	Camila
Dominika Paleta	Luciana
Humberto Zurita	Emilio

Works Cited

Ávila-Saavedra, Guillermo. 'New Discourses and Traditional Genres: The Adaptation of a Feminist Novel Into an Ecuadorian Telenovela'. *Journal of Broadcasting and Electronic Media* 50.3 (1 Sept. 2006): 383–99.

Beard, Laura J. 'Whose Life in the Mirror?: Examining Three Mexican Telenovelas as Cultural and Commercial Products'. *Studies in Latin American Popular Culture* 22 (1 Jan. 2003): 73–88.

Biltereyst, Daniel, and Philippe Meers. 'The International Telenovela Debate and the Contra-flow Argument: A Reappraisal'. *Media, Culture, and Society* 22.4 (1 July 2000): 393–413.

formulatv. 'La Primera estrena *Amar en tiempos revueltos*'. 25 Sept. 2005. Accessed 29 May 2007. <http://www.formulatv.com/1,20050925,1503,1.html>

Fox, Elizabeth. *Latin American Broadcasting: From Tango to Telenovela*. Luton: U of Luton P, 1997.

Galán, Elena. 'Las huellas del tiempo del autor en el discurso televisivo de la posguerra española'. *Razón y Palabra* 56. Accessed 29 May 2007. <http://www.cem.itesm.mx/dacs/publicaciones/logos/actual/egalan.html>.

Imparcial, El. 'Elección de *sobremesa*: ¿*Amar en tiempos revueltos* o *El auténtico Rodrigo Leal*?' 28 Sept. 2005. Accessed 29 May 2007. <http://imparcial.blogcindario.com/2005/09/00308–Amar-en-tiempos-revueltos-o-el-autentico-rodrigo-leal.html>

Kaiser, Patricia. 'Primer encuentro de la telenovela latinoamericana'. *Encuadre* 70 (1 Apr. 1998): 70–74.

laguia. '*Amar en tiempos revueltos*'. Accessed 29 May 2007 <http://www.laguiatv.com/serie_episodios_sinop.php?id=147669& t=1&e=1>.

—. 'Comentarios'. 19 December 2006. Accessed 29 May 2007 <http://www.laguiatv.com/serie_comentarios.php?id=147669&total=47&pagina_enviar=3>

—. '*Amarte* asi'. Accessed 29 May 2007 <http://www.laguiatv.com/serie_detalle.php?id=145635

—. '*Los Plateados*'. Accessed 29 May 2007 <http://www.laguiatv.com/series_resultados.php?id=147944>.

Margalló, Eugeni. Unpublished talk given at 'La televisión en España (1956–2006)'. Madrid: Universidad Carlos III, 10–14 July 2006.

Martín Barbero, J., and Sonia Muñoz. *Televisión y melodrama: Géneros y lecturas de la telenovela en Colombia*. Bogotá: Tercer Mundo, 1992.

Mayer, Vicki. 'Living Telenovelas/Telenovelizing Life: Mexican American Girls' Identities and Transnational Telenovelas'. *Journal of Communication* 53.3 (1 Sept. 2003): 479–95.

Mazziotti, Laura. *La industria de telenovela: La producción de ficción en América Latina*. Buenos Aires: Paidós, 1996.

Michelin, Gerardo. 'Informe Iberoaméricana: Un continente en movimiento'. *Cineinforme* 751 (1 Nov 2002): 35–56.

—, ed. 'Telenovelas: Desde Latinoamérica con amor'. *Cineinforme* 755 (1 March 2003): 39–48.

O'Donnell, Hugh. 'High Drama, Low Key: Visual Aesthetics and Subject Positions in the Domestic Spanish Television Serial'. *Journal of Spanish Cultural Studies* 8.1 (March 2007): 37–54.

Rodríquez Cadena, María de los Ángeles. 'Contemporary Hi(stories) of Mexico: Fictional Re-Creation of Collective Past on Television'. *Film and History* 34.1 (2004): 49–55.

Sánchez Tena, Jesús. 'Trece años de telenovela en España'. *Cineinforme* 755 (1 March 2003): 40–43.

telemundodallas. Discussion forum on *Amarte así*. Accessed 29 May 2007. <http://www.telemundodallas.com/Amarteasi/index.html>

Television Business International. 'Territory Guide to Latin America'. [Special issue] May 2007.

vertele. 'Pilar Bardem, Rodolfo Sancho, y Ana Turpin protagonizarán la nueva telenovela de TVE'. 4 Sept. 2005. Accessed 29 May 2007. http://www.vertele.com/noticias/detail.php?id=10230

CHAPTER SEVEN

Auteur TV: Case Studies in Creativity

Authorship in cinema and television

The debate around the auteur has been surprisingly durable in film studies. The editors of a recent anthology of new articles in the field (Gerstner and Staiger) argue that the 2000s have seen a 'resurgence in the analysis of authorship', which they attribute to three motives: the fact that it serves as an 'enabling tool' of study; the awareness that (even for Barthes) authors were not truly dead; and the use of authorship, however compromised by humanism and capitalism, as a 'function for social action' (1). Moreover, introductory volumes for film students in the US and UK continue to cover the debate even as they caution against it: Bordwell and Thompson (29–30) discuss the 'three distinct (and contradictory) meanings' of the term (as production worker, personality, and group of films). Patrick Phillips writes more hesitantly of the 'auteur contrast' (which offers 'insurance value' to the industry and 'trademark value' to the audience), the auteur structure, the auteur 'habitat' (or production context) and, finally, of the spectator as auteur (150–56).

Pam Cook's *The Cinema Book*, published by the BFI, devotes over 100 pages to the field, covering topics such as 'cinema as art or commodity', 'the artist as creative source', 'the function of authorship in drama' and 'authors in art cinema' (235–36). She is surprisingly positive in her conclusions, arguing that 'too often the critical assault on authorship has failed to recognize the force of these pleasures [of 'recognizing the marks of "greatness"'], [...] finding itself in the impasse of a puritanical rejection' (235). If, then, it is 'wrong to suggest that authorship as a category has ended or is irretrievably problematized', 'auteurism now' should be read within a number of new contexts:

> There is now a certain tendency to examine how particular sites and practices produce the author, a concentration on how films circulate, the contexts in which they are apprehended and the rules which govern their interpretation. This approach contends that authorship is produced through such cultural apparatuses and technologies as: interview, criticism, publicity, and curriculum, and that [...] one should try to take account of the different conditions of possibility for creative claims. (Cook 314)

Such conditions include nationality ('changed global circumstances of film production, circulation, and exhibition'), gender (the emergence of female studio heads has not helped women to become producers or directors), and cinephilia (aesthetic agendas may be determined by economics when art movies and festivals are sponsored by corporations). For Cook the 'independence' of auteurs and their 'vision' are inextricable from industrial factors (314).

These points are echoed by Catherine Grant, a Latin American specialist, in the academic quarterly *Screen*. Grant notes (in 2000) the continuing 'apparent ubiquity of auteurism' (101), but claims that Latin American directors are 'increasingly co-opted by the commerce of auteurism as they seek worldwide distribution and finance' since 'money for non-US, non-European "quality" film production continues to come from outside' (105–56). Paradoxically perhaps, auteur, quality, and art cinemas (which are characteristically identified with one another here) are thus unusually vulnerable to the external artistic influence effected by foreign funding, unlike local genre films, which can often be funded within a relatively small home market. An interview with five directors competing for the foreign-language Golden Globe in the trade journal *Screen International* (given the title 'The Auteur Side of Life') also stresses the tension around this national criterion. Spain's Alejandro Amenábar (who was to win the award) calls attention to the gulf between 'Spanish cinema culture' and the 'universal language' of Hollywood, which he attempted to 'blend' in his English-language chiller *The Others*. He tells how his film was subjected to the indignity of a test screening in the US (unthinkable in Europe) and claims there is a 'crisis in storytelling' in mainstream movies, which he is attempting to transcend (Goodridge).

Of course, similar contradictions have been voiced since the auteur debate began. As is well known, Truffaut's original 1954 article in *Cahiers du Cinéma* on a 'certain tendency' in French cinema (a phrase knowingly recycled by Cook, see above) was implacable in its attack on a 'tradition de qualité' held to be precisely the opposite of the new auteurist trend (26). Bazin's 'La Politique des auteurs' of 1957 began with an epigraph from Tolstoy on the 'mediocrity' of much work by Shakespeare and Goethe (2) and already attacked the aesthetic 'personality cult' of a theory that had barely begun (10). Moreover, Bazin proclaimed it a 'paradox' that the promoters of the new 'politique' should admire US cinema, whose directors were most 'enslaved' by the demands of the production process (11).

Fifty years later the cult of the author remains secure in Spain, at least. The quality press consistently promotes national cinema through the figures of directors, and a survey by the Society of Authors and Publishers suggests that audiences choosing a Spanish film are motivated (unlike in US movies) by their familiarity with local directors and actors (SGAE 90). When *El Mundo*'s cultural magazine covers the new season of Spanish films at San Sebastian, its cover shot is of an anonymous actor in war paint (from *Noviembre*, the disastrous second feature by critical darling Achero Mañas), but its strapline lists only the names of six directors (18–24 September 2003). *El País*'s weekly supplement presents the Goya Awards through a photo spread of seven middle-aged male directors with their (considerably younger and less-clothed) 'fetish actresses' (28 January 2007). While the cover of the magazine shows the apparently pubescent star of Bigas Luna's latest film sitting on his lap with her legs provocatively spread, there is little doubt who is on top. Most recently, *El País Semanal*'s cover shows a broodingly handsome Julio Medem, whose impressive head of black hair partially obscures the delicate face of the adolescent star of his *Caótica Ana* ('Chaotic Ana') on a poster behind him (12 August 2007). (An accompanying web page, no longer accessible, presented Medem's career, by analogy with that of Almodóvar, as a succession of 'chicas', or young leading ladies.)

In the article, Medem (31, 34) presents his 'journey with Ana' in terms that are clearly consistent with the personality cult, which fuses private and public into a single artistic mission. The new feature is said to be the result of his overcoming the twin traumas of the death of his sister and the hostile response to his previous feature, a documentary on the Basque conflict. The motif of the 'journey' thus proves capacious enough to fulfil the three criteria essential for Foucault's author function: consistency of value (all of Medem's films are equally worthy of serious consideration); conceptual coherence (however varied, they share a common theme); and stylistic unity (their aesthetic signature is unmistakable) (Foucault 108–12). Both local and global, Medem is at once Spanish and a citizen of the world, as is proved by his travels to New York and Arizona to shoot his picture. A similar rhetoric lies behind the publication of a lavish picture book illustrating somewhat tenuous written correspondence between Víctor Erice and Abbas Kiarostami, the twin auteurs of Spain and Iran, united in spite of cultural differences by the common hermeticism of their cinematic language.

Like journalists, Spanish academics are also devoted to the author function. *Archivos de la Filmoteca* may take it for granted that the auteur is dead, but it has still published substantial articles in the field (Laínez; Torreiro). Respected scholar Carlos F. Heredero has devoted books such as *20 nuevos directores del cine español* to creating a critical and discursive field for the interpretation of Spanish cinema based on directors who have barely begun their careers. Moreover, as in other higher education systems, 'Cine de autor' is taught as a course in high-profile degrees in universities such as the Carlos III in Madrid, whose students combine theoretical and practical interests in media studies (Universidad 87). It is clear that, as Cook suggested, cinematic authorship is produced in the case of Spain by the full range of cultural apparatuses (both press and academy) and that the creative claims of the Spanish auteurs thus nominated benefit from positive conditions of possibility (at once national, gendered and industrial) that are rarely taken into account when their work is the subject of analysis.

One scholar who has indeed offered a critical study of Spanish authorship is Núria Triana Toribio. In her *Spanish National Cinema* she gives a close reading of Carlos F. Heredero's construction of a narrative based on a 'hierarchical scheme [of] selection and exclusion' (148). Women directors tend to be marginalized from this narrative (positioned as 'prologues' to the main story), while those working in commercial genre cinema are branded *realizadores* (a dismissive term corresponding in French auteurist discourse to *metteur en scène*), and are held to be 'slavishly commercial' (149). However, writes Triana with some irony, 'as long as the national cinema boasts at least one [...] auteur per generation, many misdemeanors of the commercial sector [...] can be forgiven'. For Heredero that auteur was in the early 1990s, Bigas Luna, and in the latter half of the decade, Julio Medem. Triana thus presents authorship in purely functional terms: 'an instrument by which the discourse that locates the Spanishness of Spanish cinema in high art and the intellectual traditions of the country is maintained' (149). Medem is thus the 'acceptable European face of contemporary Spanish cinema and, as such, highly suitable for export' (150). Ironically Medem's crossing of national boundaries (in his narratives and in his funding) makes him especially appropriate as a representative of a modern, cosmopolitan Spain.

For Triana, authorship is here but one of many legitimating factors in the Spanish cinema apparatus, among stars, film journals, government legislation and prize-giving. But she later went on, with two collaborators (Peter Buse and Andy Willis) to propose a new model of authorship for a critically neglected filmmaker. Alex de la Iglesia, they argue, is that oxymoron, a 'popular auteur' (Buse, Triana and Willis 4). Unsettling the dichotomy between art house and genre cinema, he calls into question 'Europe's cultural rhetoric of aesthetic and cultural distinctiveness which set its products apart from the industrial "standardization" of Hollywood'. De la Iglesia also produces fractures in conventional discourse, in that he is proclaimed by Spanish critics as both 'the most accomplished filmmaker of his generation and [one who] has failed yet to make a decent film' (6). Dismissing auteurship as the (Medem-style) analysis of 'creative sensibility' and 'life experiences', and sceptical of its function ('to organize cinema for film critics and teachers' (7)) and its assumptions ('about genius and creativity, not to mention gender'), the authors propose to study instead de la Iglesia's persona and his conditions of possibility. The former is 'constructed in the para-filmic space of publicity and criticism and function[s] to shape the reception of films released under his name', while the latter comprise '[the] team that has been involved in the labour behind the images on the screen as well as a set of social structures and cultural contexts which make possible certain utterances and exclude others' (7).

Crucially, one of those structures and contexts is television, a medium to which de la Iglesia compulsively returns in his films. The authors note that, as is common in Spanish cinema, there are elements of critique here. For example, *El día de la bestia* ('The Day of the Beast', 1995) mercilessly parodies the excesses of so-called *telebasura* [trash TV] broadcast on Italian-owned Tele 5 (73). But the film does not suggest that television is 'intrinsically dangerous' and is 'unwilling to offer an easy political position for the liberal viewer [and appeals rather to a] generic hybridity which refuses the bounds of good cinematic taste' (75). De la Iglesia's features thus view television 'ambivalent[ly] [as a] crucial aspect of Spain's rapid modernization' (26). It is striking that de la Iglesia does not even condemn the Francoist monopoly of television in the 1970s. Rather, his *Muertos de risa* ('Dying of Laughter', 1999), set in that period, 'emphasizes how important television was as a shared experience and how it produced memories held in common' (113).

There is a more precise reference here also. In *El día de la bestia*, once more, de la Iglesia 'openly pays homage' to *Historias para no dormir* ('Stories to Keep You Awake'), a celebrated TV horror and suspense series first shown in the 1960s and examined in Chapter 8 of this book. De la Iglesia introduces his film on DVD in a way that directly, if ironically, cites the series' writer-director Narciso Ibáñez Serrador (61–62). Television is thus not simply treated as a topic in the films. Rather, it is fully incorporated into a cinematic project that, uniquely perhaps in Spain, addresses the medium seriously for its role in both the international modernization of the country and the construction of a distinctively national historical memory, inaccessible to foreign audiences. Moreover, the inconsistent texture of de la Iglesia's film style (which problematizes his inclusion in the ranks of film auteurs) also draws on the hybridity of television, with its rapid and frequent tonal shifts.

If television is inescapable in the work of Spain's 'popular auteur', then it is increasingly so in industrial accounts of Spanish cinema. The most recent commercial survey in *Screen International*'s Special Issue on Spain (February 2007) defines 'ambitious filmmakers' not as directors but as producers, anxious about the increasing difficulty of making films in Spain and in Spanish (2). Familiar canonic names such as Andrés Vicente Gómez are, however, juxtaposed with representatives of what has suddenly become the biggest film company in Spain: Estudios Picasso. The production arm of Tele 5 (the network so mercilessly parodied by de la Iglesia) funded the first- and the third-biggest-grossing films of 2006: 'period romp' *Alatriste* (fifteen Goya nominations); and Guillermo del Toro's historical fantasy, *El laberinto del fauno* ('Pan's Labyrinth', six Oscar nominations and three wins) (12). Although the company's aims are modest (one executive states 'our objective is not to lose money making films') and its incursion into film is enforced (a law of 2001, strengthened in 2007, compels TV channels to invest 3 per cent of their annual budget in Spanish film production), it is clear that television is rapidly changing the industrial and artistic landscape of cinema in ways that are difficult to predict. One current Picasso project mentioned is *The Oxford Murders*, an English-language feature by 'popular auteur' de la Iglesia that is shooting in Britain 'with international talent' (13). Tele 5 also stated that it aimed to 'nurture' new directors, the auteurs of the future.

In spite of this volatile situation (and isolated cases of telephilia such as that of de la Iglesia), a working hypothesis would be that auteurist cinema has traditionally contrived to retain its distinctiveness by distancing itself not only from the industrial standard of Hollywood but also from the commercialism of domestic television. Indeed, the notion of a TV auteur (like that of a popular auteur) seems oxymoronic. Industrial, theoretical and empirical studies of the medium fail to identify this figure. For example, the exhaustive account of the development of prime-time fiction in US manual *This Business of Television* (Blumenthal and Goodenough) charts the lengthy and perilous process from the concept (created either by salaried personnel within the company or freelances outside, 202), through the pitch meeting to the 'end user' by producer, writer and production company (203), treatments, scripts and development deals (207–209), to the 'package' (involving 'key participants' such as performers) and the pilot (210). In this process the director goes unmentioned. It is writers who 'drive the network television business', and who are offered producer's credits and staff capacities, serving as story editors or supervising other writers for additional fees (209).

In a very different but complementary context, John Fiske's pioneering *Television Culture* argues that television is a 'producerly' text that combines a somewhat dispersed 'authorial voice' (not, of course, to be identified with the director) with 'discursive competencies that the viewer already possesses' (95). 'Television', he writes, 'does not preserve its authorial power and privilege […] [and] offers the viewer access to its discursive practice' (237). Empirical studies have suggested the extreme difficulty of locating authorship in television. This is the case even when an independent production company achieves a clear change in artistic style, thus challenging the competence of the audience: was MTM's success in the 1970s due to its executives, actors, or writer-directors? (Feuer, Kerr and Vahimagi); or when a prestigious public broadcaster enjoyed a lengthy tradition of personally 'autographed' one-off drama: in the 1990s the BBC is said to have 'authored' not individual programmes but whole channels (Born 288–90).

Nonetheless, it is in such production contexts that claims to TV authorship tend to arise. Steven Bochco, whose *Hill Street Blues* was produced by MTM, and

Dennis Potter, whose *The Singing Detective* was aired by the BBC, are generally held to be artistically distinctive figures with consistent style and value over many years. More recently, the HBO dramas that have come to constitute a new canon in TV studies are regularly attributed to their 'creators': David Chase of *The Sopranos* or *Six Feet Under*'s Alan Ball. Such claims of authorship even extend into US network drama (we read of 'Aaron Sorkin's *West Wing*', 'David E. Kelly's *Ally McBeal*', 'Marc Cherry's *Desperate Housewives*') and selected genre serials ('Joss Whedon's *Buffy the Vampire Slayer*', 'Tim Kring's *Heroes*'). Such writers, often described as 'creators', occupy a range of positions within the complex and compromised sphere of creative control described (above) by Blumenthal and Goodenough.

In spite of the boom in domestic drama since the 1990s it seems likely that Spain offers no equivalents of the consecrated creators cited above. Manuel Palacio indirectly suggests some reasons for this. Distinguished figures of Spanish television under Franco, who vindicated the medium's distinctive potential for studio-shot weekly drama, found themselves excluded when a new and more prestigious cinematic aesthetic arrived with the glossy 'classic serials' of the new democracy (Palacio, *Historia* 86–87). Likewise, while cinema benefits from a canon based on a critical or social realism that is held to be essentially Spanish (a consensus that has lasted from Francoism to the present day), television, caught between differing definitions of the nation, has struggled to construct even an embryonic authorized list (Palacio, 'Notas sobre el canon'). Moreover, Spain has no equivalent of HBO, a premium, commercial-free cable channel that self-consciously seeks to set itself apart from the mainstream networks through artistically challenging in-house drama.

Palacio does, however, make five suggestions for further study in the field, citing general factors that have been common to the medium since its inception. Most of these are historical in nature: social modernity; pedagogy in democratic politics; 'consensus' on the Francoist past; and historical revisionism. One, however, is given as: 'series and works *de autor*'.

The rest of my chapter is devoted to two such plausibly auteurist figures who have made careers in television longer than those of any director in film. They thus make the strongest claim to the construction of a unique body of work that has helped to constitute a distinctively national historical memory, inaccessible to foreign audiences. Narciso Ibáñez Serrador and Antonio Mercero are two writer-directors who could hardly be more different from each other. The first remains notorious for the gloomy horror series beloved of Alex de la Iglesia; the second has specialized in sunnier shows, such as the much-loved teenage drama *Verano azul* ('Blue Summer', 1981–82). As we shall see, however, as putative TV auteurs occupying a contested place in the Spanish audiovisual field, they have unexpected similarities as well as differences.

Two authorial profiles

The Renoir chain of art houses, which has a dozen theatres in major Spanish cities, publishes a free, full-colour newspaper that is a vital resource for shaping and supporting cinephilia. Alluding to the auteur namesake of the cinemas, the newspaper is called *La gran ilusión*. In September 2007, to mark the new 'season' of Spanish film, which is traditionally inaugurated by the San Sebastian festival, the paper was headlined 'Spanish cinema speaks'. The cover carried pictures of five directors who gave interviews on their new releases. And here, remarkably, the implicit definition of Spanish auteurism and hence of a consecrated national cinema is unusually catholic. The five names selected to 'speak' for Spanish cinema included two women (Icíar Bollaín and Gracia Querejeta), one Catalan (José Luis Guerín), one Argentine (Marcos Carnevale) and one director most familiar from television (Antonio Mercero).

Cinephile auteurism can thus sometimes function inclusively to break down barriers of gender, nationality and medium. But if we look back at the press profiles of Ibáñez Serrador and Mercero, constructed over some forty years and collected in the form of often unattributed clippings held in files in the Filmoteca Nacional, we find a somewhat tense attempt to constrain varied and prolific careers in television and film within the dictates of the personality cult. It is not easy to reduce such disparate works to the coherent and consistent oeuvre required of the auteur.

This tension is particularly noticeable in the case of Ibáñez Serrador, of whom Alex Mendíbil says, in the only scholarly volume devoted to the subject, that histories become 'legends' when they are constantly repeated (13). Journalists seem especially concerned to establish an origin for Ibáñez Serrador, who has often said that he is thought to be Spanish in Argentina and Argentine in Spain (he was, in fact, born in Uruguay in 1935). A lengthy profile from *Gaceta Ilustrada* (no date [1970]) promises to give a full account 'from outside and inside' and is prefaced by a pensive shot of the creator in his trademark black-rimmed spectacles (47). Ibáñez Serrador claims that his work in three media (he is currently appearing in a self-penned play) is 'popular' but not 'populist', with the former term defined as social and human, as well as commercial (48). He also identifies himself modestly as a mere professional: working in minor genres (horror, farce) but attempting to 'dignify' them in spite of their low status. Ibáñez Serrador's works, according to the journalist, are generally located 'abroad', signalling a troubling foreignness that their creator ascribes to his own inheritance: having lived such a nomadic life, he is not at ease in the idiom of any particular country (49). But his 'little things' are not without merit. In episodes of *Historias para no dormir* he has treated big themes such as overdevelopment (the celebrated *El asfalto* ('Asphalt') addresses the related topic of lack of solidarity);

and, having travelled widely in Asia he claims to 'feel' for his fellow man. As a child he was 'terribly shy' and unusually prone to the twin vices of reading and writing (50). He thus forced himself to undertake a great and romantic journey (to Cairo at age 16 in pursuit of a youthful love) and to 'fabricate' the 'dummy' that he now is, the pedantic and self-assured figure who wore glasses even when he did not need them (51).

Interestingly, Ibáñez Serrador's account of his professional methodology is parallel to this self-conscious creation of a press persona who took the place of its supposed authentic original, for he claims to begin writing at the end of the story with a surprise twist and only then work back to the beginning. Defining himself as 'a writer who directs' (using the modest term *realizar*), he claims once more to be not a creative genius but rather a hard worker who has had the good fortune to make many mistakes in Argentine television before coming to Spain (53). It is this experience and his patient rehearsal of actors that have won his shows seven international prizes for TVE.

Two years later the 'apolitical' Chicho (journalists now use his nickname), heavily bearded but still wearing the glasses, is said to have sought scandal 'once more', with a violent feature film *¿Quién puede matar a un niño?* ('Who Can Kill a Child?', 1976). When interviewer Maruja Torres asks if he is 'obsessed' with children, he replied that he cannot forget the child he carries within him, indeed, that he works for that child (no source [24 April 1976]). Accused of commercialism and of pandering to the masses (vices allegedly learned in Latin American television) he again defends his works, talking up their technical quality: good lighting and acting cost money.

The unspoken background here is his current television project. In other interviews Ibáñez Serrador defends *Un, dos, tres* ('One, two, three'), the long-running and hugely successful game show he had originated, denying that it is an example of Spanish 'ignorance'. Nonetheless, he still distances himself from it, saying that the show 'means nothing in his career' (*Arriba*, 23 April 1976) and stating that film is his 'vocation', a 'university' compared to the 'high school' of TV (*Ya*, 5 June 1976). Later in the decade Ibáñez Serrador is still claiming to be not a genius but a hard worker, but now defends the 'sociological' value of entertainment for Spanish audiences in a troubled time (*Pueblo*, 10 February 1978). Some years later the press even praises him as a 'man of talent' and a 'new conquistador' when his game show format is exported around the world (*Tele-Radio*, 5–11 November 1984).

Clearly Ibáñez Serrador's stock was rising: he received a tribute at Sitges, although, pathetically, the director of the Festival said that the most important episodes of *Historias para no dormir* could not be screened, as they had been wiped by TVE (*El Independiente*, 11 October 1989). Ironically, even at a film festival Ibáñez Serrador remained best known, not for his infrequent features

(*La residencia* ('The Boarding School', 1969) and *¿Quién puede matar ...?*, 1976) but for an ephemeral, low-budget series from the early days of television that had, nonetheless, remained firmly lodged in popular memory. *Historias* would be revived in different formats and with different directors in the 1970s, 1980s and the 2000s. And in 2006 Ibáñez Serrador (along with Mercero) would be a regular guest on nostalgia shows celebrating the 50th anniversary of television in Spain.

Press clippings reveal that journalists writing on Antonio Mercero, born just one year after Ibáñez Serrador in 1936, were equally keen to establish his origin and early history, insisting in this case on his Basqueness. Where horror is the guiding thread for Ibáñez Serrador's narrative (journalists have even claimed that, seated in his gloomy office, his eyes gleam in 'the burning darkness'), humour is the consistent thematic line for Mercero. And like 'Chicho', 'Antxo' (as his friends call him) distances himself from television even as he acknowledges his mastery of the medium. When asked straight out if he is 'a man of film or television' he claims to be 'a man of sound and image' who learned his craft on TV (unidentified clipping [27 October 1973]). Fresh from an Emmy for *La cabina* ('The Phone Box', a celebrated one-off drama, to which I return later), Mercero is, again like Chicho, the consummate winner of prizes who claims to address big themes on the small screen: in his case 'the universal problem' of man's freedom and destiny. Mercero outlines his plans for a TV 'tetralogy' of single plays (thirty years later they would be published together on DVD as 'Dramáticos'), apologizing if he sounds pretentious. Using a key image (which conflicts with the avowed professionalism of the interview), the journalist signs off by saying Mercero has all 'the innocence and goodness of a child'.

One year later Mercero is proclaimed 'the man of prizes' (unidentified clipping, [1974]). Here he again emphasizes humour as a 'vital attitude'. We are told that Mercero's name remains little known to the public (unlike Ibáñez Serrador, he rarely appears on screen himself) and are privy to his own childhood trauma (the death of his father in the Civil War). This 'shyness', so typical of the budding auteur, is once more overcome by a journey, this time from provincial Guipúzcoa to Madrid's official Film School (the parish priest kindly offered to pray for him in the godless metropolis). Again like Ibáñez Serrador, Mercero gained his media apprenticeship in television (through the long-running *Crónicas de un pueblo*, 'Chronicles of a Village'); and like him he seeks to 'dignify' his chosen genre, raising its status. Yet, he claims later, images take precedence over such grand ambitions. *La cabina* may deal with the failure to communicate and human solitude, but it begins with a single, simple concept (a man trapped in a phone box) and is not 'moralizing' (*Gaceta del Norte*, 19 September 1976).

This lengthy article, significantly titled 'Coherent and Harmonic', establishes a new theme: that of the family. If Mercero is obsessed with children, it is because he has six of his own and a wife whom he met when she was a teenager and he a young student. And at a politically turbulent time (especially in the Basque Country), he takes care to point out that he belongs to no party. The adoring journalist concludes by saying that Mercero's true politics is his 'honest' and 'profound' work, his engagement with his 'creative labour and art'.

Three years later, with yet another TV play in competition at the Monte Carlo festival, Mercero is once more said to be 'between cinema and television' (*Norte de Castilla*, 9 March1979) and one of the three most profitable directors on TVE. Canonized by a critical and popular film hit – *La guerra de papá* ('Daddy's War', 1977) was based on a novel by Delibes – Mercero is praised again for his 'identification' with the world of children (which he claims is inherently dramatic), especially at this time of a 'wave of gratuitous eroticism'. His secret lies in his 'realism' and 'everydayness'.

Such articles paved the way for Mercero's greatest TV success, *Verano azul* ('Blue Summer'). In pre-publicity, he claimed he was 'passionate, interested, and concerned' about kids and that his show was 'aesthetic and ethical, but not political' in its focus (*Ama*, 1 July 1979). Mercero's own large family pose solemnly for the camera, as he inveighs against consumerism and even television itself, accusing it of making the spirit 'barren', and rendering viewers 'passive, unable to think for themselves'. Mercero, like Ibáñez Serrador, thus distances himself from his chosen medium, partly by stressing the sheer labour that goes into his TV works and thus renders them atypical. *Verano azul*, described as a 'realistic' account of 'problems in the family', was three years in the making (*Supertele*, 16 October 1981). *Farmacia de guardia* ('Night Chemist', 1991–95), his later hit for the new commercial channel Antena 3, is also said to 'bear witness to our reality, offering us characters who are near to us' (*ABC*, 22 September 1991). On another occasion Mercero describes his heroes as 'ordinary citizens who struggle against the odds to live with dignity' (*Suplemento Semanal*, 20 June 1993). Latterly 'tired of television', he remains an 'emotional man', who is aware that his career is more uneven on film than on television (*Deia*, 21 August 1998). Ironically he has experienced his greatest successes in the medium that he values so much less, a mere 'high school' compared to the 'university' of cinema.

We have seen, then, that, twin pioneers of serious drama on Spanish TV who are often mentioned in the same breath, Ibáñez Serrador and Mercero, have led parallel lives. Indeed, both were recently awarded rare Lifetime Achievement awards from the Spanish Academy of Television. These lives, at once personal and professional, are lightning rods for the traditional topics of the auteur debate, newly intensified in the context of a television medium that is ever menaced by banality and frivolity. Their careers thus stage conflicts between art and commerce (with both stressing they have been financially disadvantaged by their quest for quality at all times) and between originality and genre (with both seeking to raise the status of horror and comedy, respectively, by raising big themes on the small screen). The familiarity of series television, integrated into everyday life through the regular rhythm of its weekly episodes, is also set strategically against one-off dramas (such as the thematically similar *El asfalto* and *La cabina*) which are presented as unique media events (an interruption of the televisual flow) and duly awarded sundry international prizes that legitimate their exceptional value.

This question of prize-giving raises the further problem of nationality and canonicity. While such critically praised dramas serve the same function recently played in Spanish film by the demanding and highly crafted features of Julio Medem (that is, that of 'redeeming' the supposed commercial sins of their medium), the representativity of these two figures is repeatedly called into question. Ibáñez Serrador, who has worked in Spain for forty years, is constantly reminded of his South American origins and slight trace of an accent; Mercero, who has been resident in Madrid over the same period and whose greatest successes were set and shot in Castile and Andalusia, is also called to account for his Basqueness and, once more, persistent accent. Hence even as journalists take pride in the projection and legitimation of late Francoist TVE at foreign festivals (a unique achievement of these two avowedly apolitical auteurs), they register unease about the Spanishness of the works that are called on to represent national television, a medium that is itself held responsible for the ignorance and individualism [*incultura, insolidaridad*] held to be increasingly characteristic of the modernizing nation.

The uniqueness of the vision with which both are readily attributed is also called into question by their generosity (or strategically false modesty?) in acknowledging the collectivity of the production process in TV. Both stress above all their intense collaboration with actors, who, in the case of Mercero, are often non-professional children. Yet this theme of childhood is also underwritten by the personality cult of the author function. While Mercero may not have crafted a media persona as did Ibáñez Serrador (the former's spectacles are merely spectacles and not a theatrical prop), he shares with Ibáñez Serrador a constructed narrative of infantile trauma. If Ibáñez Serrador's celebrated actor parents divorced when he was a child, Mercero's mother was widowed just months after he was born. It is thus in the figure of the child (perverse in Ibáñez Serrador and troubled in Mercero) and the related trope of the (often broken) family, that the personality cult fuses private and public into a single artistic mission.

But if Ibáñez Serrador and Mercero fulfil the first two of Foucault's criteria for the author function, namely consistency of value (ratified by prizes) and conceptual coherence (underwritten by the guiding theme of the child), then it remains to be seen if they can satisfy the third criterion of stylistic unity in the unforgiving habitat of series television. We can now examine three episodes of their respective dramas for the trace of a unique aesthetic signature.

Historias para no dormir and *Verano azul*

Historias para no dormir
'El muñeco'
Basado en una obra de Henry James. La acción situada en Londres en 1924, relata los problemas de una niña de corta edad. Su padre ajeno al problema de su hija, es alertado por un hermano de que la niña está poseída por el espíritu de Elena, su primera institutriz.

['The Doll'
Based on a story by Henry James. The action takes place in London in 1924 and tells the story of a young girl's problems. Her father who is unaware of what is going is alerted by his brother to the fact that the girl is possessed by the spirit of Elena, her first governess.]

'La alarma'
Ante la inminente llegada de naves extraterrestres a la tierra los medios de comunicación emiten continuos mensajes para tranquilizar a la población. Sin embargo, un físico investiga algunos fenómenos extraños. La policía detiene a la joven sospechosa denunciada por el físico Javier Urrutia, que trata de localizar el origen de las radiaciones que ella emite. El comisario investiga los antecedentes de la joven quien al fin confiesa haber nacido en el año 1597 y no saber como ha llegado hasta el siglo XX.

['The Alarm'
As UFOs are about to reach earth, the media are constantly broadcasting in an attempt to keep the populace calm. Meanwhile, a physicist is investigating strange phenomena. The police arrest a young female suspect who has been turned in by the physicist, Javier Urrutia. He tries to find the source of the radioactive waves she is emitting. The police inspector investigates the young woman's background. She confesses that she was born in 1597 and has no idea how she has survived into the twentieth century.]

'NN23'
La acción se sitúa en un futuro, donde todo está deshumanizado. Queda un único poeta, a quien, en vista de una amenaza extraterrestre, la Sociedad de Naciones encarga que dirija a la Humanidad. El poeta transforma aquella horrible pesadilla organizada en algo más feliz. Pero, desaparecido el peligro, la Sociedad de Naciones vuelve a actuar.

['NN23'
The action takes place in the future, when society has completely lost its humanity. Just one poet is left and, when earth is threatened by UFOs, he is made leader of the world by the Society of Nations. The poet transforms the organized nightmare

of his society into something happier. However, once the danger has disappeared, the Society of Nations makes its move once more.]

Miguel Fernández Labayen and Elena Galán have given an account of the genesis of *Historias para no dormir*, whose more than 30 episodes were screened on TVE from 1966–68 and again in 1982 (30) (plot summaries and translations above are taken from the Ministerio de Cultura website). Their length is surprisingly varied, from 18 to 105 minutes. The first episode ('El cumpleaños', 'The Birthday', now lost) was broadcast on 4 February 1966, with an over-18 rating. While each story is independent, many are authored by Ibáñez Serrador under his well known pen-name 'Luis Peñafiel', and most star his father, Narciso Ibáñez Menta, who had a distinguished pedigree in Buenos Aires theatre and television (fifty-something Argentine viewers still remember his performance in his son's adaptation of *The Phantom of the Opera*, which so impressed them as children).

The Spanish *Historias* were often remakes of these earlier Argentine successes from the father and son team. But Fernández Labayen and Galán note the influence also of US mysteries of the period (*The Twilight Zone* and *Alfred Hitchcock Presents*) in the use of an ironic and distancing introduction direct to camera, delivered in this case by the newly celebrated Chicho. They also stress that the massive popularity of the original series gave rise to a series of books (1967–74), miniseries and feature films, and four new episodes remade in colour in 1982 (31).

In spite of the enduring strength of this brand, which remains inextricable from the trademark value of Ibáñez Serrador (the DVD collection bears a modern picture of the horror meister holding an antique chandelier), the episodes themselves are surprisingly varied, comprising three main strands: nineteenth-century Gothic romance, twentieth-century science fiction, and ahistorical absurdist or expressionist allegory (defined by Chicho in his DVD commentary as 'stories to make you think'). I will examine one example from each strand. Each begins with a flashing screen and an electronic drone (the pioneering music is composed by Waldo de los Ríos), followed by a graphic of a door creaking open. In a trademark spidery font the first title reads: 'Narciso Ibáñez Serrador presenta'. Over pounding drums a scream rings out and the door creaks closed once more. It is an opening inscribed in the memories of generations of Spanish TV viewers.

'El muñeco' ('The Doll') opens with Chicho on set in front of two cameras. Puffing on a pipe and holding a clipboard, he hides behind his dark-rimmed glasses. In schoolmasterly fashion he warns viewers that in Spain this episode was shown in full at 45 minutes, while in Latin America (the version used for the DVD) it was for commercial reasons split in two. We should thus pay attention tonight so we can pick up the narrative threads next week. After this wilfully pedantic introduction (which, nonetheless, raises the question of internationalism so vital to Ibáñez Serrador's persona) we cut to the credits proper, in this case a handsome chiaroscuro shot of a chandelier, whose six candles are slowly removed by a disembodied female hand. Narciso Ibáñez Menta's name is shown before the episode title, while the writing credit goes to the pseudonymous Peñafiel, although the idea is claimed to be adapted from Henry James (the story preserves some plot points from *The Turn of the Screw*).

The setting is said to be 'London 1924' (although the wardrobe seems to belong twenty years earlier). After a brief exterior of a severely hatted matron arriving at a domestic terraced house (a British bobby ostentatiously patrols the street outside), we cut to a lengthy scene of expository dialogue. The (oddly named) Mr and Mrs Willberg are being visited by their brother-in law's governess, who has handed in her notice. As they take (stereotypical) tea together, the latter informs them that the brother-in-law beats his young daughter and accuses her of witchcraft. Ibáñez Serrador shoots classically here, slowly cutting closer from long, to medium, and close-ups of the three speakers. There follows a brief exterior of a vintage car arriving at a country villa. Narciso Ibáñez Menta descends a lengthy staircase, puffing on a pipe (like his son in the Introduction) and, fully bearded, bearing a strong resemblance to George V. There follows another lengthy scene of exposition in the father's study, in which Ibáñez Menta drinks endless glasses of brandy and claims that his daughter communes in the attic with the ghost of a dead governess. His voice is soft, slightly accented, and benefits from actorly enunciation and dramatic pauses:

16 The devil child of 'El muñeco': *Historias para no dormir*

'Me dijo cosas … tremendas' ['She said things to me that were … terrible']. The split episode ends with a cliffhanger as the brother mounts the handsome staircase towards the ominous attic.

After Chicho has repeated his warning about the commercial demands of Latin American scheduling and we sit through a lengthy recap of last week's teasing episode, we are finally shown the diabolical child. The hitherto static camera tracks backwards before the bemused brother as he paces a lengthy corridor before craning up the final staircase to the attic. Here Ibáñez Serrador exploits framing for dramatic effect. The apparently innocent Alicia, in a prim sailor suit, plausibly argues that her father is emotionally crippled. Ibáñez Serrador pulls back to show that the daughter is herself wearing a disfiguring brace on her leg. After the brother, reassured, has left, the camera movement along the corridor is repeated, but this time we see a brief shot from the father's POV of the ghostly governess in the attic, communing with the ecstatic and immobile child. Pledging vengeance, the latter locks her father in his bedroom (we hear only an ominous clumping off-screen) and he is wracked by mysterious pains. As the brother returns, he finds Alicia innocently rocking her home-made doll, which proves to be an image of her father pierced by a pin. The trademark shock ending comes when Alicia bites into her doll's head and, with strident orchestration, we cut to a final shot of Ibáñez Menta, his forehead marked by a bloody and fatal wound from his perverse infant.

'El alarma' ('The Alarm'), another two-part episode, could not be more thematically different. Here Chicho's introduction is so wordy that an (off-screen) technician tells him to cut it short. He does so by throwing a brick into a shop window on set, thus springing the alarm that plays through the credits. Ibáñez Serrador is granted (auteurist) *dirección* and (technical) *realización* for this episode, as well as an 'original' script by his pseudonym. Once more he raises the question of nationality here, commenting ironically on the fact that Spain, now visited by so many hordes of foreign tourists, rarely receives extraterrestrial visitors, who tend to prefer the US, or even the Soviet Union, as a destination. The locale here is an unspecified Spanish city in 1968, whose requirements are only that it should be a port possessed of lower depths. The premise itself oddly combines elements of *The Makropoulos Case* and *2001: A Space Odyssey*.

We open in a traditional bar, where Ibáñez Menta, here a timid physicist whose moustache marks him as a middle-aged Spanish everyman, is watching television. The stiff announcer calls for calm as the Earth awaits a fleet of UFOs. We even see pseudo-documentary footage in which concerned citizens voice their hopes for a peaceful encounter (although a woman warns her daughter in Catalan not to leave the house). With a voice-over we flash back two weeks as Ibáñez Menta patrols the waterfront with a Geiger counter (there is a nuclear reactor nearby). Realizing that one blowsy prostitute is highly radioactive, he follows her to another impressively sleazy location, a nightclub where women with hour-glass figures and spaghetti-strapped evening gowns are paid for dances. The episode ends here once more, before any action has taken place, with Chicho drinking an innocuous glass of milk in the nightclub as another prostitute tells him her life story.

Calling attention again to broadcasting conventions, Chicho claims in his intro the next week that the girl's story was 'so long' that they are still sitting at the same table after seven days. Action moves more rapidly now. Interrogated in prison, the radioactive prostitute confesses she was born in 1597 (sic) and has not aged since she encountered a UFO at the age of 20. A surprisingly bloody operation retrieves a metal pyramid uncannily inserted into her body, which (with impressive special effects) falls into dust as soon as the object is removed. Strangely indifferent to the effects of radiation, Ibáñez Menta watches as a scientist cracks open the otherwordly object, thus inadvertently triggering the alarm of the episode title and summoning the extraterrestrials. Back in the opening bar, he muses in voice-over once more that 'men have become dangerous' and that the UFOs, alerted to this potential, have now come to destroy us. The final shot is of a starry sky set to a doomy drumbeat. But, as Ibáñez Serrador warned ironically in his presentation, perhaps the most disturbing aspect of 'La alarma' is the placing of a cosmic drama in an unusually everyday setting, far from the Gothic horrors of distant, foggy Britain: the bars, ports and brothels of provincial Spain, recreated so cheaply and evocatively in claustrophobic studio sets.

My third episode, 'NN23', is an absurdist allegory located even further from Spanish viewers in a future dystopia, overtly modelled on the Eastern bloc (Ibáñez Serrador notes in his modern commentary that this was an excellent way of avoiding the Francoist censors). Beginning with humorous drawings from the famous cartoonist Mingote, Ibáñez Serrador's voice-over sets the scene of a world so overdeveloped that no trace of nature has survived the city, and in which the compulsory use of *telencéfalo* [brain TV] ensures the Supreme Ruler's will that all citizens should not speak or think, but just be entertained. Uncannily silent and immobile on the Metro, they are, however, absorbed in current US imports familiar to viewers at the time: *Queen for a Day* and *The Untouchables*.

Distancing itself from sheer entertainment, then, the episode also favours the high art thought to be menaced by the mass medium of television. Here Ibáñez Menta, an elderly gent with grey hair and beard reminiscent of the Juan Ramón Jiménez whom he later cites, is the last poet in the world, an employee of the Bureau of Defunct Professions. He also lovingly cares for a single precious iris. As a global bureaucracy staffed by national stereotypes (the cowboy-hatted American and the turbaned Indian) argues over the vital importance of chewing gum, aliens (once more) threaten to destroy the planet. Appealing to the poet for help, the downtrodden earthlings are offered a brief glimpse of freedom beyond brain TV. But when the threat is revealed to be a hoax, the poet is executed. While the opening credits played over an image of the single precious iris, the closing credits feature a wastepaper bin, the final destination of the poet's plans for an authentic happiness founded on nature and freedom.

Ibáñez Serrador's DVD presentation notes that such allegorical episodes were aimed at securing international prizes, rather than filling the more mundane requirements of serial television schedules. But, if this episode was intended mainly for foreign consumption, it still seems unlikely that Spaniards in late Francoism would have had any difficulty decoding the satire on their own Supreme Leader that is lightly camouflaged by the whimsical art design of this episode. What interests me more is how Ibáñez Serrador strengthens his own claim to auteurism and distances his drama from the everyday flow of television by vindicating the unique value of a single poem, a single flower. The references to literary precedents elsewhere (to James and Poe) also make this claim for distinction. What is clear, however, is that Ibáñez Serrador's signature style is nonetheless a unique exploitation of the peculiar properties of the televisual medium, as is acknowledged by the frequent allusion in his intros to his series' conditions of possibility: its processes of production (the cameras placed behind him) and distribution (the regular rhythm of weekly episodes).

This studio-shot drama, still a relatively new phenomenon in Spain, thus ensured the fidelity of audiences to such an extent that it has lasted some forty years. The show also intensified through its claustrophobia and primitive means the uncanniness of its familiar narratives. Even the slowness and staginess of exposition works well in the new domestic medium. And although Ibáñez Serrador's personal autograph could hardly be more emphatic, continuity is ensured across very varied thematic material by Ibáñez Serrador's gifted team, including composer de los Ríos and, above all, his chameleonic (but instantly recognizable) father. Hence, although the shooting style [*realización*] is generally transparent (with only rare tracking and crane shots calling attention to themselves), the signature style [*dirección*] comes through loud and clear, transcending the limited means that are themselves now haloed by nostalgic memories. In keeping with Freud's definition of the uncanny, in which what is most troubling is an unfamiliar phenomenon found in a familiar place (363), it was thus highly appropriate that national audiences should be shocked and seduced by Ibáñez Serrador, an ostentatiously international auteur who found horror in (and brought horror to) the heart of the Spanish home.

* * *

If Ibáñez Serrador seasons terror with humour, Antonio Mercero combines humour with drama. Indeed in an interview on the DVD of his late feature film *Planta cuarta* ('The 4th Floor'), whose emotive theme is teenagers with cancer) he claims that the most difficult task for him as director is to find the delicate balance between these two elements. The notoriously sunny *Verano azul* (like *Historias para no dormir*, an epochal event in Spanish television) is, as we shall see, also strangely shadowed by serious themes.

Juan Carlos Ibáñez ('Verano') suggests that Mercero, whom he calls one of the 'most outstanding' figures in Spanish TV history, achieved the greatest social impact of his entire career with this serial of 19 parts of one hour each. First shown on the family-friendly Sunday *sobremesa* [afternoon] slot between 11 October 1981 and 14 February 1982, *Verano azul* was so popular that TVE, in a unique case of programming, repeated it as soon as it was over. It remained a staple of summer schedules until it appeared on DVD.

Ibáñez has no hesitation in ascribing the show's significance to its intimate connection with a nation that was itself experiencing adolescence as a democracy and exploring, like its teenage stars, how to live together in freedom. *Verano azul* thus activates 'mechanisms of identification' for both child viewers (who see themselves reflected on screen) and adults (who succumb to the myth of the 'lost paradise' of childhood). Moreover, there is an unexpected ideological message here. The young protagonists' problems are never solved by their parents. The traditional family thus gives way to the intergenerational solidarity of an elective 'gang' of friends and the 'black Spain' still in mourning for its horrific past (evoked to some extent in the gloomy and claustrophobic *Historias para no dormir*) is dissolved into the luminous blue of the Mediterranean.

Ibáñez highlights here to two crucial differences with *Historias*, shown some fifteen years earlier. Mercero, who claims to be above all a 'documentarian', shoots entirely on location and now in colour (although his black and white *Crónicas de un pueblo* uses similar techniques). In the credit sequence the dazzling sun rises behind the hills of Nerja (the unnamed Andalusian village where the show was shot) and we see seven children riding their bicycles towards the camera, whistling to the jaunty flute motif of the theme tune. In descending order of age they are teenage heart-throb and local boy Pancho, wealthy vacationer Javi, pretty Bea and her 'ugly' sidekick Desi, the curiously underwritten Quique, and the infants Piraña (named for his insatiable appetite) and Tito (a tiny born comedian). Of the actors playing these parts (some of whom were simply found on the beach) only Juan José Artero as Javi would become a professional actor, starring in police drama *El comisario* some twenty years later. The adult protagonists are not the children's parents, who remain caricatures, but their two friends, Julia (María Garralón), a kindly middle-aged woman who has come to paint in the village as 'therapy' for an undisclosed trauma (later we learn she has lost her husband and child); and Chanquete ('Whitebait', played by veteran of film and television Antonio Ferrandis), a portly fisherman who lives in picturesque eccentricity in a large boat atop a tall hill. Chanquete is perhaps the most loved character in all Spanish TV history (Ibáñez) and his death in a late episode is said to have 'paralysed' the nation (Díaz 226).

Episode 1, 'El encuentro', stages an encounter between the children, the adults and the spectator. Beginning with an aerial shot of the shimmering sea, towering cliffs and new chalets (some proudly sporting tiny swimming pools), we soon hear Julia acknowledging in voice-over her mysterious 'convalescence', which will be cured by an 'intensely lived' summer. She 'meets cute' with the kids when they trail after her during her morning session of jogging (still a novelty in the period).

More physical activity follows, ensuring a mobile camera (with some shaky zooms) that exploits the varied topography of the location. Thus the two older boys, rivals for the attentions of fair Bea, dive into the sea at the port to retrieve her lost bracelet and race down the beach in earnest competition. Meanwhile the little kids climb the hill to Chanquete's 'magical' boat and make his acquaintance. Javi's prissy parents complain about the 'bad company' he is keeping: he could be making 'important contacts' among his fellow bourgeois beachcombers. The parents are swiftly proved wrong when working-class Pancho bravely volunteers to be lowered from the cliff to the rocks below, where Javi risks drowning in the rapidly approaching tide. Some pointed editing here

17 The angel child Tito (Miguel Joven) and Julia (María Garralón): *Verano azul*

cross-cuts between the boys perilously suspended on ropes to the heedless parents eating prawns and knocking back drinks at a disco bar on the beach. When, finally, the parents arrive, they refuse an offer of grilled sardines from Chanquete, who has just helped save their son's life. But Julia and the seven kids do turn up that evening on his landlocked deck, to eat dinner and be serenaded by Chanquete's accordion. A final zoom takes us into the glare of the sun setting over the sea.

But as 'No matéis mi planeta, por favor' ('Don't Kill My Planet, Please', the second award-winning episode) reveals, this sensual paradise is threatened by man. The episode begins with a folky protest song on the theme of ecology set to a montage of babies, puppies, and flowers on the beach. Soon, risking cliché, Julia is running in slow motion by the sea. But when she throws a letter in a bottle into the waves, Chanquete as Neptune emerges, admonishing her for soiling his realm with her rubbish. This scene is then revealed to be a dream sequence. But when the two smallest children fly a kite on the beach (there are some vertiginous high angle shots from the cliff above) they discover the sea is indeed a sewer: dead fish festoon the shore. When Julia tells Chanquete the news at a crowded marketplace, he correctly identifies a chemical company as the culprit. The whole gang visit the mayor who declares, in a group shot, 'This country lacks civic sense' and 'We are not citizens but individuals'. Chanquete also wisely weighs in on the side of 'solidarity'.

Having learned their lesson, the kids march on the beach with a banner proclaiming 'The beach is everyone's: don't mess it up' and disgust Javi's conservative parents by picking up other people's rubbish. There is some visual comedy here as little Tito eyeballs adult litterbugs, daring them to drop their beer bottles in the sand. One unsympathetic polluter, who has come to the beach to leer at bikinied babes, is surrounded by rubbish as he sleeps, the heap surmounted by a home-made sign saying: 'I'm a pig – I like shit'. This somewhat disturbing sight of moralizing blond infants gives way to a final sing-a-long with Julia and Chanquete. While the didactic charge of this episode is now too explicit (earlier audiences were no doubt less familiar with the ecological theme), its importance lies in the fusion of natural location and social action: Spanish adolescents (of all ages) are being trained in the democratic art of sharing common space and preserving common resources.

The third episode has a more diffuse moral, one suggested by its Cervantine title 'Pancho Panza'. It begins with perhaps the most documentary-flavoured sequence in early episodes, as the small boys stalk lizards in an abandoned building, trapping them with fragile grass nooses. As they discuss how to feed their captives (do lizards prefer ants or mortadella?), Mercero exploits depth of field: the older Pancho slowly disappears into the distance between them. When Pancho is knocked off his bike by a car that is going the wrong way down a one-way street, a policeman pronounces in his favour (all should respect the law). But now Pancho can no longer deliver the groceries from his uncle's shop. His new vacationing friends take on the task for him, once more to the horror of their snooty parents. Lecturing his generous son, Javi's unsympathetic father comments that 'everyone should help themselves and know their place'. Chanquete, on the other hand, observes that 'all jobs have equal value, irrespective of their wage'. The former's authoritarianism is clearly no longer a match for the latter's egalitarianism. Indeed, even Bea's father quotes Cervantes in support of the kids' generous actions: we are all the children of our own deeds. Soon his daughter, in red gown and flowing locks, is sharing a romantic ride on the beach with working-class Pancho, who has procured a handsome white mare for their first date.

Verano's sense of luminous light and space could not be further from *Historias*' lugubrious studio-bound sets. And its pseudo-documentary technique (already found in Mercero's late Francoist *Crónicas de un pueblo*) is the antipodes of Ibáñez Serrador's classic TV shooting. Although Mercero coached his novice actors extensively, the sense of improvisation is striking, enhanced by a cinematic grammar that remains rare in TV drama: where possible (and clearly this is difficult with inexperienced child actors) he favours long, leisurely takes that permit action to flow in real time. Crowded group shots also give a sense of dynamic, social process. It is a clear artistic signature from a creator who shares a screen-writing credit with two colleagues, but claims for himself the role of 'dirección'. And the candy floss insubstantiality of the series, which can be as fragile and fey as a hippy chick's gauzy gown (see Episode 4), is undercut by its attempt to address vital issues that are not just voiced in sometimes overexplicit dialogue but embodied in a now mythical landscape (Nerja) and archetype (Chanquete).

We can now go on to see how Ibáñez Serrador and Mercero treat an identical topic (lack of solidarity) in their own distinctive styles in two prize-winning one-off dramas of the same genre: the absurdist allegory. It is the clearest of test cases for television auteurship.

El asfalto (1966) and *La cabina* (1972)

Narciso Ibáñez Serrador and Antonio Mercero each directed and scripted one of the best-known short-form single dramas in the history of Spanish television. *El asfalto* and *La cabina* share a similar premise (a man is trapped – in sticky asphalt/a phone box), genre (absurdist farce), and theme (existential alienation, urban isolation and lack of solidarity). However, the tone is uncharacteristic of each. Indeed, they seem here to have swapped places. *El asfalto* is humorous (albeit tinged with tragic pathos, especially at the close), while *La cabina* culminates in horror (albeit relieved in early scenes by comic detail). Initially, the locations also seem to be inverted. Ibáñez Serrador's *El asfalto* takes place in a street (a favourite location for Mercero from *Crónicas* to *Verano azul*), while Mercero's *La cabina* is confined to a claustrophobic setting more typical of Ibáñez Serrador's *Historias* (such as the Poe-based 'El tonel de Amontillado' ('The Cask of Amontillado'), where a man is immured in a cellar; or the original story 'La cabaña' ('The Cabin'), where two women are confined to a mountain cabin cut off by the snow).

Both dramas refuse to limit themselves to a simple or single meaning, even through their veiled political critique now seems clear. What interests me more is that they are event-programming (the first screening of *La cabina* proved to be a sensation) and were successfully devised to win international prizes (the first at Montreux and Monte Carlo; the second a unique Spanish Emmy). These two dramas thus seem at first to contradict the auteurist criteria of conceptual coherence and stylistic unity, even as they provide the strongest evidence for the distinctive value of the unique oeuvres to which they belong.

Yet there is continuity here in the authors' 'habitat', or production context, a continuity that would have been recognized by contemporary Spanish TV audiences. Thus, Ibáñez Serrador is deprived of his opening monologue to camera, but is granted an immediately recognizable voice-over, which plays through *El asfalto*'s opening sequence of humorous drawings (the personified asphalt sleeps in winter and then awakes under the fiery summer sun). These are by the cartoonist Mingote, who also contributed to 'NN23'. The flagrantly theatrical set design is by Fernando Sáenz and the eclectic soundtrack (from jazz and military bands to classical piano) by Waldo de los Ríos, both frequent collaborators of Ibáñez Serrador. But the clearest sign of continuity is, of course, the presence of Narciso Ibáñez Menta, in the central role of the anonymous gent who sinks slowly into the asphalt until only his pathetic boater and cane remain visible. With this very special episode (no fewer than 25 actors are credited), Ibáñez Serrador still vindicates the potential of the studio-shot series drama that he had already made his own, exploring a uniquely televisual style elaborated to make the most of strictly limited means.

Mercero, on the other hand, makes lavish use of the cinematic medium (known significantly in Spanish as '*soporte* cinematográfico'), to which he had appealed from the start of his career. He shoots, as ever, in authentic locations (an anonymous urban square, modern highways, country roads, and a huge facility, reminiscent of a nuclear shelter, hollowed out of a mountain). His soundtrack is often classic and his casting prestigious (José Luis López Vázquez had already enjoyed one of the most distinguished careers in Spanish film). Indeed, Mercero's opening sequence revels – ironically, perhaps, given the theme of his drama – in the mobility and flexibility of cinematic space. To the sound of birdsong,

18 Narciso Ibáñez Menta, trapped in *El asfalto*

Mercero tilts down from modern high rises to a high-angle shot, which shows a truck delivering a phone box far below. Cutting to an extreme close-up of a hand tightening bolts in the box, he then smoothly tracks right as the men return to their truck before craning up and tracking left once more to offer a new view of the box, shown from above and framed between the picturesque branches of the trees in the square. It is a virtuoso camera movement that clearly announces Mercero's ambitions to cinematic auteurship.

Using their very different decors and techniques (Mercero's colour photography enables his red box to stand out against the sterile setting of modern urbanism), both directors stage a series of encounters between the trapped everymen and their fellow citizens. Significantly, in both, children come first. Ibáñez Menta first tries vainly to attract the attention of a child at a window, who returns to torment him with his friends. López Vázquez, on the other hand, is shown saying goodbye to his young son before he enters the box, and is later mocked by jeering children when he is first enclosed. Both protagonists subsequently meet indifferent bourgeois (who in the first dismiss the man's plight as a political protest or an advertisement, and in the second treat his situation as a welcome entertainment), while in both dramas once more police and firefighters are unable to free the increasingly desperate victims.

19 José Luis López Vázquez, trapped in *La cabina*

The contrast between the two parallel dramas again comes at the level of mise en scène. Ibáñez Serrador is ostentatiously anti-naturalist here, with costumes changing from scene to scene between the eighteenth and the twentieth centuries (a pair of wigged fops sniff haughtily at the flailing Menta; a mini-skirted telephonist, absorbed by gossip, fails to put through his urgent call for help). When an elderly war veteran does try to help Menta he is stymied by bureaucracy, caught in a queue in a huge office where a civil servant looms omnipotently over downtrodden citizens. Where Ibáñez Serrador had struggled to provide impressively realistic sets for other episodes of *Historias* (even claiming in his intro to 'El tonel' that he has waived his salary so as to permit a more extensive cast of extras than was normally allowed), here he strategically enhances the theatricality of the TV studio. He thus distances this episode from the naturalism that is so typical of the medium and remains the basis of *Historias para no dormir* (after all, the uncanny is dependent on its disruption of everyday domesticity to achieve its shock effects). The absurdist premise and theatrical decor seem to cite distinguished precedents. As Menta slowly disappears beneath the street, his predicament is most reminiscent of the plucky, but pathetic, buried protagonists of Becket's *Happy Days*, which had premiered four years earlier.

Mercero, likewise, heightens his habitual signature style on this special occasion. When, halfway through *La cabina*, López Vázquez's box is placed on a lorry, the film becomes extravagantly mobile. Travelling shots from the lorry (often from the hero's point of view) give way to aerial photography (a mysterious helicopter circles overhead) and, in a final sinister form of transport, the crane that transports his box to a kind of telephonic cemetery. Here, fellow victims are reduced (in brief shots more typical of Ibáñez Serrador than the homely Mercero) to wizened corpses or suicide victims, strangled by the phone cord. Such scenes not only take advantage of an unusually large budget, granted by a TVE that, since the triumph of *El asfalto*, now recognized the economic and symbolic value of prizes. They also, pragmatically perhaps, exchange confinement for movement, rescuing viewers from a too static premise, even as they impress them with cinematic resources never before seen on television.

We have seen, then, that the effects of the one-off prizewinning drama are mixed for the oxymoronic TV auteur. On the one hand, these plays preserve aspects of their directors' respective aesthetic signature, readily recognizable from their familiar weekly shows. But on the other the plays highlight the discontinuity of that TV corpus, even as they legitimate its value through their unique distinction. After all, it must have been somewhat disconcerting for viewers to see Ibáñez Serrador dabbling in humour and Mercero in horror. What is clear, however, is that two writer-directors could emerge with legitimate claims to auteurship at the same time and in the same place, but with diametrically opposed signatures and personae.

I would argue that this is because Ibáñez Serrador and Mercero embody not only a unique personal vision but also a distinct collective ecology of Spanish television. Hence Ibáñez Serrador represents the culmination of a prestigious tradition of studio drama (the plays known as 'dramáticos', screened in strands such as *Estudio 1* in the 1960s) that was now coming to an end. Mercero, on the other hand, trained in film school and apprenticed in documentary, points forwards to the new wave of 'classic series' shot on film by cineastes in the new democracy of the 1980s. While one testifies to the past and another points towards the future, both served once as the uniquely acceptable European faces of Spanish television, highly suitable for export. Republished on DVD, their works still display marks of 'greatness', which today's spectators take considerable pleasure in recognizing and sharing.

Memorable television

It seems possible that creators other than Ibáñez Serrador and Mercero deserve consideration as potential television auteurs. For example, Pilar Miró's distinguished career as a director of nine feature films before her untimely death in 1997 was preceded by a lengthy apprenticeship in television, including milestones such as the *Estudio 1* drama strand (1965, mentioned above) and the classic historical drama of the transition, *Curro Jiménez* (1977). Moreover, under the first Socialist government she was a director in both cinema and television. But it seems more difficult to argue in her case for an artistic or thematic signature running through that diverse oeuvre and across two media.

Ibáñez Serrador and Mercero, Miró's contemporaries, benefited perhaps from the unacknowledged advantage of being men, especially in that time and that place. Indeed, it seems likely that their sexual politics are conservative. In interview, the former once compared abortion to murder, and the latter confessed that (as his large family would suggest) he has never in his life purchased condoms. The two may also have benefited from a certain production context. The early days of the new medium seem to have been relatively open to foreigners, especially those such as Ibáñez Serrador or Valerio Lazarov, the Romanian often named as the third pioneer of early Spanish television, who came with experience from abroad. Mercero, on the other hand, acquired the imprimatur of the new national film school and gained valuable documentary experience in Francoist newsreel. However, in the case of nationality (the third unacknowledged factor in access to auteur status), the pair were not so lucky, both being called to account for their supposed origins in Argentina and the Basque Country, even as they worked for decades in Madrid. Their status as artists was, of course, also reduced by their chosen genres and audiences. Ironically, both the horror that was restricted to adults and the humour that was primarily intended for children were equally devalued in status, initially at least.

If Ibáñez Serrador has the single strongest brand in Spanish television (the rebaptized *Películas para no dormir* was remade by reverent young filmmakers as late as 2006), then his career as a whole is more discontinuous and less distinctive than that of Mercero. The presence of game show *Un, dos, tres* is especially anomalous. On film *¿Quien puede matar a un niño?* perhaps has the status of a cult movie. Certainly, its demon-seed seaside kids, satanic siblings of the murderous child of 'El muñeco' (or, indeed, Mercero's gang in *Verano azul*), are constants of Ibáñez Serrador's creative imagination. In spite of the more graphic violence (remarked on by Spanish press at the time), the film is, however, much less effective than the TV dramas, deprived as it is of Ibáñez Serrador's habitual modes of production and distribution. It inevitably lacks the intimacy and immediacy of *Historias*, with their claustrophobic sets, the regular date with the faithful viewer, and (crucially) the familiar intro from the creator straight to camera.

Mercero has had more success on film, with a recent feature such as *Planta cuarta* (2003) achieving considerable commercial success. Here, the collective child protagonists (feisty cancer patients confined to a hospital) clearly connect with Mercero's television work as far back as *Crónicas de un pueblo*. The problem is that Mercero's sentimentality and didacticism (the latter aspect being the one that Palacio finds most characteristic of Spanish television as a whole) seem more intrusive and less palatable on the big screen than on the small, even when dealing with the same topics. And again, his features come close to television in those topics, risking identification as 'disease of the week' TV movies. There is some pointed continuity of casting here too. More than thirty years after *La cabina*, Mercero cast José Luis López Vázquez once more in *¿Y tú, quién eres?* ('Who Are You?', 2007) as another everyday victim, now confined to the living hell of Alzheimer's.

In spite of their common disdain for the medium, then, both Ibáñez Serrador and Mercero have had more distinguished careers in television than in film. While Ibáñez Serrador explored to lasting renown the specificity of the television medium, Mercero introduced a cinematic idiom that might have seemed unremarkable in feature films, but was highly innovative on the small screen. With three everyday milestones to his credit (*Crónicas*, *Verano*, and the studio-shot *Farmacia de guardia*), Mercero stumbles only when he consciously aspires to dignify television. The conspicuous trucks, helicopters, and cranes of *La cabina* point towards the more modest and engaging children's bicycles of *Verano azul*. The 'tetralogy' of one-off dramas inaugurated and announced with *La cabina* today seem alternatively fey (the elderly bird-loving couple of *Los pajaritos*, 'The Birdies', 1974) or preachy (the Mona Lisa weeping over the human condition in *La Gioconda está triste*, 'The Mona Lisa is Sad', 1977). Ironically Ibáñez Serrador's low-budget 'dramáticos' have aged much better. In the cases of both creators, it seems that financial limitations can lead to creative innovations.

These two bodies of work also bear witness to the surprising insistence and persistence of media hierarchies over four decades. It seems film is ever fated to lord it over its more popular, if not populist, medium. Yet I have made an argument for Ibáñez Serrador (like his admirer Alex de la Iglesia) as a popular auteur; and for Mercero (like the very different Medem in film) as a unique visionary. While the very term 'TV auteur' seems likely to remain oxymoronic, few Spanish filmmakers can lay claim to such extended and productive careers. If auteurship is by no means dead, not even in the contested and conflictive medium of television, then authorship remains significant as a critical enabling tool for the exploration of these valuable and neglected audiovisual oeuvres.

Historias para no dormir ('Stories to Keep You Awake', TVE, 1966–82)
Creator, director, executive
producer, and senior writer
(as 'Luis Peñafiel')   Narciso Ibáñez Serrador
Art direction   Fernando Sáenz
Music   Waldo de los Ríos

Regular Cast   Narciso Ibáñez Menta

Verano azul ('Blue Summer', TVE1, 1981–82)
Creator, director   Antonio Mercero
Writers   José Angel Rodero, Horacio Valcárcel, Antonio Mercero
Producer   Eduardo Esquide
Music   Carmelo Bernaola

Cast

Antonio Ferrandis	Chanquete
María Garralón	Julia
Pilar Torres	Bea
Cristina Torres	Desi
Juanjo Artero	Javi
José Luis Fernández	Pancho
Gerardo Garrido	Quique
Miguel Ángel Valero	Piraña
Miguel Joven	Tito

Works Cited

Bazin, André. 'La Politique des auteurs'. *Cahiers du Cinéma* 70 (April 1957): 2–11.

Blumenthal, Howard J., and Oliver R. Goodenough. *This Business of Television*. New York: Billboard, 1998.

Bordwell, David, and Kristin Thompson. *Film Art: An Introduction*. 3rd ed. New York: McGraw-Hill, 1990.

Born, Georgina. *Uncertain Vision: Birt, Dyke, and the Reinvention of the BBC*. London: Vintage, 2005.

Buse, Peter, Núria Triana Toribio and Andy Willis. *The Cinema of Álex de la Iglesia*. Manchester: Manchester UP, 2007.

Cook, Pam, ed. *The Cinema Book*. 2nd ed. London: BFI, 1999.

Díaz, Lorenzo. *50 años de TVE*. Madrid: Alianza, 2006.

Erice, Víctor, and Abbas Kiarostami. *Correspondences*. Barcelona: Diputació, 2006.

Fernández Labayen, Miguel, and Elena Galán. 'Historias para no dormir'. *Las cosas que hemos visto: 50 años y más de TVE*. Ed. Manuel Palacio. Madrid: RTVE, 2006. 30–31.

Feuer, Jane, Paul Kerr and Tise Vahimagi. *MTM: 'Quality Television'*. London: BFI, 1984.

Fiske, John. *Television Culture*. London and New York: Routledge, 1987.

Foucault, Michel. 'What is an Author?' *The Foucault Reader*. Ed. Paul Rabinow. Harmondsworth: Penguin, 1986. 101–20.

Freud, Sigmund. 'The Uncanny'. *Art and Literature*. Ed. James Strachey. Harmondsworth: Penguin, 1985. 335–76.
Gerstner, David A., and Janet Staiger, eds. *Authorship and Film*. New York and London: Routledge, 2005.
Goodridge, Mike. 'The Auteur Side of Life'. *Screen International* 1489 (18 Feb. 2005): 6.
gran ilusion, La. 'Habla el cine español'. Sept. 2007.
Grant, Catherine. 'www.auteur.com?' *Screen* 41.1 (2000): 101–108.
Heredero, Carlos F. *20 nuevos directores del cine español*. Madrid: Alianza, 1999.
Ibáñez, Juan Carlos. 'Verano azul'. *Las cosas que hemos visto: 50 años y más de TVE*. Ed. Manuel Palacio. Madrid: RTVE, 2006. 86.
Laínez, José Carlos. 'Trobar leu, trobar clus'. *Archivos de la Filmoteca* 14 (1993): 60–69.
Medem, Julio. 'Mi viaje con Ana'. *El País Semanal* 12 Aug. 2007: 28–40.
Mendíbil, Alex. *Narciso Ibáñez Serrador presenta...*. Valencia: Fundació Municipal de Cine, 2001.
Ministerio de Cultura. Accessed 3 November 2007. <http://www.mcu.es>
Palacio, Manuel. *Historia de la televisión en España*. Barcelona: Gedisa, 2001.
—. 'Notas sobre el canon cinematográfico y televisivo en España'. Unpublished paper.
Phillips, Patrick. 'Genre, Star, and Auteur'. *An Introduction to Film Studies*. Ed. Jill Nelmes. London: Routledge, 1996. 122–66.
Screen International. Special Issue on Spain. Feb. 2007.
SGAE. *Hábitos de consumo cultural*. Madrid: SGAE, 2000.
Torreiro, M. 'Europa: el guión en la crisis del "auteur"'. *Archivos de la Filmoteca* 5 (1990): 74–79.
Triana Toribio, Núria. *Spanish National Cinema*. London: Routledge, 2003.
Truffaut, François. 'Une Certaine Tendance du cinéma français'. *Cahiers du Cinéma* 31 (Jan. 1954): 15–29.
Universidad Carlos III de Madrid. *Licenciatura en Comunicación Audiovisual*. Madrid: Universidad Carlos III, 2004.

CHAPTER EIGHT

Sitcom Cinema: Case Studies in Convergence

Specificities of humour

Predictions of the death of situation comedy have proved premature. Indeed, the trade press has reconfirmed the vitality of that undervalued television genre, stressing innovations in technology, audience and format. Thus *Broadcast* reported that the BBC was said to be commissioning a comedy tailored to a range of multimedia platforms (White) and claimed that social networking websites such as MySpace offered newly exposed comedy talent a route to the broadcast sector (Keighron). Meanwhile, the BBC had identified four categories of comedy audience: traditionalists, new mainstream, jokers, and progressives or early adaptors (Anonymous). While *Emmy* made much of the transnational adaptation of innovative British formats such as *The Office* (O'Steen), *Broadcast* reminded readers once more that comedy could be truly local: the BBC invested £9 million in regional production beyond the metropolis (Campbell). Academic studies have also stressed the connection between transnationalism and innovation in formats: Barbra S. Morris compares news parodies in the UK and the US; Steven Peacock gives a rare close analysis of form (of setting, dialogue, gesture, cut, ellipsis and sound) in the new subgenre of pseudo-documentary comedy. Brett Mills argues that the sitcom, once more held to be essentially stable and conservative, has been subject to a radical mutation or reappraisal with shows such as *The Office* (Mills, 'Comedy Vérité').

By coincidence, that same year, 2005, saw the publication of two book-length studies of the neglected genre, a US collection edited by Mary M. Dalton and Laura R. Linder, and a British monograph by Mills. Their approaches are tellingly different. After a first section on 'conventions', Dalton and Linder's contributors address the broad social issues – family, gender, race, sexual orientation and class – studied in earlier US collections on the genre (e.g. Morreale's *Critiquing the Sitcom*). The volume ends with a section on ideology, which is arguably unnecessary as the previous sections already offer critiques or decodings of the various social paradigms held to be depicted on and promoted by television.

In their introduction, the editors make a case for sitcom as 'one of the oldest and most ubiquitous forms of television programming' which, nonetheless, has left a 'void' in academic television literature (1). They also begin by noting the 'contestation' of those structural conventions once held to identify situation comedies as a distinctive genre: 'thirty-minute episodes, photographed in a three-camera studio set up in front of a live audience and built around the situations within the programme' (2). The 'perimeters of the form' have been pushed by shows like *Ally McBeal*, an hour-long single-camera programme shot on sets without a live audience (2). Elsewhere 'transgressive' or 'oppositional programming' (such as the animated *South Park*) is juxtaposed with the 'theatrical comedy of manners genre', where *Seinfeld* is seen as a 'worthy descendant' of and 'modern variation' on the English Restoration comedies of Congreve and Sheridan (3).

These broadly positive accounts of innovations in conventions are contrasted with more negative analyses of the social issues listed earlier. Thus for sitcom families 'the more things change, the more they stay the same', even as the nuclear familiar has given way to non-traditional versions. And while 'compared to other forms of mass media, notably Hollywood cinema, television today offers a wide range of roles for women, particularly leading roles for women in their thirties and forties', sitcoms are held to reinforce, as well as intermittently to challenge, 'the hegemony of gender in historical and contemporary culture' (5). Similarly, depictions of African Americans may have moved on from 'gross stereotypes', but are still mainly confined to 'niche programming' on minor networks (6). And the emergence of openly gay characters on, say, *Will & Grace* is said to be counteracted by 'normalizing' or 'heteronormative narrative strategies' (8, 9). Meanwhile the theme of social class explored in workplace comedies of the 1970s waned with the shift to the family in the 1980s, although they returned in the 1990s with *Seinfeld* as a 'self-reflexive' or 'carnivalesque' reflection on the television industry itself (11).

The final section of the collection, on ideology, justifies the study of comedy on the grounds that 'competing messages [are] embedded in popular texts' (11). One essay here, by Christine Scodari, offers an ambivalent verdict on the 'sexcom'. According to the volume's editors this is:

> [...] a subgenre defined by its curious privileging and trivializing of concerns of the private (feminine) sphere. This leads to increasing audience segmentation by gender while the programmes purport to celebrate an emancipated, multifaceted, millennial woman. Scodari argues that the net result of this trend in terms of audience and programme content, is to further dissociate the masculine sphere from the feminine sphere. (Dalton and Linder 11)

Sitcom, it would seem, is its own worst enemy. No sooner does it raise an innovative issue (and it is assumed that such issues are essential to the genre's importance and its academic interest), than it neuters or neutralizes that issue's potential for social change. Conversely, it would seem that the more socially conservative sitcoms are prized by academics, keen to display their ingenuity in ferreting out the 'competing messages' secreted or 'embedded' in such suspiciously popular texts. One dissonant voice in the volume is Robert S. Brown, whose celebration of *Cheers* reads the bar-based sitcom as an example of Habermas's ideal public sphere, in which 'the most heavily contested ideas are discussed and debated until participants have arrived at a peaceful conclusion' (Dalton and Linder 12). It is striking that this persuasive argument is based on a process that is evident to the least attentive viewer and thus requires no ideological decoding at all from the critic.

Brett Mills's monograph *Television Sitcom* is strikingly different in both structure and approach, with chapters devoted not to social issues but to discursive categories: genre (as in Dalton and Linder), performance, representation and consumption. In his introduction Mills also notes that 'surprisingly little academic work' has been carried out in the field (2). He attributes this to the fact that the (British) Cultural Studies tradition held the 'regimes of power' in sitcom to be 'transparently obvious' and that academic priorities in popular fictional television lay rather with soap opera, which reflected the 'ethnographic and feminist dominance' of the field. The comparison with film studies, which exhibits both 'a variety of methodological approaches to funny films' and 'closer analyses of particular subgenres' is telling (3). Unfortunately, such approaches are, according to Mills, not easily transferable to broadcasting (3).

Mills also stresses differences between the UK and the US. In Britain, sitcom never achieved the ratings dominance that it did in America, with no equivalent of NBC's scheduling phenomenon of 'Must See' Thursday line-ups (5). Special Christmas editions of the British shows have, however, intimately tied comedy to the national calendar (6). While Mills acknowledges that representation is vital in sitcom (and that it has frequently been studied for its 'disruptive' or 'transgressive' potential), he argues that representation becomes complex because of the 'specificities of humour' (7). While Humour Theory cites three broad categories in this context (superiority, incongruity and relief), one culture's sense of humour is 'often incomprehensible' to another. This empirical observation is demonstrated by the fact that 'while American programmes are broadcast across the globe, they are usually scheduled and understood as "mere interlopers"' (9). Self-identifications may prove unreliable, however. The 'black humour', or 'intermingling of serious and comic subjects', which Mills takes as typically British, is also held by many Spaniards to be uniquely their own.

Turning to anthropology, Mills analyses the paradigms of humour as 'group bonding' (10) and a 'social interaction and familiarity' that transcends mere communication (11). But he argues that humour does not just have 'some relationship with social structures and power' and that jokes do not merely exist within social and national discourse. Rather 'they constitute a specific discourse of their own, in which the humour intention results in specific inflections of communication' (12). Anthropologists further suggest that the social role of humour may be to serve as 'a tool of conflict avoidance' or to function through 'permitted disrespect'. Here, insults are unthreatening because 'joking relationships rest [...] on an equal balance of power' (12). Again, however, such models are difficult to transfer to television, given the massively institutional nature of television and its power over the audience. Broadcasting standards in the UK thus recognize that while comedy has a 'special freedom', it also has a unique capacity for 'potential offence' to those joked about (13).

For Mills, one of the major problems in studying sitcom is the fact that vital specialist terms (laughter, joke, humour, and comedy itself) come with everyday meanings that are rarely explored (13). Attempting to define such terms academically (and noting in passing the rise of the hybrid 'comedy-drama' (18)), he finally arrives at a functionalist approach: sitcom is 'a form which is as distinct as possible from seriousness, upholding the validity of the serious in the process' (19). The anxiety over the 'academic value in studying both comedy and television' thus leads to the paradox (clearly visible in Linder and Mills) that 'comedy is only of interest – and of worth – if it is doing something else at the same time as being funny, for being funny is not in and of itself worthy, and certainly not worthy of understanding' (20). Seriousness is thus 'not only prioritized, but normalized' (22) and 'the constant criticism of television for its failure to present a required public sphere' (23) reflects a social bias that not only sees sitcom as trivial but also 'like[s] to see it that way'. Mills argues, then, for a new textual approach to the genre:

> [...] demonstrating that while sitcom can be seen as representative of broader concerns about representation, globalization and power structures, it is so in ways which are not only specific to the genre, but also inflect the meaning and importance of those concerns in particular ways. That is, analyzing what sitcom *says* is pointless unless we have a fuller understanding of what sitcom *does*. (24)

Significantly Mills distinguishes this situation of neglect and scorn with that of comedy in film, thus: 'Film Studies, with its sense of history and complex theoretical underpinning [...] has enough self-confidence in its own worth to risk being tainted by the silliness of studying comedy' (20). We can now proceed in the body of this last chapter to explore the specificity of humour in Spain and the ambivalent relationship between comic film and television, in which the former comes to be dependent on the latter, while insisting, still, on its pre-eminence.

Under the radar: Sitcom cinema

El juego de la verdad (dir. Álvaro Fernández-Armero, 2004)
Alberto y Susana son la pareja perfecta. Guapos, con una intensa vida social, con un trabajo reconocido y con grandes planes a la vista: una casa nueva y una boda por todo lo alto. Alberto es subdirector de un enorme supermercado. Y Susana es la presentadora más sexy del telenoticias en una cadena de televisión local. Ernesto y Lea son sus mejores amigos. Pero a ellos las cosas no les van tan bien. No tienen dinero, no tienen futuro, y desde luego no tienen planes. Él repite monótonamente las ofertas en un supermercado por megafonía en lugar de trabajar en la radio. Y ella tiene que hacerse pasar por sordomuda para hacer la traducción para sordos en un informativo en lugar de ser presentadora. Pero todo cambia un buen día, en el que los peores presagios de Ernesto (hipocondríaco incorregible) se hacen realidad: a causa de un error médico que él mismo propicia sin darse cuenta, le diagnostican un tumor incurable, y le dan tres meses de vida como máximo. A partir de ese momento, las vidas de todos ellos dan un vuelco espectacular y salen a relucir las mentiras y las medias verdades en las que viven inmersos. Susana descubre que Alberto en realidad no quiere casarse con ella. Lea se destapa como una chica fantasiosa que se inventa amantes para suplir la falta de estímulos en su vida. Y todos escuchan por boca de Ernesto cuál es el verdadero deseo que le gustaría cumplir antes de morir: acostarse con Susana, la novia de su mejor amigo.

['The Truth Game'
Alberto and Susana make the perfect couple. Attractive with good jobs and big plans for the future: a new house and a wedding in grand style. Alberto is sub-manager of an enormous supermarket and Susana is the sexiest newsreader on a television channel. Ernesto and Lea are their closest friends but they have no money, no future and certainly no plans. He shouts out the offers in a supermarket over the loudspeaker instead of working on the radio and she has to pretend to be deaf and dumb to do the translations for deaf people on the news. But everything changes when, through a medical error, Ernesto is diagnosed as having an incurable tumour and is given three months to live at the most. All their lives change drastically and all the lies and half-truths in which they live come to light.]

El penalti más largo del mundo (dir. Roberto García Santiago, 2005)
Fernando es el portero suplente de un equipo de fútbol de Tercera Regional. En toda la temporada no ha jugado ni un solo minuto. Pero, en el último partido de la Liga, el portero titular se lesiona y el árbitro señala un injusto penalti en contra. La afición, indignada, invade el campo y el partido se suspende. Hay que repetir el penalti una semana después, y Fernando, el portero suplente, tiene que ponerse bajo los palos. Ahora todo depende de él. Si para el penalti, el equipo subirá de categoría por primera vez en su historia. Si no, todo el esfuerzo de un año no habrá valido para nada. El penalti más largo del mundo es la historia de esa semana. Siete días en los que Fernando se convierte en el héroe del barrio y consigue que por primera vez la chica de sus sueños le dé una oportunidad.

['The Longest Penalty in the World'
Fernando is a substitute goalkeeper for a football team in the Regional Third Division. He hasn't played for a single minute in the whole season. But, in the last game of the League, the regular goalkeeper is injured and the referee calls for an unfair penalty against the team. Indignated [sic], the fans pour on to the field and the game is cancelled. The penalty has to be repeated a week later, and Fernando, the substitute goalie, will have to stand between the posts. Now it all depends on him. If he stops the penalty, the team will rise to second division for the first time. Otherwise, a year's efforts will have gone down the drain. *El penalti más largo del mundo* is the story of this week. Seven days in which Fernando becomes the local hero, for the first time getting a chance with the girl of his dreams.]

Reinas (dir. Manuel Gómez Pereira, 2005)
A veces parece que la vida se ponga de acuerdo con el destino y juntos se dediquen a propagar las más improbables coincidencias. Que se lo pregunten a Magda, Ofelia, Helena, Nuria o a Reyes, cinco madres de armas tomar, curtidas en la velocidad de una vida urbana y moderna, a quienes el destino sitúa a un palmo de la boda de sus respectivos hijos, con los preparativos por montera y un montón de imprevistos. Las cinco deberán pulsar a fondo el acelerador para acudir al matrimonio colectivo que se disponen a contraer sus herederos: ni más ni menos que la primera ceremonia gay de la historia de España.

['Queens'
Sometimes life seems to join hands with fate to jointly create the most improbable coincidences. Just ask Magda, Ofelia, Helena, Nuria or Reyes, five mothers to be reckoned with, weathered in the speed of an urban, modern life, all just inches away from their respective sons' wedding, with hilarious preparations and all sorts of last-minute hitches. All five have to hit the gas to get to the collective wedding of their respective heirs: no more no less than the first gay ceremony in the history of Spain.]

Semen, una historia de amor (dir. Daniela Féjerman and Inés París Bouza, 2005)
'Semen, una historia de amor' es una comedia romántica en la que el azar juega con el destino de todos sus protagonistas: Serafín, el cuadriculado biólogo atado a la razón. Ariadna, la trapecista convencida de que sólo la magia y la pasión pueden mover el mundo. Y el estrafalario padre de Serafín su particular compañero de piso. Todo comienza cuando Serafín conoce y se enamora de Ariadna, una paciente de la clínica donde trabaja, que se está sometiendo a un tratamiento de inseminación artificial. Tras varios intentos fallidos por lograr que Ariadna quede embarazada, Serafín locamente enamorado decide utilizar su propio semen sin contar a nadie una palabra, convirtiéndose así en el padre de la futura criatura.

['Semen, A Love Story'
'Semen, a Love Story' is a romantic comedy in which chance juggles with the fate of its protagonists: Serafin, a square biologist who never oversteps the bounds of reason; Ariadna, a trapeze artist convinced that only magic and passion can move the world; and Serafin's outlandish father, his particular flatmate. The whole thing

starts when Serafin meets Ariadna, a patient attending the artificial semination clinic at which he works. Following several failed attempts by Ariadna to become pregnant, and having fallen seriously for the girl, Serafin decides to use his own semen without telling anyone, thus becoming the father of the future creature.]

The mid-2000s marked a historic high point for Spanish cinema. According to the official figures given at the website of the Ministerio de Cultura (www.mcu.es, from which I also take the plot synopses and translations above), total figures for feature production rose from a low of 47 in 1990 to a high of 150 in 2006. The proportion of co-productions within that global figure also increased from 10 to 41 in the same period. Exhibition kept pace with production, peaking at 4,401 screens in 2005 (up from 2,627 in 1997), with admissions to Spanish films reaching 21.29 million in the same year (up from just 13.9 in 1997). From 2004 to 2005 the market share taken by domestic films rose from an already unprecedented 19.83 per cent to 20.35 per cent, while the US share fell from 39.61 per cent to 35.49 per cent. The Ministry of Culture's survey (or 'Balance') also noted the increase in distribution of Spanish films, from 106 to 120. Government support for the industry had also risen from €32.5 million to €58.5 million. It was a remarkable achievement for a European national cinema in its own territory.

But what exactly were the Spanish features that struck a chord with local audiences? The biggest-grossing film of 2004 was, of course, *Mar adentro*, with almost 4 million admissions, followed by the gross-out comedy *Isi & Disi* with 1.5 million. In 2005 the leader was *Torrente 3*, the third in the franchise of knowingly coarse farces from Santiago Segura. While such 'new vulgarities', as Triana-Toribio calls them (151–55), gained much press coverage (overwhelmingly hostile, of course), critically supported social realist dramas also brought up the rear. Icíar Bollaín's harrowing story of domestic abuse *Te doy mis ojos* ('Take My Eyes') reached number eight, with 1.7 million admissions in 2004 and Fernando León de Aranoa's tale of urban prostitution, *Princesas* ('Princesses'), a high number three with around 1.2 million the following year. The genres with the lowest and highest cultural cachet are thus well represented in the rankings at this crucial time for Spanish cinema.

Hovering between a quarter of a million and a million admissions, however, are a number of films that are easily passed over and yet, when taken together, constitute a large proportion of the audience for these milestone years of peak attendance for local production. For what we might call, by analogy with television scheduling, the 2004–2005 'season', they reached the positions of four, fifteen, and sixteen in their respective years. These films elicited neither indignant protests nor servile praise from the quality press, and they were rarely nominated for awards or distributed abroad. Soon after their release they tended to be on sale at bargain-basement prices in Spanish stores, sometimes collected in 'packs'. For all these reasons they constitute a distinctive corpus of work that deserves to be studied. They are, of course, the romantic comedies, or comedies of the sexes (the distinction is taken from Bruce Babington and Peter William Evans), whose official synopses I reproduce at the start of this section.

As a genre, the cinematic comedy of the sexes (all four titles are defined simply as 'comedia' on the Ministry website) is remarkably capacious. Each film displays unique distinguishing marks. For example, *El juego de la verdad*'s comedy of consumerism and coupledom is shot between Buenos Aires and Alicante (although its nationality is given as 'Spanish'). *El penalti* (the most successful of the corpus with over a million admissions) is clearly an ensemble comedy, based around an overextended football match, but with the goal of a perfect girlfriend for the goalkeeper protagonist as a parallel plot hook. *Reinas* is the only film to boast an established director with a track record in the genre (Manuel Gómez Pereira) and a glittering gallery of experienced female stars (Verónica Forqué, Carmen Maura, Marisa Paredes) to put the young male principals in the shade. In spite of the fact that it is also the only film in the group to feature a specific national event (the granting of marriage rights to same-sex couples), it is a co-production (with the aptly named Italian company of Fortissimo). Finally *Semen*, self-defined in spite of its graphic title as a 'romantic comedy', is a co-production with the UK and boasts an Argentine co-director (Daniela Féjerman) and father and son pair of actors (Héctor and Ernesto Alterio), playing mismatched flatmates.

Most of these films can be read within the film tradition of *comedia madrileña*, explored by Jordan and Morgan (68–71), although the setting is so generalized in *El juego* that Buenos Aires can pass for the Spanish city, and so particularized in *El penalti* that the distinct, gritty urbanism of the southern suburbs is clearly recognizable. The comedy corpus shares loaded urban and suburban locations and motifs, such as the supermarket (which stands for alienated consumerism in *El juego* and exploitative labour in *El penalti*), or Japanese cuisine (which is a reliable index of class and savoir faire: grande dame Marisa Paredes assumes that her gardener is unfamiliar with the use of chopsticks in *Reinas*; sheltered scientist Ernesto Alterio asks for his tuna sushi 'well done' in *Semen*).

The social issues debated in Dalton and Linder are thus explored in each of the films, but are often placed in combination or in conflict with one another. *Juego* juxtaposes rich and poor couples, but shows that the former's wealth (including fancy house with swimming pool) comes only as a gift from parents anxious to encourage the youngsters to marry. *El penalti* boasts a supporting Arab character who is a deadbeat dad (he has had a child with the goalie's sister) and in a running gag refuses offers of ham, but only because of cholesterol. In *Reinas*, Paredes' great actress (later mistaken by star-struck neighbours for 'la Carmen Maura') is distressed not so much by her son's marriage to a man as by the fact that her gardener will now become her in-law. *Semen* boasts the most elaborate new form of family: by the end, the strait-laced scientist (a romantic stereotype since at least *Bringing Up Baby*, 1938) has hooked up with kooky twin sisters and babies, one biological and the other not.

Most striking is the theme of immigration, in its more accessible Latin American version (Muslims, whether ham-eating or not, seem more difficult to assimilate). *Reinas* includes a striking Cuban chef (Jorge Perugorría from *Fresa y chocolate* ('Strawberry and Chocolate', Tomás Gutiérrez Alea, 1994)) with whom hotel-owner Carmen Maura is having an affair. *Semen* features the scientist's comically and chronically pessimistic Argentine father. Beyond stereotyping (*Reinas* is hampered by the broadest of performances from Bettiana Blum as an impossible Argentine mother), at their best these films manage to integrate social issues into the substance of their humour. For example, in *Reinas* once more, one gay couple's lovemaking is not frustrated but rather enhanced when the Argentine partner accuses his Spanish lover of treating him like a *sudaca* (a racist term for a Latin American migrant). As in Mills's anthropological model, then, insult is safely neutralized and potential conflict resolved through table-turning: the gardener in *Reinas* will prove fully proficient with chopsticks; the poor couple in *El juego* will turn out to be highly successful in their unpromising and undervalued jobs.

Sexual relations, however, remain consistently and persistently ambivalent. It is striking that all these films refuse the conventional conclusion of a wedding. *El juego* reveals with an unexpected shot/reverse shot in the chapel that it is the 'wrong' couple that is getting married (rich supermarket manager Óscar Jaeneda and poor sign-language interpreter María Esteve). *El penalti* charts Fernando's farcical attempts at seduction (trying to make his beloved drunk, he succeeds only in drinking himself under the table) and ends, even after his footballing success, with the couple still dreaming of a romantic trip to Paris that has not taken place. *Semen*, as mentioned earlier, finishes with a very modern ménage of adults and children. Only *Reinas* concludes with a satisfactorily glamorous ceremony. But here the white-costumed *novios* are, of course, of the same sex and are married by a female judge who is one of their mothers. As her colleagues note, somewhat cynically, this is surely the most visible of signs that Spain is finally up to date.

Modernization is thus signalled by homosexuality and artificial insemination. And it may be no coincidence that these same two plot lines featured prominently in the most influential TV sitcoms of the period, *7 Vidas* ('Nine Lives', Tele 5, 1999–2006) and *Aquí no hay quien viva* ('No-one Can Live Here', Antena 3, 2003–2006). But modernization also means television, improbably prominent in the fictional world of this film comedy corpus. *El juego*'s Natalia Verbeke works as a newsreader, *Reinas*' mothers and sons are pursued by the *telebasura* paparazzi, and *Semen*'s father was once an unlikely and inaccurate Buenos Aires-accented weatherman. *El penalti*'s more modest, working-class media ambition extends only to coverage in *Marca*, the football daily.

These TV thematics are inextricable from TV aesthetics. Picturesque locations go unexploited (in *El juego*, Buenos Aires simply stands in for Madrid) and composition is compatible with the traditional TV format. Only *Reinas*, exploiting the wider cinematic ratio, breaks out into split screen to show its multiple mothers and has them vamping for the opening credits in front of vibrant rainbow-flag graphics. But even here cinematic references are downgraded. Paredes' diva ('I worked for Almodóvar!') is cut down to size when she is misrecognized by fans as real-life rival Maura. Moreover, it is in *Reinas* again that Tito Valverde reprises and riffs on his familiar role in TV's *El comisario* (Tele 5, 1999–), here playing a policeman once more, but now one who is the father of a gay groom.

It seems likely, then, that the distinctive feature of these films, what made them so attractive to audiences, is their modesty and contemporaneity, or, in other words, their televisuality. Indeed, it was the most modest of all, *El penalti*, with its working-class setting, which proved most successful at the box office. And it was surely no accident that this film starred the superficially unattractive Fernando Tejero in a role not dissimilar to that of his then celebrated caretaker in *Aquí no hay quien viva*, Spain's number one sitcom at the time of the film's release.

Having examined the middle ranks of sitcom cinema, then, we can now move on to a rare exceptional case in the genre, a feature whose phenomenal success remains inexplicable, unless we pay proper attention to the televisual trace embedded in it.

El otro lado de la cama ('The Other Side of the Bed', Emilio Martínez Lázaro, 2002)

Sonia y Javier llevan varios años viviendo juntos y varios más siendo novios. Pedro y Paula no viven juntos pero sí son novios desde hace varios años. O eran, porque ella se ha enamorado de otro y le dice aquelllo de 'prefiero que seamos amigos'. Esta frase, sin duda una de las más duras que puede decirnos alguien en nuestra vida, precipita todos los acontecimientos que se cuentan en esta comedia musical que habla del amor, del sexo, de la amistad, y sobre todo de la mentira.

[Sonia and Javier have lived together for several years as well as several years going out together. Pedro and Paul don't live together but they have been going out together for quite a few years. Or rather were, because she has fallen in love with someone else and has told him the usual thing 'I'd rather just be good friends'. This sentence, which must be one of the most devastating things anyone could ever say to anyone else, sets off all the events in this musical comedy, which deals with love, sex, friendship, and above all lies.] (Ministerio de Cultura)

It is instructive to compare the studies of sitcom I analysed earlier with Bruce Babington and Peter William Evans's *Affairs to Remember*, an academic reading of the film comedy of the sexes. Writing in the late 1980s, the authors still feel the need (like the television scholars) to defend their chosen subject, 'assert[ing] the centrality and importance of comedy' (1). But the definition of contemporary romantic comedy is not easy in a period when 'sexual love is felt as the highest good, not merely [...] a ground of social life' (267). Indeed, commentators had already claimed that because of social and political changes (given as 'growing divorce, single-parenting, feminism, gay rights and, above all, the rise of the working woman'), romantic comedy might now be 'impossible' (268).

Yet comedy of the sexes, a broader category, can embrace both the repression and the celebration of the pleasures and meanings of sexuality, often, indeed, combining the two (269). Meanwhile, the optimism of earlier romantic comedies (defended by the authors as not naive but rather 'an art of the ideal') has given way to a scepticism, even nihilism (271), which offers 'a defence of the couple, not so much in terms of morality as of expediency' (272). While once 'displacement and sublimation into metaphor [were] the grounds of the art of the romantic comedy of the past, producing the delicate "libidinal glow" of comedies like *Bringing Up Baby*', the current 'lowered threshold of the forbidden' (or sexual explicitness) means that comedy 'is suited to display the erotic base, but not the superstructure of feelings deriving from it', thus reversing the presuppositions of classic romances (274). Moreover, contemporary narcissism may suggest that 'transcendence [comes] through the self rather than the couple' (275). For Babington and Evans the main 'reparative fictions' (281) for the new circumstances (*Tootsie* and *Victor Victoria*, both 1982) appealed to transvestism in an attempt to heal the wounds of a new and frankly unpleasurable battle of the sexes.

Veteran director Emilio Martínez Lázaro's *El otro lado de la cama* was the biggest-grossing Spanish film of 2002, with a huge 2,825,194 admissions. At a time when the Spanish film industry was experiencing one of its frequent crises, this comedy with musical interludes thus set the stage for a revival of both the industry and romantic comedy (or, more properly in this case, 'sexcom'), a renaissance that no doubt facilitated the production of the corpus examined in the previous section of this chapter. *El otro lado* can clearly be read within Babington and Evans's cinematic paradigm above. A tale of two couples who swap partners and are then driven to farcical deceits, it is clearly founded on the assumption that sexual love transcends fidelity and friendship. And if its twenty-something stars cannot testify to divorce or parenting, they certainly register debates over feminism, gay rights and women in the workplace. All of the principals, both male and female, seem to have comfortable jobs in the professions or the arts. The most *machista* [sexist] of the men, the foul-mouthed supporting character Rafa (Alberto San Juan), is swiftly reduced to tears when his girlfriend dumps him. And when Paz Vega's Sonia rebukes errant boyfriend Javier (Ernesto Alterio) for reading the sexist *Playboy*, he replies that the magazine is also aimed at a lesbian readership. As in the best sitcom, such comments are, of course, integrated into and inflected by plot and characterization. When Javier makes his remark it is by no means innocent: he wrongly suspects Sonia of infidelity with a lesbian friend. And when he informs best buddy Pedro (Guillermo Toledo) that 'we are all bisexual', it is to protect himself by implying that Paula could be having an affair not with him but with a friend who is known to be gay.

Later, Pedro will repeat the same line to Javier with the same bad faith (he wants his friend to think Sonia is sleeping with the lesbian, not with him). And the complex plot is full of such symmetries, suggesting a 'reparative fiction' both within and between the sexes. At one point, cheating lovers Paula and Pedro are given identical voice-overs, each ruefully commenting on a secret love that they have concealed from each other. Yet this attempt at reparation, sometimes surprisingly tender, is combined with a contemporary lowering of the threshold of the forbidden. The film is notably graphic in the display of attractive young bodies, both in and out of underwear. And those bodies are fully unsublimated: Pedro blames Sonia's affair on menstrual tension, while Paula farts when she is in bed with Javier. When Sonia gives Pedro ratings out of ten for lovemaking, he is naively delighted that he gets a better grade the second time around.

What is striking, however, is that *El otro lado* combines this new explicitness (the sexual base) with the old romance (the amorous superstructure). Here, the crucial innovation is the appeal to musical numbers inserted throughout the film. On the one hand these numbers are incongruously situated in everyday locations (a tennis court, a taxi, an office, or a bar) and are voiced and danced by the principals with endearing amateurism. But on the other hand, the numbers speak still to the optimism, even utopianism, shared by those two now historical genres, the classic musical and the romantic comedy. Thus, when Javier visits Paula to profess his love to her in her office, the initially sober setting gives way to coloured gels, which glow glamorously blue, green, and red, and to a choreography that wittily exploits office furniture (chairs on castors prove surprisingly versatile). While the lyrics merely tell us 'There's something I want to say to you', the film form directly shows us the utopian, transformative potential of romance, even a romance that is, as here, provisional and temporary. This is not something the comedy just says, but something it does.

Another touching sequence has sexy, assured Sonia schooling blokeish, dishevelled Pedro in love, asking him to pretend he is his own girlfriend while she plays Pedro himself: '¡Estás guapísima!' ('You're gorgeous!') she coos, addressing him in the feminine gender. As the role reversal continues, the two slowly become intimate. Here the soundtrack (elsewhere reliant on rock and pop songs of the 1980s calculated to engage the nostalgia of the film's young adult target audience) is reduced to a few delicate piano phrases, as hesitant as the new couple's slow rapprochement. Such expertly realized romance is, as ever, gently undercut by humour (Pedro keeps murmuring about wanting a bedtime glass of milk even as Sonia kisses him) and by our knowledge that with such shallow and narcissistic characters this new relationship is unlikely to transcend the narcissistic demands of the modern self (next morning Sonia will indeed say it was 'just one of those things'). Such quiet scenes contrast with the knockabout visual gags elsewhere, as when Javier and Pedro take out their secret resentments against one another in a tennis match that spirals into a fully fledged fist fight. While no one in the film will come out a winner, it is clear that it is men, posturing and immature, who are most maimed by sexual stereotyping.

But what seems unique about *El otro lado* (especially compared to the lesser efforts that followed it) is that, like its characters, the film has it both ways, fusing romance and cynicism, classic and contemporary, and, most importantly, cinema and television. This registers even at the level of casting, where of the

20 Laura (Paz Vega) on the small screen: *7 Vidas*

21 Sonia (Paz Vega) and Pedro (Guillermo Toledo) on the big screen: *El otro lado de la cama*

two principal couples, Alterio and Verbeke are best known for film – although Verbeke also starred in the short-lived workplace drama *Al filo de la ley* (TVE, 2004) – while Toledo and Vega were familiar only as TV stars. Transcending the televisual trace so visible to viewers, and most unusually for a comedy, the film was nominated for best picture at the Goyas (it won only for sound); and the most prestigious critic, Angel Fernández Santos, waxed lyrical on its merits in *El País* (5 July 2002), claiming it was a film not of jokes ('gracias') but of humour ('gracia'), even aspiring to a state of grace ('estado de gracia'). He goes so far as to invoke the luminous rhetoric of the 'libidinal glow' of classic romance. Citing illustrious cineastes such as Joseph L. Mankiewicz, 'Jacques Demi' (sic), Woody Allen and even Alain Resnais as precedents, he writes that this shift from joke to humour is an 'elevation' from 'spark' to 'blaze' that makes the film an example of cinema that is 'alive' and 'important'.

Such effusive cinematic abstractions are barely visible to two caustic commentators on the supposed 'crisis' of Spanish cinema in the year of *El otro lado*'s release. Josep Lluís Fecé and Cristina Pujol argue that the 'phenomenon' of the film was achieved through 'extra-cinematic' means (158), notably a unique Spanish star system in which young faces and the media in which they appear are interchangeable. Whether they are featured in films, TV series, commercials, weekly supplements, or on the cover of glossy magazines, such figures represent only a 'lifestyle'. They go further. A 'character' like 'Paz Vega' (the scare quotes are theirs) embodies a sanitized image of rebellion and feminism adapted to sell tourist guides and fashion trends with equal efficiency (159). Moreover, the role played in *El otro lado* by curly-haired, hangdog 'Guillermo Toledo' is incomprehensible unless the audience is familiar with his character in the sitcom *7 vidas*, on which he made his name with Vega herself. As series television has become the launch pad for cinema, so a successful feature film has become (has become reduced to) a vehicle for the legitimation of stars whose popularity was first established in the minor medium.

It seems that this televisual connection was even visible to some foreign critics (*Hollywood Reporter*'s Michael Rechtshaffen branded the film 'sitcom-y'). But more interestingly, Fecé and Pujol extend their functionalist critique to embrace a genre normally thought to be at the opposite pole to romantic comedy: the earnest social realist films which are held to be unambiguously serious. The second-biggest-grossing film of 2002, with 1,602,946 admissions, was *Los lunes al sol* ('Mondays in the Sun', Fernando León de Aranoa, 2002), which treated unemployment. This second success was based, they write, more on necessity than quality (155), a media 'event' constructed by critics averse to too many trivial comedies (156). 'Realism' has thus become just another stylistic exercise, one that can be as well attuned to potential profits as any other genre (155). As Mills wrote in his analysis of sitcom, then, seriousness is thus not only prioritized but also normalized, and comedy, the form that is as distinct as possible from seriousness, serves simply to uphold the validity of the serious. It is a dynamic Mills identifies in Anglo-American television that Spanish scholars have thus also found in film.

Serial cinema

In the 'making of' included as an extra to the sequel of *El otro lado*, director Emilio Martínez Lázaro claims that he himself has no idea why the first film was such a success. Unfortunately *Los dos lados de la cama* ('Both Sides of the Bed', 2005), proved a relative disappointment with 1,540,101 admissions, more than a million less than the first. Confirming the Spanish saying that 'second parts are worse' (a prejudice that the sequel's tagline unwisely attempted to refute), *Los dos lados* coarsely exaggerated the plot lines of the original, heightening the implausibility of a newly farcical 'sexcom'. Typically the lesbian theme, invoked earlier as a smokescreen for heterosexual fidelity, is here made fully explicit with the two new female stars (Vega and Verbeke had declined to return) playing secret lovers from the beginning. With truly staggering implausibility, the unrepentantly *machista* males (Alterio and Toledo once more) even reconfirm their long-time friendship by sharing a passionate kiss at the conclusion. The musical numbers, once attractively everyday, are now blowsily overblown: *Los dos lados* makes one of the new characters a professional singer, opening with her sprawled on a grand piano in a swish nightclub. It is notable that techniques that work well in TV sitcom, where familiarity is a virtue (the repetition of situations and reprise of catchphrases such as 'Everyone's bisexual!') fall flat here in a film sequel. Although Hollywood can establish franchises of superheroes (as can Spain in the unique case of Santiago Seguro's gross-out comedy), the attempt failed for the innovative genre of the musical romance. 'The Three Sides of the Bed', invoked perhaps jokingly by the films' producer, has not been sighted.

The same went for another comedy success of the time. *Días de fútbol* ('Football Days'), based, like *El penalti*, on soccer as a metaphor for male comradeship (and with a supporting romantic theme) achieved over 2.5 million admissions in 2003 (the year after *El otro lado*). But follow-up *Días de cine* ('Cinema Days') flopped with just 100,000 in 2007. And this in spite of the fact that all four films shared the familiar brat-pack cast of the young Spanish star system (Alterio, Verbeke, Tejero). Two other continuities are less apparent. David Serrano was screenwriter for the two *Lado* films and director of the two *Días*, thus ensuring a reassuring similarity of character, plot and tone. More importantly, perhaps, all four were produced by Estudios Picasso, the production arm of Tele 5. No doubt the experience in creating long-running sitcoms such as *7 vidas* (the finishing school or launching pad for so many young actors) was indispensable in this production line of comedy on film. Certainly Tele 5 achieved notable success with humour in both media.

There is a further connection specific to Spain that prepared the ground for TV viewers venturing beyond their living rooms to see their small-screen stars graduate into theatres (what Fecé and Pujol called their 'elevation'). The familiar conventions of sitcom in the US (30–minute episodes, photographed in a three-camera studio set-up in front of a live audience) are rare in Spain. Single episodes of *7 vidas* and *Aquí no hay quien viva*, the most important examples of the genre during the time when what I have baptized 'sitcom cinema' was at its height, were at least 60 minutes long and played for a feature-length 90 minutes with commercials. New episodes were followed by repeats running back to back deep into the night. It was thus no great novelty to see Paz Vega and Guillermo Toledo, say, in long-form comedy fictions that barely discriminated in their form and content between one medium and the other. Viewers were already well accustomed to spending whole evenings in their company.

Yet even these two landmark shows, which I have studied at length elsewhere (see Smith, *Spanish Visual Culture*; *Television in Spain*), were surprisingly different from each other. *7 vidas* ran for over 200 episodes and boasted a large number of talented players (veteran Amparo Baró harked back to *Chicas en la ciudad*; Javier Cámara, Toni Cantó and Blanca Portillo all later starred in features for Almodóvar). *7 vidas* made much of its studio audience, with returning cast even performing a special live show to mark the 200th episode. *Aquí no hay quien viva*, on the other hand, which ran for a similar extended length, had no laughter track or single set-up, cutting dizzily between the many and varied locations of its shared apartment building.

Thus, while US sitcom only belatedly hybridized with drama in long-form, single-camera shows without a studio audience, the formal division between comedy and drama in Spain was always unclear. Indeed, as I mentioned earlier, the 'black humour' that blends the comic and the serious is held in Spain (as in the UK) to be typical of a nationally specific regime of humour. Spanish sitcom thus continues to be formally diverse and experimental. This is illustrated as I write (November 2007) by two shows that could not be more different from one another. *Los Serrano* (2003–) is based on a *Brady*-like blended family (new spouses bring sets of children with them) that is clearly conservative in its ideology, appealing to traditionalist audiences. And it boasts dramatic elements that climaxed with the death of the blended family's mother, played by *Mar adentro*'s Belén Rueda. The more recent *Cámera café* ('Coffee-Cam', 2005–), based on a pan-European format, owes something to the mock-documentary subgenre of *The Office*, and thus targets progressives or 'early adopters'. Workers' antics are spied on in minimalist style by a single camera located in a coffee-dispensing machine. But perhaps the greatest innovation in a Spanish context here is the length: *Cámara café* fills a skimpy 30–minute slot. The fact that both shows are broadcast by Tele 5 once more reminds us that a single corporation can embrace a broad range of audiovisual products, aesthetic styles and cultural values.

We have seen that Spanish sitcom (on film and television) seeks to make reparation for the battle of the sexes by attempting to ensure an equal balance of power, even when (as is inevitable in comedy) offence is given. Unlike the US 'sexcom', *El otro lado*'s sometimes graphic humour takes care to leave a place for straight male viewers, who can identify with actors who remain endearing in spite (or perhaps because) of their considerable limitations. It is not clear if there can be a reconciliation between cinema and television, as there has been between the sexes. Just as drama defines seriousness (defines its seriousness) as the opposite of humour, thus normalizing itself, so film attempts to distance itself from television, even as the two media converge both aesthetically and industrially. Rather than dismiss this relationship as an example of cynical exploitation (Fecé and Pujol's thesis of the merchandising of 'lifestyle'), we should investigate it attentively and without prejudice. Sitcom, whether on the big or the small screen, is not or not merely of value because of the undoubted evidence it gives of changing social attitudes. Rather, it is a prime example of those artistic and industrial innovations that can arise from cross-fertilization between cinema and television and that I have attempted to document through the course of this book.

El otro lado de la cama ('The Other Side of the Bed', 2002)
Director	Emilio Martínez Lázaro
Production companies	Telespan 2000, Impala; with Vía Digital, Tele 5
Screenwriter	David Serrano
Cinematographer	Juan Molina
Art direction	Julio Torrecilla

Cast
Ernesto Alterio	Javier
Paz Vega	Sonia
Guillermo Toledo	Pedro
Natalia Verbeke	Paula
Alberto San Juan	Rafa
María Esteve	Pilar

El juego de la verdad ('The Truth Game', 2004)
Director	Álvaro Fernández Armero
Production companies	Morena Films, Dea Planeta; with Antena 3, Canal + España, Forta, De Palacio
Screenwriters	Alvaro Fernández Armero and Roberto Santiago
Cinematographer	Aitor Mantxola
Art direction	Mercedes Alfonsín

Cast
Tristán Ulloa	Ernesto
Natalia Verbeke	Susana
María Esteve	Lea
Óscar Jaenada	Alberto

El penalti más largo del mundo ('The Longest Penalty in the World', 2005)
Director and screenwriter	Roberto García Santiago
Production companies	Tornasol, Ensueño; with Antena 3, Canal + España, Forta
Cinematographer	Juan A. Castaño
Art direction	Federico García Cambero

Cast
Fernando Tejero	Fernando
María Botto	Ana
Marta Larralde	Cecilia
Luis Callejo	Khaled

Reinas ('Queens', 2005)
Director — Manuel Gómez Pereira
Production companies — Warner Bros España, Lucky Red with Canal + España, Antena 3
Screenwriters — Joaquín Oristrell, Yolanda García Serrano, Manuel Gómez Pereira
Cinematographer — Juan Amorós
Art director — Carlos Conti

Cast
Verónica Forqué — Nuria
Carmen Maura — Magda
Marisa Paredes — Reyes
Bettiana Blum — Ofelia

Semen, una historia de amor ('Semen, A Love Story', 2005)
Directors and screenwriters — Daniela Féjerman and Inés París Bouza
Production companies — BocaBoca Producciones, Future Films
Cinematographer — Néstor Calvo
Art direction — Luis Vallés

Cast
Ernesto Alterio — Serafín
Leticia Dolera — Ariadna/Penélope
Héctor Alterio — Emilio

Works Cited

Anonymous. 'Are You a Joker?' *Broadcast* 5 May 2006: 7.
Babington, Bruce, and Peter William Evans. *Affairs to Remember: Hollywood Comedy of the Sexes*. Manchester: Manchester UP, 1991.
Campbell, Lisa. 'BBC Puts £9m into Regional Comedy'. *Broadcast* 25 Feb. 2005: 6.
Dalton, Mary M., and Laura R. Linder, eds. *The Sitcom Reader: America Viewed and Skewed*. Albany: SUNY Press, 2005.
Fecé, Josep Lluís, and Cristina Pujol. 'La crisis imaginada de un cine sin público'. *Once miradas sobre la crisis y el cine español*. Ed. Luis Alonso García. Madrid: Ocho y Medio, 2003. 147–65.
Fernández Santos, Angel. 'Camas revueltas'. Review of *El otro lado de la cama*. *El País* 5 July 2002. Accessed 11 Nov. 2007. <http://www.elpais.com/articulo/cine/Camas/revueltas/elpcinpor/20020705elpepicin_2/Tes>
Jordan, Barry and Ricky Morgan. *Contemporary Spanish Cinema*. Manchester: Manchester University Press, 1998.
Keighron, Peter. 'Laughter Tracks'. *Broadcast* 16 March 2007: 20–21.
Mills, Brett. 'Comedy Vérité: Contemporary Sitcom Form'. *Screen* 45.1 (1 April 2004):

63–78.

—. *Television Sitcom*. London: BFI, 2005.

Ministerio de Cultura. 11 Nov. 2007. Accessed 3 November 2007. <http://www.mcu.es>

Morreale, Joanne, ed. *Critiquing the Sitcom: A Reader*. Syracuse: Syracuse UP, 2003.

Morris, Barbra S. 'Come and Get It! Television News Criticism: American and British TV Comedy Versions'. *Journal of British Cinema and Television* 3.1 (1 June 2006): 47–58.

O'Steen, Kathleen. 'Brit Wit'. *Emmy* 27.2 (1 March 2005): 23.

Peacock, Steven. 'In Between Marion and Geoff'. *Journal of British Cinema and Television* 3.1 (1 June 2006): 115–21.

Rechtshaffen, Michael. 'The Other Side of the Bed'. *Hollywood Reporter* 20 Aug 2003. Accessed 11 Nov. 2007. <http://www.hollywoodreporter.com/hr/search/article_display.jsp?vnu_content_id=1962117>

Smith, Paul Julian. *Spanish Visual Culture: Cinema, Television, Internet*. Manchester: Manchester UP, 2006: 39–48.

—. *Television in Spain: From Franco to Almodóvar*. London: Boydell and Brewer/Támesis, 2006: 82–112.

Triana-Toribio, Núria. *Spanish National Cinema*. London: Routledge, 2003.

White, Geoff. 'BBC Looks to Find Mobile Comedy'. *Broadcast* 16 Sept. 2005: 5.

Index

Page references in *italics* indicate illustrations.

7 Vidas 30, 31, 34, 183, *187*

Abril, Victoria 49, 50
Aguirresarobe, Javier 110, 119
Al filo de la ley 12, 91
    comparisons with *Hospital Central* 89–91, 93–94, 101–02, 102–03
    production details 103
    specimen episode 95, 98–100
Allinson, Mark 24
Ally McBeal 32, 81, 151, 176
Almodóvar, Pedro 17–37, 39–40, 51, 60
Alvarez, Marcial 72, 74, 82
Amar en tiempos revueltos 12, 15, 126, 132–42
    production details 142
    synopsis of 132
Amarte así 126, 127, 133, 134, 142
    production details 143
    specimen episode 128–30
Amenábar, Alejandro **105–21**
    and *Mar adentro* DVD documentaries 108–09, 118
    motive for *Mar adentro* 110
    review of work of 107–08
    on Spanish cinema and Hollywood 146
    televisual connection 111–12, 119
Antena 3 34, 123, 155
    funding for films 80
    Lobos 98
    Periodistas 117

Policías 65, 71
    as production company 192, 193
Aparicio, Rafaela 46, 63
Aquí no hay quien viva 34, 183, 184, 190
Armiñán, Jaime de 18, 38, 42–45, 46, 47
Arroyo, José 22, 24, 35
Artero, Juan José 72, 74, 82, 163, 173
Asfalto, El 152, 156, 166–67, *168*, 170
auteur TV **145–174**
Ávila-Saavedra, Guillermo 124
Ayaso, Dunia 17, 19, 20, 27, 36

Babington, Bruce 182, 185
Baeza, Fátima 89, *90*, 103
Bailey, Steve 89, 100, 102
    on 'professional television' 87–88, 91, 97, 98, 99
Banderas, Antonio 36, 48, 49, 50
Barbero, Martín 124–25, 129, 133, 139
Baró, Amparo 44, 46, 60, 63, 190
Barranco, María 36, 50
Barroso García, Juan 76
Bazin, André 43, 146
Beard, Laura J. 123
Benet, Vicente 105
Berkman, Lisa F. 89
Biltereyst, Daniel 124
Blumenthal, Howard J. 150, 151
Bordwell, David 145
Born, Georgina 150
Bradshaw, Peter 108
Brissette, Ian 89

Britts, Melissa 86–87
Brunsden, Charlotte 66
Bryant, Jennings 67
Buezo Armiñán, Catalina 42, 43, 44
Buonanno, Milly 13, 126
Buse, Peter 148

Cabina, La 154, 156, 166–67, 169, 170, 172
Caffarel, Carmen 34, 54, 55
Calle 13 70, 73, 74–75
Campbell, Lisa 175
Caparrós Lera, J. M. 22
Caughie, John 35
Chávarri, Jaime 50, 51, 63
Chicas en la ciudad 18, 38, 39, 42–48, 50
    comparison with *Mujer de tu vida* 39
    production details 63
    reality show 60
    social change, evidence for 60–61
Chicharro Merayo, María del Mar 14
Chory-Assad, Rebecca 86
Cineinforme 122
Climent, Joaquín 74, 83
Coixet, Isabel 18, 20
Comisario, El 12, 13, 15, 72
    comparisons with *Policías* 65, 72–73, 74–75, 80–81
    production details 82
    series concept 70
    specimen episode 75, 78–80
Con dos tacones 13, 18, 34, 54–59, 57, 60–62
    comparison with *Chicas en la ciudad* 38
    production details 63
consumers, viewers as 14, 45–46, 133, 155, 162
    and cultural contexts 48, 96–97
    and television drama 80, 86–87, 101
    women 40, 54, 58, 61
convergence 11, 105–06, **175–94**
    and auteurs 145–74
Cook, Pam 145–46, 147–48
Cormier-Rodier, Béatrice 66
Coronado, José 49, 112, 113, 115, 120
Costa, Jordi 15

Dalton, Mary M. 175, 176, 177, 182

de la Iglesia, Alex 18, 20, 59, 150, 151
    and authorship 148–49
del Toro, Guillermo 18, 20, 149
¡Descongélate! 19–20
El Deseo 11, 20, 36, 60
    business mission of, 18–19
    and Mediapro 33–34
    and *Mujeres al borde de un ataque de nervios* 20, 22
    and TV series *Mujeres* 17, 27, 32, 33, 34–35
Desperate Housewives 32, 34, 54, 62, 151
Díaz, Lorenzo 164
diversification 18, 19, 20, 33
    of Spanish sitcom 191
    and telenovelas 122
D'Lugo, Marvin 20, 21
Dow, Bonnie J. 40–41
dreams 22–24, 27, 30, 165
Durkheim, Emile 66, 118
    and collectivity 80, 81–82, 119
    and suicide 106–07
    and understanding of crime fiction 67–70

Écija, Daniel 113, 116, 120
Economist, The 35
Eory, Irán 46, 63
ER 87, 88, 102
Estudios Picasso 11, 149, 190
    production company for drama 70, 103, 120
ethics 113, 115, 117–19
    in workplace drama 87, 88, 97–98
Eurofiction Working Group 13
euthanasia debate **105–21**
Evans, Peter William 24, 35, 182, 185

Fecé, Josep Lluis 188, 189, 190, 191
Fernández, Adolfo 73, 82
Fernández, Ana 70, 73, 77, 80, 82
Fernández, Chiqui 17, 25, 36
Fernández Labayen, Miguel 158
Feuer, Jane 150
Fiske, John 150
Flores, Rosario 50, 51, 62, 63

formulatv.com 55, 56, 89, 91–92, 93, 134
Forqué, Verónica 49, 182, 193
Fox, Elizabeth 124
Franco era, the 38, 42, 132, 149
   and *Amar en tiempos revueltos* 133–42
   and Ibáñez Serrador 151, 161, 162
funding 19, 85, 146
   of films 13, 80, 118, 149

Galán, Elena 132, 134, 158
Galería de esposas 43, 46
Galería de maridos 43
García, Esther 25, 34–35, 36
Garrow, Kirsten 85–86
Gatti, Juan 20, 22, 23, 24, 36
Gautier, Fanny 90, *91*, 103
Gerstner, David A. 145
Glass, Thomas 89
González de la Vega, Marta 54, 62, 63
Goodenough, Oliver R. 150, 151
Goodridge, Mike 146
Grabe, Maria Elizabeth 67
Grant, Catherine 146
Gran Wyoming, El (José Miguel Monzón) 50, 51, 53, 63
Guardian, The 108
Guiones de TV 43
Gutiérrez Caba, Emilio, 89, 94, 103

Hable con ella 18, 111
HBO 30, 39, 151
Heredero, Carlos F. 147, 148
Hergueta, José 22
Hermida, Alicia 46, 63
Hill Street Blues 76, 114, 150
Historias para no dormir 149, 152–53, 154, 171
   compared with work of Mercero 163, 166, 167
   episodes of 157–62, 167
   production details 173
Holden, Stephen 108
Holmwood, Leigh 65
Hospital Central 12, 13, 15, 90, 91–93
   comparisons with *Al filo de la ley* 89, 91, 93, 94, 99–103
   production details 103
   specimen episode 94, 95–98

Ibáñez Menta, Narciso 158, 159, 160, 161, 167, *168*, 169
Ibáñez Serrador, Narciso 12, 15, 151
   and Antonio Mercero 155–57, 166–70, 171
   profile of 152–54
   work of 158–62
Iglesia, Alex de la, *see* de la Iglesia, Alex
Irueta, Elena 74, 83
Islas, Mauricio 128, 143

Jacobs, Jason 87, 93
Jones, Robert Alun 106, 119
Journal of Broadcasting and Electronic Media 85, 95
Journal of Communication 67
Juego de la verdad, El 179, 182, 183, 184, 192

Kaiser, Patricia 122
Keighron, Peter 175
Kerr, Paul 150

Laínez, José Carlos 146
L. A. Law 76, 88, 114
Landman, Margaret 86–87
Law & Order franchise 66, 86–87, 100
Lenz, Timothy O. 66
Linder, Laura R. 175, 176, 177, 178, 182
Litzy 127, 128, 143
López Izquierdo, Javier 48, 49
Lozano, Teresa 17, 33, 36
Lunes al sol, Los 34, 189
Lury, Karen 41–42
Lyford, Joanna 85

Mala educación, La 21, 109
Malvar, Aníbal C. 118
Mann, Denise 40, 63
Mar Adentro 12, **105–21**, *111*, 181
   production details 119–20
   televisual trace 107–12, 118
Margalló, Eugeni 141, 142
Marlow, Jane 65

Marsillach, Adolfo 44, 62
Martel, Lucrecia 18, 20
Martel, Paula 46, 63
Martínez Lázaro, Emilio 50, 184, 185, 189, 192
Mason, Gary 65
Massey, Doreen 41–42, 63
Maura, Carmen 17, 48, 182, 183
   Mujeres al borde de un ataque de nervios 24, 36
Mayer, Vicki 123–24
Mazziotti, Laura 124
Medem, Julio 74, 147, 148, 156
Mediapro 24, 34, 36
Meers, Philippe 124
melodrama 11, 87, 97, **122–44**
   in *Amar en tiempos revueltos* 134–35, 138–39
   Latin American model of 125–26, 129, 139, 141
   in *Mar Adentro* 105, 107
   motifs of 130, 142
Mendibil, Alex 152
Mercero, Antonio 12, 15, 152
   and Ibáñez Serrador 151, 155–56, 166–70, 171
   profile of 154–55
   work of 100, 162–66, 171–72
Michelin, Gerardo 122–23
Mills, Brett 175, 177–78, 183, 189
Ministerio de Cultura 12–13, 80, 181, 182
Montserrat, Tamara 127, 143
Monzón, José Miguel, *see* Gran Wyoming, El (José Miguel Monzón)
Morreale, Joanne 175
Morris, Barbara S. 175
Mujer de tu vida, La 48–54, 52, 62
   production details 63
Mujeres al borde de un ataque de nervios 11, 14–15, 20–24, 35
   and *La mujer de tu vida* 48, 50–51
   production details 36
   and TV series *Mujeres* 17, 27, 29
Mujeres (television series) 11, 13, **17–37**
   El Deseo, concepts of 17, 19, 27, 32, 33–35

   familiarity and repetition 33
   historical tradition 18
   opening sequence of 24–27
   plot synopses, first three episodes 28–29
   production and distribution context 33–35
   production details 36
   similarities with *Mujeres al borde* 29–30
   social and urban issues 30–31
Mullen, Lawrence J. 85–86
Mundo, El 55, 60, 117–18, 146–47
Muñoz, Sonia 124–25
musical prompts 32, 59, 116, 128, 129

New York Times 108

O'Donnell, Hugh 125–26, 129, 130, 138, 139, 142
O'Steen, Kathleen 175
Otro lado de la cama, El 12, 15, 185–89, *188*, 191
   production details 192
   synopsis of 184

País, El 31, 33, 93, 105, 188
   supplements of 11, 147
Pajuelo Almodóvar, Diego 18–19, 33
Palacio, Manuel 55, 61, 151, 172
   on female-centred dramas 34, 54
Palma, Rossy de 22, 36
Pardo, Angel 89, 90, 102, 103
Peacock, Steven 175
Penalti más largo del mundo, El 179–180, 182, 183, 184, 192
Perdona, bonita, pero Lucas me quería a mí 19, 20
Periodistas 12, 15, 71, 114, 115
   and the euthanasia debate 106, 107, 112–19
   production details 120
Pfau, Michael 85–86
Phillips, Patrick 145
Planta cuarta 100, 162–63, 171–72
Plateados, Los 126–27, 127–28, 130–32, 136, 142

production details 143
police drama on television **65–84**
Policías 12, 65, 71, 80, 81
    comparisons with *El comisario* 72–75
    production details 82
    series concept 70
    specimen episode 75, 76–78
Potter, W. James 66
Pou, José María 70, 73, 82
    in *Mar Adentro* 111, 118–19, 120
Princesas 34, 181
production in film and television 18–22, 43, 150, 156
    and Almodóvar 22–25, 33–35, 39–40
    Amar en tiempos revueltos 132–34, 138–39
    and authorship 145–46
    and humour 181–82, 190
    and Ibánez Serrador 162, 167
    Mar Adentro 110–11
    medical and legal drama 89, 93–94
    Periodistas 112–13
    and police drama 65–66, 71, 74, 76, 77
    and telenovelas 124, 128–31
    television context 49, 54
Pujol, Cristina 188, 189, 190, 191

Qué he hecho yo para merecer esto? 19, 29

Raney, Arthur A. 66, 67
Rapping, Elayne 66
Rebellón, Jordi 89, 103
Reinas 180, 182, 183, 184, 193
Reith, Margaret 67
Rodríguez Cadena, María de los Angeles 124
Rodríguez Zapatero, José Luis 54, 55, 61
Rogers, Jon 85
Rueda, Belén 15, 105, 106, 110–11, 118
Rueda Laffond, José Carlos 14

Sabroso, Félix 17, 19, 20, 27, 36
Sampredo, Ramón 105, 106, 107, 117–18
    and *Mar adentro* 107, 108–10, 111–12, 118–19
    and *Periodistas* 112, 114–15, 116, 117, 118

Sanchez Tena, Jésus 123
Sbaraglia, Leonardo 90, 91, 94, 102, 103
Screen International 146, 149
Semen, una historia de amor 180, 182, 183, 184, 193
Six Feet Under 30, 151
Smith, Paul Julian 112, 113, 190
Sociedad General de Autores y Editores (SGAE) 146
Soriano, Arturo 32, 36
Sparks, Richard 67
Spigel, Lynn 40, 63
Staiger, Janet 145
Sumser, John 68
Sutton, David L. 86–87

Tamborini, Ron 86
Tele 5 30, 74
    7 Vidas (drama) 34, 183
    broad range of products, styles and cultural values 191
    critique of TV in films 149
    El comisario (drama) 82
    and funding for films 13
    Hospital Central (drama) 89, 92, 96, 103
    and media convergence 11
    Periodistas (drama) 12, 71–72, 120
    Periodistas (drama) and Ramón Sampredo's story 106, 112–13, 117
    production company with others 192
    and social engagement (official website) 101
telenovela 12, 14, **122–44**
    Amar en tiempos revueltos 132–42
    Amarte así and *Los Plateados* 126–32
    methodology and melodrama 122–26
televisuality 18, 54, 65, 101
    exploitation of 162, 167
    and film comedies 184, 188–89
    in *Mar Adentro* 105–06, 107–08, 110–12, 118, 119
    style of 30, 32, 33, 45
    and workplace fiction 75–76, 97, 100
textuality 100, 124–25, 150
    comparisons of film and television 17–37

and composition 129, 130–31, 139, 142
and sitcom 178
and social issues 52
on television 41, 48, 87
Thompson, Kristin 145
Thompson, Susan 85
Toro, Guillermo del 18, 20, 149
Torreiro, Mirito 107, 147
Triana Toribio, Núria 148, 181
Trueba, Fernando 38, 48, 50, 62
TVE 12, 35, 46, 51, 55, 60, 74, 89, 127, 128, 133, 136, 153, 155, 156, 158, 163, 170
 authentic reflection of society 93, 132, 142
 and films 118
 and gender politics 54, 61
 and private competition 49, 71, 123
 and private production companies 34, 100
 production values 93, 100, 141
TVE1 12, 32, 33, 34, 49, 54, 94, 123, 129, 133
TVE2 17, 30, 33, 36

Ulloa, Tristán 74, 79, 83, 192

Vaca Berdayes, Ricardo 70–71, 100
Vahimagi, Tise 150
Valverde, Tito 74, 79, 82, 184
Van den Bulck, Jan 67
Verano azul 74, 151, 155, 163, 164
 production details 173
Verbeke, Natalia 183, 188, 192
 in *Al Filo de la ley* 90, 91, 94, 103
viewers as consumers 14, 45–46, 133, 155, 162
 and cultural contexts 48, 96–97
 and television drama 80, 86–87, 101
 women 40, 54, 58, 61
Vilches, Lorenzo 13, 15
Volver 17, 29, 35

White, Geoff 65, 175
Williams, Raymond 62, 101
Willis, Andy 148
Wilson, Sherryl 62
Wilson, Vicky 107
women in work of Almodóvar **17–37**
women, urban, on television **38–64**
workplace fiction on television **85–104**

Zurita, Humberto 127, 143